FUNDAMENTALS OF
VALUE METHODOLOGY

"The text brings the reader up to date on the practice of VM, as well as the application of Value Metrics that emphasizes the importance of measuring improvements in project performance as being of equal or greater importance than just the realization of cost savings. This book will also become a valuable addition to colleges and universities who are looking for a classroom text or reference on the topic."—*Ronald J. Tanenbaum, PhD, CVS, PE, GE, F. ASCE, President, GeoVal, Inc.*

FUNDAMENTALS OF VALUE METHODOLOGY

"This book is a "must" for those desiring an introduction into Value Management. Each part of the VM process is simply explained, and presented from a project management point of view. The author easily slips between the construction and manufacturing industries to demonstrate the validity of the Value Methodology as applied to these and other market segments. As a long time Value Practitioner, I welcome Rob's book on my bookshelf...."—*J. Jerry Kaufman, CVS-Life, Fellow, Recipient of the Lawrence D. Miles Award, SAVE International's Highest Honor*

Robert B. Stewart

Copyright © 2005 by Robert B. Stewart.

Library of Congress Number: 2005903045
ISBN: Hardcover 1-4134-9194-4
Softcover 1-4134-9193-6

All rights reserved. No part of this publication may be stored in a retrieval system, transmitted, or reproduced in any way, including but not limited to photocopy, photograph, magnetic, or other record, without prior agreement and written permission of Value Management Strategies, Inc.

Cover Art from Photodisc® by Getty Images®

Caricature sketches were created by Patrick Sterno of the Caricature Zone and are used by permission. Please visit the Caricature Zone on the World Wide Web at *www.magixl.com* if you are interested in the artist's work.

Author photograph by Jamie Bosworth.

This book was printed in the United States of America.

To order additional copies of this book, contact:
Xlibris Corporation
1-888-795-4274
www.Xlibris.com
Orders@Xlibris.com

28409

CONTENTS

Acknowledgements 9

Chapter 1—Introduction 11

Chapter 2—Value 38

Chapter 3—Value Methodology Job Plan 67

Chapter 4—Preparation 86

Chapter 5—Information 117

Chapter 6—Function 161

Chapter 7—Speculation 206

Chapter 8—Evaluation 230

Chapter 9—Development 249

Chapter 10—Presentation 268

Chapter 11—Implementation 285

Chapter 12—Value Leadership 304

Appendix A—Glossary 333

Appendix B—Value Study Management Plan 351

Appendix C—Case Studies 370

Index 435

To Robert H. Mitchell, who set things into motion long ago. You have been my mentor and inspiration, both in work and in life. I am filled with pride to be your grandson.

—Robert Bruce Stewart

Acknowledgements

There are many people who contributed to this text and I would like to extend to all of them my sincerest appreciation. Firstly, I would like to thank R. Terry Hays, Robert H. Mitchell, and Stanley R. Kelley, all of whom had a direct hand in helping me write this book—their knowledge, guidance and influence throughout my career has been enormous. I am deeply thankful to both Ginger Adams and Jill Woller for allowing me to incorporate portions of their technical papers. Special thanks to George Hunter for his help and support in developing and applying Value Metrics. Thanks to all at the Miles Value Foundation for their excellent work and for granting me permission to use excerpts from Reflections, a biographical account of the founder of the Value Methodology, Lawrence D. Miles. To Ted Fowler, Art Mudge and Jerry Kaufmann, who have done much to deepen my understanding of the Value Methodology (I plead for your forgiveness for including all of your names in the same sentence!) Thanks to everyone at VMS, Inc. for their support, dedication and hard work—especially to Jan Parker for her help in proofreading and editing this text. And finally, I would like to thank Jamie and Kaillen for their love and support, and for tolerating all the days I have been away from them in pursuing my career.

Chapter 1—Introduction

Lawrence D. Miles—Engineer, Creator of the Value Methodology

If I can't get the product, I've got to get the function. How can you provide the function by using some machine or labor or material that you can get?

—Larry Miles

All cost is for function.

—Larry Miles

Lawrence Delos Miles was born in 1904 to Delos Miles, a public school superintendent, and Vinetta Miles, an elementary school teacher in Harvard, Nebraska. Miles was very bright, and graduated from high school in three years rather than the usual four. He attended Nebraska Wesleyan University in Lincoln, Nebraska with a degree in Education. In 1925, he was a teacher and high school principal in Winnebago, Nebraska. In 1926, he made a career change and moved into banking. Dissatisfied with this, he returned to college to study engineering. In 1931, Miles graduated from the College of Engineering at the University of Nebraska with a degree in Electrical Engineering.

In 1932, Miles began a long and productive career at General Electric Co. in Schenectady, New York. His first assignment at GE was that of a design engineer in Vacuum Tube Engineering Department. Over a six-year period in this position, he earned 12 patents for vacuum tubes and related circuitry. During this time, Miles developed awareness for unnecessary costs and began seeing the need for developing better ways of doing things.

This sensitivity to cost earned him a transfer to GE's purchasing department, and in 1938 he moved to the position of purchasing engineer. During this time, Miles worked closely with vendors to reduce costs associated with electronic components, eventually moving on to precision-machined parts. In 1944, Miles was transferred to a subsidiary of GE called Locke Insulator. While at Locke, he began the development of the process that has now evolved into the function-oriented problem solving methodology known today as Value Methodology.

Miles was instrumental in the development and spread of Value Methodology. In 1959, he helped create the Society of American Value Engineers and served as its first president between 1960 and 1962. He was the author of the first book on the subject, *Techniques of Value Analysis and Engineering*, which was published in 1961. He taught seminars and lectured extensively throughout the U.S. and the rest of the world.

Larry Miles received many accolades and awards during his career, but none were greater than the honor bestowed on him by Japan. In 1984, he was posthumously awarded the Third Order of Merit with Cordon of Sacred Treasure by the Emperor of Japan. The Japanese bestowed this honor on Miles due to the major impact the Value Methodology had on making Japan an industrial and economic powerhouse. He received additional international recognition from Germany and South Africa for his contributions.

The story of Larry Miles is a fitting introduction to this book. Without him, the writing of this text would not have been possible. Larry Miles also exemplified the role that Value Leadership can play in improving the value of products, services and facilities. While other leaders in business improvement like Dr. W. Edwards Deming and Phillip Crosby have received greater notoriety, the work of Larry Miles has created a quiet legacy that endures today.

VALUE METHODOLOGY

This text is written to provide a basic understanding of the fundamentals of Value Methodology. It is addressed to those new to the discipline with emphasis placed on the practical application of Value Methodology techniques to improve the value of facilities, products and processes. The Value Methodology exists under several different names, such as value engineering, value analysis and value management. There are no essential differences between these designations and they are, for all practical purposes, interchangeable. The term value engineering (VE) has been traditionally used whenever the Value Methodology is applied to the construction industry or industrial design; the term value analysis (VA) for concept planning or process applications; and the term value management for administration or management applications. Value Methodology is the term most commonly used today and refers to the comprehensive body of knowledge related to improving value regardless of the area of application. Value Methodology is formally defined as:

> *The systematic application of recognized techniques which seek to improve the value of a product or service by identifying and evaluating its functions, and provide the necessary functions to meet the required performance at the lowest overall cost.*

Value Methodology (VM) is an organized process that has been effectively used within a wide range of industries to achieve their continuous improvement goals, and in government agencies to better manage their limited construction budgets. The success of the VM is due to its capacity to identify opportunities to remove unnecessary costs from facilities, products and services while assuring that performance, and other critical factors, meet or exceed the customer's expectations.

The improvements are the result of recommendations made by multi-disciplined teams under the guidance of a skilled VM facilitator, commonly referred to as a value specialist. The multi-disciplined teams can be comprised of those that were involved in the design and development of the project, technical experts that were not involved with the project, or a combination of the two. There are two essential elements that set the Value Methodology apart from other techniques, methodologies, and processes:

♦   The application of the unique method of function analysis and its relation to cost and performance.
♦   The organization of the concepts and techniques into a specific job plan.

These factors differentiate Value Methodology from other analytical or problem solving methodologies.

Value Methodology can be applied to products, manufacturing processes, administrative procedures, and construction projects. The VM process is applied in basically the same way for each type of study; however, there are some differences in how you prepare for the different types of studies and how some of the VM techniques are applied.

VM is often confused with cost reduction; however, cost reduction and VM are distinctly different. Cost reduction activities are part-oriented. This usually means altering construction techniques, substituting less expensive systems, relaxing tolerances, and/or thinning or changing of material. Normally, this will produce savings without an alteration of the design concept. Value Methodology is function-driven, and generally leads to new or refined concepts that perform needed functions more simply with higher quality and more economical manufacturing processes or construction techniques. In procedural studies, the general question is, "How can the process be modified to reliably accomplish the

FUNDAMENTALS OF VALUE METHODOLOGY

required functions more efficiently?" This line of thinking often leads to new concepts that improve the performance of the functions while reducing costs.

TODAY'S CHALLENGES

Most people today would agree that long-term profitability is the main objective of privately held companies, while the timely delivery of efficient services would describe the goal of public agencies. They would also quickly point out that the products and services these organizations produce must be competitively priced and meet or exceed the performance expectations of their customers to achieve these goals. The coordination and communication to accomplish this complex task is often difficult. To keep pace with the ever-changing business climate, organizations must better use their most important resource, their people!

This has been demonstrated through the quality revolution that has been experienced in recent times. Management has learned that by involving the entire organization in the decision making process and committing the organization to a goal, significant improvements can be realized. The quality revolution has paved the way in business for even further improvements, as it has demonstrated that waste and inefficiency are unacceptable anywhere in the organization. We have also learned that organizations must offer the customer products and services that satisfy their needs in a timely and responsive manner.

Managing the change that is necessary to compete is a difficult challenge. However, the more successful we become at managing change, the better we become in meeting the customer's needs, reducing waste and inefficiencies, and controlling costs. These changes not only result in improved profits and better efficiency today, but continue to pay dividends for years to come. In today's economic environment, cost control, a focus on performance, responsiveness to change, and increasing operational efficiencies are critical attributes for long-term profitability in any organization.

WHY USE VALUE METHODOLOGY?

The economic health of an organization relates to the efficient use which is made of available resources. As our society evolves we are confronted with increasing awareness that resources appear to be shrinking. No longer do we have unlimited choice in materials, types of energy, or sources of labor. The availability of capital is also limited, especially when we consider that the cost of borrowing is ever fluctuating, and the purchasing power of the dollar seems to be steadily diminishing. Further, the quickening pace of technological advances may find us using designs or methods which are far behind the leading edge of scientific progress. The owner, whether an individual, a corporation, or a tax-supported public body, cannot afford the luxury of paying for design or performance features that contribute nothing to the basic purpose or function of the object being acquired. Such unneeded features are often introduced into designs either because there is inadequate communication between the owner, who controls the budget, the user, who identifies the requirements, and the designer who transforms these requirements into plans and specifications.

To achieve maximum benefits from our limited resources we must make full use of our only unlimited resource—our ability to think creatively. By taking advantage of technological advances in materials and methods of production, and by applying our creative ability to each project, we can in some measure offset the rapid rise in the cost of acquiring goods and services. These costs have risen sharply in the past decade, and in almost any year the rise in costs exceeds that of the preceding year. For example, within the construction industry, the cost of building materials has spiked sharply for essentials such as steel, concrete, and lumber *Fig. 1-1*[1]. In order to acquire the projects, products, and processes within available funds, we must use every possible means to attain the required functions at minimum cost. This is precisely what Value Methodology attempts to accomplish through a systematic, organized approach.

It is also worth noting that Value Methodology is currently mandated in the United States by federal law. These laws generally apply to the design and construction of facilities, but are also applied for the procurement of some types of equipment and supplies. These laws and regulations include:

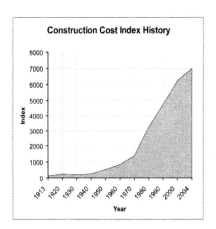

Fig. 1-1

- The Defense Authorization Act (Public Law 104-106) states that each executive agency must establish and maintain cost-effective VM procedures and processes.
- The 1995 National Highway System Designation Act requires states to carry out a value study for all federal-aid highway projects with an estimated total cost of $25 million or more.
- The 1986 Water Resources Development Act (Public Law 99-662) requires a review of costs (i.e., value study) on all federally funded water and wastewater treatment projects with a total cost in excess of $10 million.
- The Office of Management and Budget's Circular A-131 requires federal agencies to use the Value

Methodology as a management tool to reduce program and acquisition costs.

As a result, not only is VM required at a federal level, but also at the state and local levels due to the fact that federal funding is an integral part of most major capital improvement projects. In addition, many state and local governments have enacted legislative policy of their own mandating the application of VM for a wide variety of projects at various budget thresholds.

PROJECT MANAGEMENT AND VALUE METHODOLOGY

Value Methodology is a body of knowledge related to improving the value of a product, whether it is a new facility, a manufactured item, or a management procedure. The application of Value Methodology occurs within the context of a value study.

Experienced project managers, especially those with a thorough understanding of the Project Management Institute's Project Management Body of Knowledge, will appreciate the similarities between the management of a value study and the management of a project. In fact, a value study is a project! It meets all of the criteria of a project:

- *Is it unique?* Yes, a value study is a unique endeavor having the goal of improving the value of a product, regardless of whether it is a new product or an existing one.
- *Is it temporary in nature and have a definite beginning and end?* Yes, a value study typically involves an intense expenditure of resources within a very short time, usually occurring over a few weeks or months.
- *Is there a way to determine when it is completed?* Yes, the value study is completed when the formal study

process has been completed and oral and written reports have been submitted detailing the specific value improvements developed by the value team.
- *Is there a way to determine stakeholder satisfaction?* Yes, stakeholder satisfaction is determined by holding a formal implementation meeting, which will allow the project team and vested stakeholders to determine the acceptability of the value improvements recommended by the value team.

Value studies can be conducted as a part of an ongoing project, or they may be completely free-standing projects in and of themselves. Throughout this text, reference will be made to additional links to project management as both a career path and a body of knowledge. Project managers, as you will learn, have a special role to play in the application of Value Methodology.

THE ROLE OF PROJECT MANAGERS IN VALUE STUDIES

Project managers are generally positioned within an organization where they may take either a direct or indirect role in the performance of value studies. In projectized and matrix-based organizations, there may be a VM department where value specialists are assigned to facilitate value studies for specific projects. This involvement of a project manager in a value study may take on a variety of forms:

- The project manager may act as a value specialist in facilitating a value study. For some projects and organizations, this may make the most sense, especially if the project is still in the initiation phase.
- The project manager may request and/or sponsor a value study to be performed for a project he or she is actively managing. In this case, the value study may be

led by a value specialist from a different department within the organization, by a consultant value specialist, or by a value specialist from an external project stakeholder.
♦ The project manager may be the recipient of a value study on a project he or she is actively managing. Another entity within the organization, or perhaps an external stakeholder, will have requested that a value study be conducted for the project. In this case, the project manager may be an "unwilling" participant and will be required by the organization to cooperate with the value specialist in participating on the value team directly or in a support role.
♦ The project manager may be a primary decision maker with respect to the acceptability of value alternatives developed as part of a value study.

It is not uncommon for some project managers to take on more than one of the roles identified above. Regardless of which role they will play, it will be an important one in determining the success of the value study. Project managers in all organizations should have a fundamental understanding of VM and be aware of how it can improve the cost, performance, and value of their projects.

It is important to understand that Value Methodology, unlike many management fads, is more than just a concept. VM provides an actual means of achieving improved value. The universality of its application to any project makes it an ideal project management tool. No project manager should be without it!

VALUE METHODOLOGY AND TEAMWORK

The successful application of Value Methodology, as originally conceived by Larry Miles, has always focused on the importance of multi-discipline teams. In fact, VM was one of the first disciplines to recognize the value of drawing upon the group synergism of individuals representing different technical backgrounds. VM is therefore a team process and, as such, requires that members of the value team work together harmoniously and in unison if its output is to exceed the sum of the individual efforts. Genuine teamwork should always be value-based. In other words, it should be behaviorally rooted in mutually shared values. The value specialist will exert considerable influence over the values that will fundamentally affect teamwork. It must be further emphasized that the value specialist's sphere of influence must extend beyond the boundaries of the value team. The value specialist should think of the value team as an extension of the project team. Further expanding on this idea, the value specialist must seek to include the customer or user, the project team, and the project stakeholders as part of the total team effort as illustrated in *Figure 1-2*.

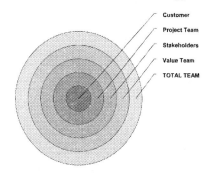

Figure 1-2

There are a number of values and principles that must be followed in creating successful teams *(Fig. 1-3)*. These include:

- Innovation requires an open discussion about things that are "wrong" about the current project. This is achieved by validating assumptions, strengthening the understanding of the problems that are trying to be solved, and improving communication amongst team members. Therefore, it is important to establish a basic level of trust amongst the team members that is based

upon the understanding that the goal of the value effort is the overall improvement of the project. It is not about criticizing team members for perceived shortcomings.
- No one individual must ever intentionally be praised or rewarded for looking good at the expense of another. When team members sense that such behavior is rewarded, they will use information about the project in ways that will subvert the value effort and prevent teamwork. Team players are committed to the success of the project, which in turn will make everyone a success.
- Large organizations and bureaucracies tend to shield individuals from conflict through policies and procedures. Discomfort with conflict runs higher in these environments for this reason. Therefore, the value

Values that Support Teamwork
- No looking good at another's expense.
- It is okay to be wrong.
- Respect facts, data, and objective analysis.
- All team members are equally valuable.
- Individuals must welcome constructive criticism.
- It is okay to evaluate the team's efforts.
- Rewards must be based on the team's output.

Fig. 1-3

specialist needs to develop strong facilitation skills inorder to make people more comfortable resolving conflicts in team settings. The value effort by nature should be a process of consensus rather than an autocratic one.
- Managers within a bureaucracy generally understand that clarifying responsibility is necessary in order to prevent the paralysis that can develop when there is uncertainty within a team about who is responsible. Within the context of the value effort, teams, rather than individuals, must be empowered to solve problems.
- Individuals must have respect for facts, data, and objective analysis in order to foster teamwork. Members of a team are more willing to create interdependencies

involving trust and vulnerability when they feel that facts and neutral data are valued.
- All members of the team that are part of the value effort must be valued equally, no matter how far down within an organization's hierarchy they are. The value specialist should seek to solicit information and ideas from everyone. Oftentimes, those within the lower echelons of an organization will hold important information that is usually overlooked.
- It is not at all unusual for there to be both superiors and subordinates from the same organization participating simultaneously within the context of the value effort. The value specialist must emphasize the importance that team members demonstrate tolerance in the acceptance of constructive criticism of their own ideas. Teamwork improves when people can be critically evaluative of the group's efforts without fear of reprisal, and when superiors become more "hands on" and less authoritarian.

A "teamwork culture" must acknowledge interdependencies that exist in a complex organization. Values about "equity" must support the interdependencies within the total team comprising the value effort; otherwise, teamwork is undermined and the outcome will be compromised. Teambuilding is further discussed in *Chapter 4—Preparation*.

HISTORY OF VALUE METHODOLOGY

The genesis of the Value Engineering methodology was during the period of World War II, from 1938 to 1945. Lawrence Delos Miles, regarded as the father of Value Analysis/Engineering, was an engineer for General Electric Company[2]. During this time every facility was scheduled to the hilt, with priorities running higher and higher, up to AAA and higher. Steel of all types was totally scheduled. Also were copper, bronze, tin, nickel, ball bearings, roller bearings, electrical resistors and capacitors, and all vital products and materials. Miles was assigned the task of "finding, negotiating for and getting" a number of these vital materials, such as materials to expand production of turbo-superchargers from 50/week to 1,000/week for B-24s, capacitors and resistors for skyrocketing military electronic needs, armament parts for expanding production of B-29s, etc. In this environment it was not possible to stop short of achieving the essential results.

Frequently, suppliers, already over-extended, said "No" to increased schedules or new necessary products. In this desperate situation Miles was forced to basics. "If I can't get the product, I've got to get the function. How can you provide the function by using some machine or labor or material that you can get?" Time and again there was a way to do it. Engineering tests and approvals were rushed and schedules met. Thus "function" grew in vitality and was to later mature into the development of the VA techniques.

To assure materials for these and other vital programs, Miles usually worked two days in the vendors' plants, one to two days in GE plants, one day in the Pentagon keeping priorities suitable, and Saturdays and Sundays in his own office. One exact incident will illustrate the function emphasis which pressed itself upon him.

A production manager gave Miles a schedule calling for thousands of a few dozen types of resistors and capacitors to be delivered weekly starting in one week. Manufacturing schedules at the time were 9 months out, with 6 months firm. He was told it was an absolute requirement. Miles asked, "Who agrees with you that this must be secured regardless?" The manager said, "Tom Garahan, overall production manager of GE." Miles asked, "Does Harry Erlicher (Vice President of Purchasing) agree?" The manager said yes.

The resistors and capacitors were secured. They were for Oak Ridge Tennessee. Much later it was learned they were for atomic bomb research and development. Their priority overrode everything; still the others were vital too. Miles went to vendors, made schedule changes, but told each he would find some way to provide the essential functions of resistance and capacitance through a different shape or type or material or equipment, which would keep other vital electronic equipment on schedule for the military. The function approach proved to be so effective that he was never to abandon it.

Critical years passed. In 1944 Erlicher asked Miles to become Purchasing Agent of a GE plant. Miles experienced more benefits from the functional approach in buying.

In March of 1944, he was transferred to Locke Insulator, Baltimore, Maryland, a subsidiary of GE, as Manager of Purchasing. He took line responsibility for delivery and cost of millions of dollars worth of materials and products per year. During nearly the next four years, he developed patterns of engineering, laboratory, and purchasing teamwork which limited costs and improved products. He learned first-hand both the productive and the destructive force of human attitudes and practices, and their effect on appropriate designs and appropriate costs. His thinking was becoming more and more "What FUNCTION am I buying?" rather than "What material am I buying?"

In 1947 Miles wrote a letter to Erlicher saying that he believed that much good could come to GE if he were relieved of line operation responsibilities and assigned full-time to cost reduction work in the central purchasing office. Mr. Erlicher bought the idea and moved him back to Schenectady in late 1947, where his activity was named the Purchasing Department Cost Reduction Section, PDCRS.

So in late 1947, back in Purchasing on Mr. Erlicher's staff, his schedule was cleared so that he could research and develop workable techniques which would secure more cost effective achievement by the decision-making employees in a plant or business.

The early technique, as described by Larry Miles:

> To an exceptional degree it focuses on what is important, develops knowledge about it, and then causes great creativity in that area. You select from the creative approaches, answers that may not have come in years with other thinking methods. When the system was put to work the first time, it resulted in replacing a bronze clip holding a cover on a refrigerator control (that could flex millions of times without breaking) with a lower cost brass clip (that would flex thousands of times). Quality was not sacrificed because the clip would be flexed only about six times in the lifetime of the refrigerator. The $7,000 per year savings may seem like nothing, but when the same technique was applied to everything in the control box, the yearly savings jumped to $1.25 million.

The new functional approach was introduced to Mr. Winne, Vice President of Engineering. Mr. Winne listened, understood, and said, "This is the best method I have seen to get competitive costs and retain quality. What are you going to call it? Proper quality at proper costs equals VALUE. Why not call it VALUE ANALYSIS?" Thus the new methodology was named. Then he said, "The Vice President of Manufacturing, Mr. DuChemin, will be most interested in this." Mr. DuChemin set up a 20-minute appointment with Miles. After two hours of listening and understanding, he said "Train 1,000 men per year." With the support of these men, Miles set up training programs which were available to GE's plants. He accepted men and products from different plants—applied the techniques, and showed them how they could increase earnings and maintain competitive positions. He learned that great benefits were derived when technical people used the VA system and geared training to them.

For the next three years, Larry continued training men and doing work for the plants. He did this using a revolving team of six to eight people. Training was moved into plant locations with a goal of 1,000 per year to be trained. Later GE often exceeded that number. Larry and his training team learned that greatest benefits come when customers and vendors also know and use the VA functional and methodical thinking approaches. On his advice, GE agreed to provide VA training to other industries as well. During the four years from 1948 to 1952, $10 million in benefits were reported.

In 1950, GE gave Larry Miles its highest award—the Coffin Award. This is given in honor of their first president, for benefits to the company resulting from the creation and use of the VA System.

This highest GE award, at that time, went to less than one in each 10,000 employees. Larry Miles was the first and only purchasing man to ever receive it. The citation was:

In recognition of his outstanding accomplishment through the establishment, organization, and development of a Value Analysis Program, which has resulted in substantial cost reductions.

In 1954 the U.S. Navy Bureau of Ships implemented the first Federal Government program with the assistance of Miles and his staff. There followed a period of gradual growth in Federal agencies until 1963 when the Department of Defense established specific requirements for a formal program within the three military services. This involved their design and construction activities as well as suppliers, and mandated incentive-sharing clauses in construction contracts. Contractors were permitted to propose Value Engineering changes and share in net savings. It also introduced full-time Value Engineers within agency staffs to promote and administer the program. The high level of success achieved by the Department of Defense led to further recognition in civil agencies. Great expansion followed in the next fifteen years. Today every

Federal agency with a significant construction or purchasing program employs VE in some form. In addition to defense, such agencies include General Services Administration, Environmental Protection Agency, U.S. Forest Service, Veteran's Administration, the Federal Highway Administration, and the Department of the Interior. This was further expanded during the 1980's by the Executive Branch, with the support of Congress, to include requirements for the application of Value Engineering to all agencies within the Federal Government. In addition, a few states and city governments have directed, through legislative action, that value methodology be applied to all capital expenditures. Thus the value technique, born of necessity in a single company, has become a widely used technical methodology for effective utilization of resources.

SAVE INTERNATIONAL

SAVE International, originally founded in 1959 as the Society of American Value Engineers, is the premier international society devoted to the advancement and promotion of the Value Methodology (also called value engineering, value analysis or value management). Value Methodology benefits include decreasing costs, increasing profits and improving performance.[3]

Society members practice the Value Methodology in the public and private sectors for organizations in more than 35 countries. VM applications span a variety of fields, including construction, corporations and manufacturing, transportation, health care, government and environmental engineering.

SAVE International offers member services such as education and training, publications, tools for promoting Value Methodology, certification, networking and recognition. The SAVE International certification program is linked to a number of value societies in other countries. Additional information concerning professional certification is provided in *Chapter 12—Value Leadership*.

MISSION

To lead and expand the value profession by:

- Fostering education.
- Communicating VM news and activities.
- Promoting the ideals of professional practice.
- Broadening the application of VM use.
- Recognizing significant VM contributions.

Core Values and Beliefs

The following core values and beliefs give SAVE International boundaries in the pursuit of its vision.

- Foster an environment for personal and professional growth.
- Embrace honesty and integrity.
- Celebrate the accomplishments of members.
- Advance the profession worldwide.
- Concentrate on strengthening the knowledge of members.

PROJECTED ROLE FOR THE FUTURE

- Because of SAVE International's influence the problem-solving value methodology, including function analysis, is intimately familiar to chief executive officers and chief financial officers of corporations and government agencies worldwide for achieving stellar results in adding value to products, services, construction projects and business operations.
- SAVE International is known as the premier value organization, with highly skilled members providing value-based leadership in every facet of VM application.

- Opportunities abound as SAVE International members enjoy top career advancement and business success due to the variety of educational and value-based research offered by the society at universities, symposia, on the Internet, and in collaboration with societies of similar interests.
- SAVE International is the repository of all value and related improvement methodologies, as well as information knowledge databases, for people everywhere.

Current VM Applications

Today, Value Methodology is widely used within the public sector and private industry to improve the value of their outputs. Value programs have been instituted in order to ensure that value improvement occurs as a matter of choice. Profiles of three of the most prolific users of VM at the federal, state and local levels are provided below. Each of these entities has found unique ways in which to apply the Value Methodology to improve the value of their facilities and services to the public.

U.S. Army Corps of Engineers

The U.S. Army Corps of Engineers has one of the longest running programs within the construction industry and has been a leader in applying the Value Engineering to construction projects since 1964, solidly demonstrating the Corps' cost effectiveness. Historically the program has returned 20 dollars for each dollar spent on the VE effort, and has documented over $3.1 billion in savings and cost avoidance since its inception.

The basic thrust of the program is to provide the required project at the lowest life cycle cost while maintaining or enhancing project performance. Although not documented, savings are repeated many times by incorporating proposals into similar follow-on projects. These increases in design quality and cost effectiveness have been substantial. The Office of Federal Procurement Policy Act (41 U.S.C. 401 et seq.), as amended in 1996, requires each executive agency to establish and maintain cost-effective Value Engineering procedures and processes. The Office of Management and Budget (OMB) Circular A-131, requires Federal agencies to apply VE procedures to all projects with estimated costs of $1 million or more. The Corps utilizes Value Engineering to:

- Solve technical problems
- Prepare project scopes
- Negotiate environmental contracts
- Provide optimization in planning
- Provide project review
- Ensure project coordination with sponsors, customers, and users
- Ensure that projects meet their intended need and purpose

The Corps regularly helps other Federal agencies initiate their value programs by advising their headquarters offices, exporting its established training workshops, and furnishing teams to perform VE studies. The Corps maintains a centrally headquartered team of technical experts, referred to as OVEST, which the various Districts can employ to conduct VE studies on an as-needed basis.

Over the past decade there has been an increasing use of charrettes (intense design workshops focused on developing the conceptual design of a project) by U.S. Army Corps of Engineers (USACE) Districts to initiate the design process for military construction. Many Districts within the Corps are now utilizing the Value Methodology in the form of a "value based design charrette" to ensure that a project meets its scope, schedule and cost targets at the earliest stage in the design concept.

California Department of Transportation

The California Department of Transportation (also know as Caltrans) uses Value Methodology, where it is referred to as Value Analysis. Caltrans uses VA for a variety of reasons. These include:

- *Maintain Federal Funding*—Value analysis studies are now required on all projects greater than $25 million (construction, right of way, and capital outlay costs) on the National Highway Systems (NHS). The project is defined by the environmental document and may include multiple contracts over many phases. The NHS Act of 1995, the subsequent Federal Rule (February 1997—Subpart 627) and the Federal Aid Policy Guide, which added a new Chapter 6—Value Engineering to define the application of this regulation.
- *Building Consensus with its Transportation Partners*—is becoming the way we do business in Caltrans. Federal and state legislation over the last several years has given the local authorities a greater role in deciding local transportation issues. Value Analysis is an effective tool to break down the conflicts and build consensus with project stakeholders and partners.
- *Solving Difficult Transportation Projects*—The steps and tools of Value Analysis provide an excellent tool to focus on and solve our most difficult transportation problems. The more complex a project in terms of geometry, staging, environmental impacts, etc. the more opportunity it provides a skilled, well-led VA team to provide an in-depth analysis and subsequent innovative solutions for the project.
- *Cost Reduction while Maintaining or Improving Product Quality*—is becoming a big part of the Project Development process, as the public is demanding more for less cost. Project costs should include the total cost

of ownership, which includes both the original (construction) cost and subsequent operation and maintenance costs. VA recommendations should not include cost reduction at the expense of project functions.
- *Elimination of Detrimental Design Influences*—There are many influences that can negatively affect a project's design, ranging from a lack of information to the unwavering adherence to design standards. The VA review process can overcome the above influences by use of an objective, multi-disciplined team of individuals applying the VA methodology in a controlled environment.

Caltrans regularly conducts three types of value studies:

- *Highway Construction Projects.* Performing value studies on highway projects is the primary focus of the Caltrans VA Program. Caltrans typically conducts over fifty value studies per year on the design of highways, bridges and other supporting facilities, resulting in implemented cost savings averaging over $100 million per year.
- *Product Studies.* The VA process can be used to improve the quality of highway products. Typically, engineering products are items and systems as described in Caltrans' standard plans and specifications. Value Analysis can help identify products that need to be updated due to changing technology, outdated application, or any other changes that affect our standard engineering products.
- *Process Studies.* The VA process can be used to improve the quality of Caltrans' processes, such as policy and procedures and business practices

Caltrans experienced a major boost to their Value Analysis program in 1995, when the FHWA began mandating that value studies be conducted on all projects involving the National Highway System. Between 1996 and 2001, the implemented savings have been considerable (nearly $700 million). Caltrans continues to be the leader in the use of Value Analysis for transportation.

City of New York, Office of Management and Budget

The New York City Value Engineering/Value Analysis (VA/VE) Program began in 1983 as a response to a series of capital projects which had become very public embarrassments for the Mayor. He asked the Budget Director for a capital project cost management tool to ensure that agencies would catch problems at an early stage, before costs escalated and construction schedules and public perception were affected.

The Program has evolved and expanded over the past twenty years to focus on more than just cost management. OMB's VE objectives include getting a full reality check on a capital project's cost, program and schedule, and offering alternative proposals to improve the project's cost effectiveness, functionality, and schedule. The routine use of VE has become linked to OMB funding approval for large capital projects. Agencies use these reviews as an opportunity to get a second opinion from relevant experts to confirm or modify the technology choices and functional arrangements for their projects, and to identify ways to make them more cost effective, especially in times of fiscal constraints.

Additionally, VA has been used successfully to streamline or redesign agency operations or processes. Agency staff becomes the team of experts who suggest improvements and changes to upper management, using the structured VA Job Plan and professional VA facilitation. This tool is much in demand, as agencies must do more with less and deal with changes in technology. Often, "business as usual" is not an option anymore.

OMB has reviewed hundreds of capital projects of great diversity and complexity using VE. Subjects have included schools, hospitals, jails, water pollution control plants, bridges (movable and fixed, roadway and waterway), computer systems, parks, museums, zoos, garages, courts, health and social services facilities, police and fire facilities, vehicle maintenance facilities, corrections food services, combined sewer overflow facilities, water treatment plants, sludge and ferry boats and ferry terminals, landfill closures, lab buildings, data centers and environmental projects.

The scale and variety of projects reviewed in the NYC Program is unique, as almost all City agencies are administered by OMB. The wide range of projects demands that OMB undertake extensive outreach for appropriate and credible team expertise. In addition, OMB has used VA to recommend improvements to operational processes or delivery of services. Examples of subjects reviewed include the City's procurement process for professional design services or human services contracts, leasing and space acquisition, daycare contracting, mail handling, the construction change order process, the emergency housing intake process, information technology services, social services payment and case documentation, and hospital revenue enhancement processes.

The VE Program reviews the largest, most complex or important capital projects from within the City's capital program ($7.7 billion in Fiscal 2004). From 2001 to 2004, OMB has reviewed 60 major projects. The NYC VE Program has been a model for other government agencies, and it continues to evolve in response to the needs of its demanding stakeholders.

Major Corporations

Numerous major corporations throughout the world representing all spheres of manufacturing, construction, and professional services maintain active VM programs. A representative list of these includes:

- Bechtel
- Bristol-Meyers Squibb Inc.
- Ford Motor Co.
- General Dynamics
- General Motors Corp.
- Ingersoll-Rand Company
- Kellogg Brown & Root
- Kraft Foods Inc.
- Pratt & Whitney
- Raytheon Systems
- Samsung Electro-Mechanics Co., Ltd.
- Teco-Westinghouse Motor
- TRW Automotive
- URS Corporation

While the scope and focus of the application of Value Methodology within these organizations varies widely, all maintain formal VM programs.

SUMMARY

In today's global economy, Value Methodology is being used to improve the value of construction projects, consumer and industrial products, manufacturing processes, and business practices around the world. Value Methodology achieves is this by:

- Identifying areas of poor project value
- Developing innovative ways to better perform key project functions at less cost
- Maximizing the use of our most valuable resource—people!"

[1] Construction Cost Index History, Engineering News-Record, McGraw Hill, 2004 - 200 hours of common labor at the 20-city average of common labor rates, plus 25 cwt of standard structural steel shapes at the mill price prior to 1996 and the fabricated 20-city price from 1996, plus 1.128 tons of Portland cement at the 20-city price, plus 1,088 board-ft of 2 x 4 lumber at the 20-city price.

[2] O'Brien, James J. (1987) Lawrence D. Miles Recollections, Miles Value Foundation—Excerpts relating to the historical development of Value Analysis, included by permission of the Miles Value Foundation.

[3] SAVE International—Material on SAVE International included by permission.

Chapter 2 — Value

Adam Smith—Economist

Consumption is the sole end and purpose of all production; and the interest of the producer ought to be attended to, only so far as it may be necessary for promoting that of the consumer.
—Adam Smith

Labor was the first price, the original purchase—money that was paid for all things. It was not by gold or by silver, but by labor, that all wealth of the world was originally purchased.
—Adam Smith

Adam Smith is perhaps the most well-known advocate of capitalism in history. He was born in Kirkcaldy, Scotland, in 1723. Smith was educated at Glasgow University and Balliol College in Oxford, England. He later lectured at Edinburgh and became a professor at Glasgow University. After a time, Smith went to France to tutor the Duke of Buckling. While in France, he began work on his famous economic treatise *The Wealth of Nations* and continued writing it upon his return to Scotland. This influential work was published in 1776. In 1778 he followed in the footsteps of his father as a customs official. He died in Edinburgh.

The light of higher learning has shone brightly on Adam Smith's contribution to the field of economics. As a result, his views of religion and morality have been eclipsed. In the *Theory of Moral Sentiments,* he discussed the role of sympathy in connecting self-interest with virtue. One of the primary themes of this work was his view that if the free market is allowed to function and people are affluent, they will have time to worry about the plight of the indigent. In contrast, he argued that in a primitive society, people primarily focus upon survival. Smith also postulated that a free market promoted virtues such as responsibility, honesty, frugality, ability, and self-control. In the quest for acquisition of wealth and power, he believed these virtues were needed to succeed. In the past, there was no such channeling mechanism or incentive of the market to harness virtue. The rich and powerful depended upon deception and privilege in the pre-commercial era, Smith wrote.

Besides the market, other institutions such as the church and public society would reinforce virtue. Smith asserted that religion is the manifestation of humanity's need for justice and benevolence in the material world and "enforces the natural sense of duty." Despite this, Smith wrote that the funding of religion through taxation, would remove its proclivity for evangelism in spreading the faith. He also argued that in society, association with like-minded people would foster like effects. If one chose to affiliate with good people, good results would tend to occur.

Adam Smith spent much of his life's work dedicated to the research and analysis of the concept of value on both an individualistic and societal level. Smith made direct correlations between the properties of value as it relates to morality and the economy, which were radical for its time. The writings of Adam Smith provide the foundation for our contemporary understanding of value, which introduces us to the primary focus of this chapter.

THE CONCEPT OF VALUE

The objective of any Value Methodology study is to improve the *value* of whatever is being studied. Unfortunately, we all have our own opinions regarding what affects the value of a product or service, which may vary greatly depending on our own perspective. Too often decisions are based on just one criterion such as cost, performance, or schedule. This leads to less than optimum decisions. A decision that improves performance but increases the cost to a point where the product is no longer marketable is just as unacceptable as one that reduces cost at the expense of performance! It is also important to avoid confusing cost with value. Added material, labor or overhead increases cost—but not necessarily value. Value is lessened if added cost does not improve the ability to perform the necessary functions.

Key to understanding the value concept is an awareness of several other critical terms and their definitions as used in Value Methodology:

Function   The natural or characteristic actions performed by a product or service. That which a product, facility or service does as it is currently designed or conceived.

Performance   Performance describes the capacity of a product to fulfill its intended function. Ideally, performance should be defined by the intended customer or user. Appropriate performance requires that the product, facility or service have a predetermined level of quality, reliability, interchangeability, maintainability, producibility, marketability and deliverability. These performance levels must match the customer's requirements and vary depending upon the nature of the project.

Product   The end result of our work—a generic term given to the creation of any facility, product, service or process.

Project   The Project Management Institute defines a project as—*a temporary endeavor undertaken to create a unique product or service*[1]. The word

FUNDAMENTALS OF VALUE METHODOLOGY

"temporary" implies a finite beginning and end. For the purposes of this text, a project refers to any endeavor whereby a product is brought into being. A project begins at the inception of a concept, into its design and/or development and through its production, construction or implementation.

Customer The word "customer" refers to anyone who receives a product "downstream". Customers are also sometimes referred to as a "user," depending on the application.

There are three basic elements that provide a measure of value to the user. To use project management terms, these are *scope, schedule* and *cost*. These three elements provide the basic building blocks on which all projects are managed.

Scope There are two aspects of scope that must be considered: product scope and project scope. Every successful project produces a unique product: a tangible item or a service. This could be a new highway, a better mousetrap or a new management process. Customers or users typically have expectations about the features of products they seek to acquire. *Product scope* describes the intended performance and features of the product. *Project scope* describes the work required to deliver a product or a service within the intended product scope. Although product scope focuses on the customer or user of the product, project scope is mainly the concern of the people who will execute the project.

Schedule The customer requires acceptable delivery, usually at a specific place within a given time. The best products or services are of no value if they cannot be provided to the customer in a timely fashion. Schedule is also referred to as "time."

Cost   Similar to the previous definition, costs include all the resources required to deliver the project. Cost includes the people and equipment that do the work, the materials they use, and all the other circumstances that require an expenditure of resources.

Project managers will be able to instantly relate to these three elements, as it is their job to strike a balance between them in order to achieve the best possible value to the customer or user. Maximizing the relationship of these three elements is important to satisfying the customer *(Fig. 2-1)* and achieving "best value." From this relationship it is easy to see that value can be enhanced by improving either scope or schedule or reducing cost. While most value studies have specific objectives such as performance improvement, cost reduction, or improved delivery, the value relationships identified here require a balanced approach. A properly facilitated value study should seek to optimize all three elements of value.

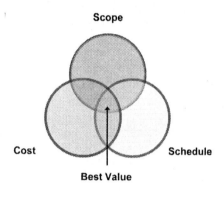

Fig. 2-1

VALUE THEORY

The evolution of the concept of value has been a long one. The philosophical groundwork for the concept of value was first established in ancient Greece in Plato's dialogue *Protagoras*. Closely following this philosophical work, in 350 B.C., Aristotle identified seven classes of value that are still used today. These include ethical, judicial, religious, political, social, aesthetic, and economic. Value Methodology is primarily concerned with economic value. There are four types of economic value:

- **Cost**—The total cost involved in producing a particular item—the sum of labor, material and overhead.
- **Exchange**—The continuing value of properties or qualities of an item that enables us to trade it for something else.
- **Esteem**—The properties, features, or attractiveness that makes its ownership desirable.
- **Use**—The properties or qualities that accomplish the work or service.

Our present understanding of the concept did not begin to fully take shape until the 18th Century. During this period Adam Smith published *Wealth of Nations*, his landmark economic treatise, while Immanuel Kant's *Critique of Pure Reason* provided the humanistic basis for value—that value is uniquely assessed by the individual. The economic theory of value continued to develop through the early 20th Century in Europe and the United States, until in 1947, Larry Miles firmly established the concept of value as a field of study unto itself. In 1961, Miles published his *Techniques of Value Analysis and Engineering*, which laid forth the concept of function as an integral part of value.

Miles' codification of function as a component of value has had far-reaching implications within the sphere of human industry. It spurred a new wave of thinking with respect to the value of goods and services. Miles defined value in terms of the relationship of function and cost. This was eloquently stated in his now famous axiom, "All cost is for function."[2] Of equal importance, he stressed that value is established by the user's, or customer's, needs and wants. This basic understanding of value is essential if we are going to set about improving it.

Building upon Miles' theory of value, Carlos Fallon further refined these concepts. Fallon recognized that while function lay at the heart of value, it was the manner in which the function performed that allowed it to be quantified. Through his work with RCA, Fallon developed a methodology for quantifying performance, which he described using the word *utility*. Although Fallon credits numerous philosophers and economists, most notably Daniel Bernoulli and Jon Von Neumann, for developing the concept and mathematical approximations of utility, he appears to be the first to concisely define a practical method for its quantification. Utility, as Fallon describes it, is "the non-linearity between performance, on the one hand, and the effect of performance, on the other."[3]

In a monograph published for RCA in 1965, Fallon outlined a process, also known as *Combinex*, for measuring the utility of manufactured goods.[4] This process consisted of 1) defining the product's objective; 2) defining key utility factors and related measurement scales; 3) identifying the relative importance of the utility factors; 4) quantifying net value. Fallon's method for weighing the relative importance of utility factors is simple, yet direct—the customer (user) directly assigns them.

David De Marle provides several simple equations to define value.[5] The first is based upon Miles' understanding of value *(Fig. 2-2)*, where F = function and C = cost.

Fig. 2-2
$$V_{max} = \frac{F}{C_{min}}$$

The next equation is an expression of Fallon's theory of value where the term *utility* is defined as the product of a need (n) and the ability to satisfy that need (a) *(Fig. 2-3)*.

Fig. 2-3
$$V = \frac{n \times a}{c}$$

Finally, he proposes a simple equation for value that also captures the idea that the customer or user determines value (*Fig. 2-4*).

Fig. 2-4 $$Customer\ Value = \frac{performance}{price}$$

This equation addresses several observations made by Miles on value. Miles stated that a product or service is considered to have good value if that product or service has appropriate performance and cost. He also made the following observations:

- Value is always increased by decreasing costs (while, of course, maintaining performance)
- Value is increased by increasing performance *if the customer needs, wants, and is willing to pay for more performance.*[6]

There are indeed other ways, however, to improve value. One way is to increase performance while increasing costs such that the improvement in performance is greater than increase in cost. Another way is to decrease performance while decreasing costs such that the decrease in cost is greater than the decrease in performance. The two methods of improving value described here are less obvious, and require specific techniques to measure performance in order to evaluate the relationship of cost and performance.

Where does the concept of function fit into these notions of value? The equation suggested by Miles states that maximum value is achieved by providing the function for the lowest possible cost. The term "function," as it is commonly understood within the context of Value Methodology, is defined as the means by which an expressed need or want is fulfilled. When we discuss the concept of value, what we are really expressing is a measure of how well that need or want is being fulfilled relative to the cost to do so. The "how well" part really refers to the performance of the function rather than of the function itself. Function is tied directly to value such that it provides us a framework for establishing value. It could thus be said that Value Methodology is a body of knowledge focused on improving *functional value (Fig. 2-5)*. Functional value forms the basis for *Value Metrics*, a process for measuring value improvement, which is introduced in *Chapter 3—The Value Methodology Job Plan*.

Fig. 2-5
$$V_f = \frac{P}{C}$$

In other words, "The value of a function is equal to its performance divided by its cost." From this relationship the following definition for value has evolved:

> **VALUE:** *A qualitative or quantitative expression of the relationship between the performance of a function, and the cost of acquiring it. Hence the term "best value" refers to the most cost effective means to reliably accomplish a function that will meet the performance expectations of the customer.*

Building upon this concept, we can tie this equation to the previous discussion concerning scope, schedule and cost if we think of performance as being the sum of scope and schedule *(Fig. 2-6)*.

Fig. 2-6
$$Value = \frac{Scope + Schedule}{Cost}$$

Finally, it has been postulated that value can be interpreted as a form of energy with properties similar in nature to other convertible forms of energy. This "value force," though subjective in nature, can be measured and modeled.

FUNDAMENTALS OF VALUE METHODOLOGY

De Marle argues that it is, in fact, the driving force behind the evolution of products, services, and societies to meet human needs[7]. For those wishing to delve into these more philosophical aspects of value theory, De Marle devotes an entire Chapter in his book, *Value: Its Measurement, Design and Management*.

Ultimately, Value Methodology must focus on functional value, that is, the value of the function the customer or user is seeking to acquire. At this level of understanding, Value Methodology provides a framework in which we can measure the components of value, identify where there are value deficiencies, and direct our efforts at improving it.

WORTH

There is usually some confusion in discussing the concepts of worth and value. The two words are often used interchangeably, though they do have different meanings. Within the context of Value Methodology, worth is the least cost method for performing the function. Worth generally refers to the valuation of a product as perceived by an individual and tends to reflect subjective perceptions of esteem they hold for things. Value refers to an average worth that a group of people attribute to a product. For example, a particular customer might purchase a very expensive suit for a $1,000 because he feels the image he is able to convey while wearing the suit is well worth the price. On the other hand, another less style conscious customer may feel that paying a $1,000 for the same suit is ludicrous! The manufacturer of the suit, on the other hand, should be less interested in these individual perceptions of worth and more interested in what the entire market's perception of value is. Good market research should provide data on what exactly this is. The following equation illustrates the relationship between individual worth and total customer value (Fig. 2-7)[8].

Fig. 2-7 $\quad Customer\ Value = \dfrac{\Sigma\ (worth\ 1 + worth\ 2 + worth\ n)}{n}$

CUSTOMER VALUE

The concept of customer value is built on the idea that people make buying decisions based on the relationship between price and performance. The primary variable is overall value; or, simply said, is the customer getting the most for his or her money? The other two variables are what have been determined to be the main components of value: overall price (cost) and overall performance. The impact of price versus performance is very different depending on the industry or products being measured. Customer value is clearly illustrated using a Customer Value Map (Fig. 2-8).

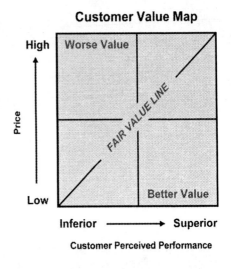

Fig. 2-8

Once again, it is important to remember that customer value relates directly to the function or functions the customer is trying to acquire. The fair value line represents the points at which price and performance are "in balance." A service, product or facility falling to the right of the line (superior performance, lower price), would be perceived as offering "better value" to its customer or user. A service, product or facility falling to the left of the line (inferior performance, higher price) would be considered as offering "worse value" and stands to lose the confidence and/or size of its customer base.

The study of customer value has developed into an entire body of knowledge unto itself called Customer Value Analysis (CVA). CVA is generally a marketing oriented discipline that focuses on identifying, measuring and improving customer value for the purpose of improving the profitability of an organization. Customer Value Analysis focuses on how people choose among competing suppliers of goods and services. This approach leads companies to search for the answers to a number of important customer value questions:

- What are the key buying factors that customers value when they choose among a business and its toughest competitors?
- How do the functions support customer "wants and needs?"
- How do customers rate a business' performance versus competitors on each key buying factor?
- What is the percentage importance of each of these components of customer value?

By highlighting the best performer on each key buying factor, marketers can obtain important data regarding the customer value position for their organization and that of their competitors. Often the view from the marketplace differs from the organization's internally developed perception of customer values. Although it is not the intent of this text to review the way in which organizations market their products, it is important that those seeking to apply Value Methodology develop an appreciation of just how important it is to understand the wants and needs of its customers in improving value.

CREATING VALUE

Ultimately, the success of an organization will depend on how well it satisfies the needs of its customer. The key criterion in measuring this is value. The Value Methodology, as described in the chapters that follow, will provide you with a means of creating and improving value for the products, services or facilities your organization provides. An organization must strive to see value through the eyes of their intended customers or users. This is the first, and most important, step in:

- Understanding what customers value from your facilities, products and services
- Measuring value and communicating it to the customer
- Prioritizing what a customer wants as value and delivering it
- Retaining existing customers (the cost of finding a new one is typically 5 to 10 times that of servicing an existing customer)
- Converting unknown customers to known ones
- Creating a competitive advantage through the development of a customer-focused organization

REASONS FOR POOR VALUE

Value seems to be something most organizations strive for in delivering their products and services to the customer; however, seldom is optimum value achieved. Based upon observations in the marketplace, the level of customer satisfaction (which is a good indicator of perceived value by the consumer) for goods and services for many industries is in decline (Fig. 2-9)[9]. Why is this so? There are many reasons why poor value occurs. Some of the more common ones are identified in the list below:

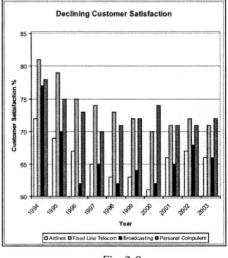

Fig. 2-9

- Focus on internal value rather than customer value

FUNDAMENTALS OF VALUE METHODOLOGY

- Poor communication or lack of consensus in developing project scope
- Changes in the customer's needs or wants
- Outdated design standards or changing technology
- Incorrect assumptions based on poor information
- Fixation with previous design concepts
- Temporary circumstances
- Honest wrong beliefs
- Habits and attitudes

The first three bullets identified above are the primary contributors to poor value. The first reason is universal in nature and relates to virtually every organization, regardless of whether they are involved with products, services or facilities. The second and third reasons apply primarily to businesses and organizations involved in the development of facilities and services.

Focus on Internal Value rather than Customer Value

Too many companies and organizations use internal value measurements in choosing product development projects to fund. They look at whether they can create a new product based on an existing product or whether they possess the technology and capabilities to produce a new product easily.

Too few companies use customer value as a parameter in managing their portfolios. In his book "Product Leadership,"[10] Robert Cooper found that nearly 90 percent of the 35

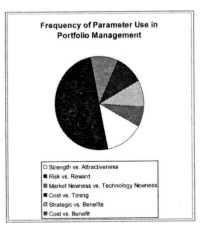

Fig. 2-10

companies he studied did not include customer value in their portfolio management process, and only one of seven bubble charts explicitly analyzed value to the customer *(Fig. 2-10)*. *Even then, many organizations took an internal view, looking at how attractive the market was to their own company, rather than how attractive the products they offered were to their customers.*

Basing important decisions related to product development on internally derived values can produce disastrous results, for an individual company or, as in the case of the U.S. automotive industry, an entire business sector. In the 1980s, automakers focused on just such internal value measurements. In order to minimize up-front design costs and produce a greater variety of models in a shorter time period, they extended "platforms" by modifying body styles but leaving the basic structure unchanged by basing new models on existing ones. The problem was that customers didn't want more cars in a shorter time period. They wanted models with unique characteristics that captured their imaginations and made it easy to differentiate between models. While companies met their internal goals, they lost the differentiation of their products, resulting in customer confusion, which ultimately damaged sales.

The application of VM techniques and processes, such as Value Metrics, brings together key project stakeholders and develops consensus regarding the project's performance and value measurements to develop the best value solutions.

Poor Communication or Lack of Consensus in Developing Project Scope

Most projects, especially those dealing with facilities and management processes, involve multiple stakeholders. Nowhere is this more evident than within public organizations where there are typically a number of regional and local government entities, regulatory agencies, special interests and citizen groups involved in the project development process. Many times, these stakeholders will hold radically different views with respect to the importance of a project's objectives. Typically, the dominant stakeholder (usually the project's "owner") will place its values and objectives ahead of all others. This bias often leads to the development of a project scope that does not provide good value to all stakeholders.

Related to this phenomenon is the relatively poor level of communication that exists between owners and users in developing project scope requirements. This trend has been recognized by many public agencies, and there has been a conscious movement toward performing value studies early in the project planning process in order to improve the level of communication and correctly translate the user's needs and wants into project scope requirements.

The application of VM within the context of a value study is an intense, focused effort where members of the value team, project team, owner and user representatives come together in the same room as a single team possessing a single goal—that of improving project value. In addition, the VM techniques applied at each step of the Job Plan gathers, organizes and develops information regarding the project; draws meaningful conclusions from it through the application of Function Analysis and Value Metrics; and fosters direct communication between the team members through a consensus driven process.

Changes in the Customer's Needs or Wants

Changes in customer needs or wants can occur within a relatively short timeframe, often right under the noses of a project team. Examples of this phenomenon abound in virtually every type of project. Even in the design and development of facilities, user requirements can change quickly. With respect to public facilities, which can take many years to deliver, population growth can make the original design criteria obsolete by the time the design is ready for construction. Many local departments of transportation struggle with this issue where highway improvements cannot keep pace with the growth of traffic. The project scope cannot keep pace with the changing scope of the problem and is therefore unable to satisfy the users' needs.

Value Methodology can be used to accelerate the project delivery process by bringing together the project stakeholders, who will often hold differing wants and needs with respect to the project's outcome, and helping them see the broader picture. The key to doing this is to distill complex organizational and technical issues into simple, easy to understand elements and to identify their relationship within the context of the broader framework of the total project. Furthermore, the application of the processes of Function Analysis and Value Metrics will provide a means for identifying and defining incomplete or overlooked project issues, risks and objectives. With a well-defined project at the onset, the project delivery can be better focused and accelerated, thereby providing better value by addressing stakeholder needs as quickly as possible.

Outdated Design Standards or Changing Technology

In today's world, technological change is an accepted part of life. Despite this, organizations still fall prone to maintaining outdated standards or relying upon aging technology. Much of this resistance is rooted in a belief that new technologies are unproven and inherently flawed. With this line of thinking, individuals and organizations can quickly fall behind the competitors. History has provided us some excellent insights of this phenomenon relevant to several of the world's most significant technological breakthroughs.

- *The Locomotive*—George Stephenson worked in a colliery near Newcastle, England for a number of years, during which time he developed what he called a "traveling machine" for handling coal along the tramway from pithead to the canal. In 1814, after two years of intensive work, the locomotive was completed. It pulled eight trucks loaded with 30 tons of coal up a slight grade at 4 miles per hour. After further development, an engine was produced which would attain speeds of 12 miles per hour. The cities of Manchester and Liverpool applied to Parliament for permission to build a railroad line. Stephenson went to Parliament to appear before the committee his ideas, claims and Calculations were ridiculed. The scheme was called "the most absurd that ever entered the head of a man." It was claimed that the terrible spectacle of a locomotive rushing by would affect people and animals—ladies would have miscarriages, cows cease to give milk, and hens lay no more eggs; the poisoned air from the engine would kill all livestock in the district and the birds in the trees; houses along the line would be set on fire by sparks from the locomotive; there would be no more work for horses, which would die out as a result, and coachmen and innkeepers along the deserted roads would become beggars while highwaymen would roam the countryside; the engine boilers would burst and scald the passengers to death—after they had gone mad because no human could stand the speed of more than ten miles per hour ... and so on.

- *The Electric Light*—In the middle of the 19th century the gaslight industry had achieved enough acceptance to be regarded as the only practicable system of lighting the city of London, despite early objections. However, the city council was becoming concerned about increasing the level of illumination in order to cut down on crime. Means of improving gaslight technology were sought, and much time and effort were put into crash programs for increasing the heat content of artificial gas, producing better and bigger mantles, increasing pressure, etc. This effort was funded by the establishment with great gusto and many affirmations of goodwill and inter-company cooperation. Unfortunately, the results were unspectacular or downright failures, and the streets of London continued to be bathed in flickering semi-darkness. At precisely the same time, an obscure professor in an English university applied for a modest grant to aid him in his research into a phenomenon called "electromagnetism." He admitted to the university authorities that his researches were entirely within the realm of pure science and that he could not see any immediate practical application for his work. He was unable to obtain a penny and had to limp along with the meager resources of his own pocket for several years. His name was Michael Faraday, and electric power and light didn't arrive until much later in the 19th century.

- *The Telephone*—Early efforts to sell stock in the fledgling Bell Telephone Company were hounded off the streets of New York by a crusading journalist who "exposed" the activities of a securities salesman. This man, the story ran, was attempting to fleece innocent buyers by claiming that the human voice could be transmitted over a wire, lie compounded the felony by naming this device the "telephone," an obvious allusion to the word telegraph, which was a practical and proven method of communication. The journalist advised his readers to beware, as the scheme was impossible and doomed to failure.

Value studies that are initiated by an organization are conducted under the premise that innovation is necessary in order to improve value. In light of this, VM provides an excellent vehicle for presenting the ideas and technologies of tomorrow, and challenging yesterday's standards, within an environment that is conducive to introspection and thoughtful consideration.

Incorrect Assumptions Based on Poor Information

A basic lack of information can lead to some amazingly bad decisions. History books are literally filled with countless examples of the world's greatest leaders and thinkers making faulty assumptions based on poor or outdated data. An excellent example of this concerns a value study the author recently facilitated.

In a recent project for a new highway facility, four potential alignment options were initially developed. Three of these bisected a wetlands area according to project documentation that was not less than a year old. Based on this information, the project team selected the alignment option that avoided this area due to concerns related to obtaining environmental clearances from regulatory agencies. During the course of a value study for this project, the value team noted that the three alignment options that had been eliminated from consideration all impacted the same wetland area. Furthermore, all three of these alignment options offered numerous significant advantages over the "preferred alignment." In light of this, the value team decided to further investigate the nature of the affected wetlands to see if there might be ways to mitigate the impacts.

After contacting a number of individuals that had knowledge of the wetlands area, a rather surprising discovery was made—the wetlands no longer existed! Apparently, the "wetlands" were a series of manmade ponds which were fed by the outflow of a nearby wastewater treatment plant and used by local sportsmen to hunt ducks. These ponds had not been formally designated as emergent wetlands at the time of the initial environmental studies and, in the meantime, a local developer had purchased the land and filled them in. Ironically, the developer had also constructed new ponds in the direct path of the "preferred alignment"! In light of these findings, the three alignment options that had been previously eliminated instantly became viable options.

What is today's good information often becomes tomorrow's bad information. Conditions can change quickly and without our knowledge, as was the case in the preceding example. In this respect, an accurate assessment of value is only as accurate as the information upon which it is based.

All projects generally begin with a number of basic assumptions. Too often as project's progresses, these assumptions become "criteria" or "requirements" if they are not challenged and either verified or changed. Value studies provide a structured way to question original assumptions, identify their cost and performance impacts, and replace or challenge them with facts.

Fixation with Previous Design Concepts

There is a natural tendency for humans to resist change, especially in relation to long-time solutions that appear to be working just fine. We are all familiar with the mantra, "If it ain't broke, don't fix it!" While there is an undeniable common sense to this phrase, we should not let it dull our creativity and the desire to find a solution that works better.

The noted American geologist, Thomas C. Chamberlin (1843-1928), addressed this concept as it applies to the application of the scientific method. He had observed that there was a strong tendency among scientists and researchers, in their desire to reach an interpretation or explanation, that commonly lead them to a tentative interpretation based on an initial examination of a single example or case. He realized that this tentative explanation, as such, was not a threat to objectivity, but if it began to be trusted without further testing, it could blind us to other possibilities that were ignored at first glance. This premature explanation can become a tentative theory and then a *ruling theory*, and subsequently, our research becomes focused on proving that ruling theory. The result is a blindness to evidence that disproves the ruling theory or supports an alternate explanation. Only if the original tentative hypothesis was by chance correct does our research lead to any meaningful contribution to knowledge.

Through these observations, Chamberlin developed the Method of Multiple Working Hypotheses[11]. The method of multiple working hypotheses involves the development, prior to research, of several hypotheses that might explain the phenomenon to be studied. Many of these hypotheses will be contradictory, so that some, if not all, will prove to be false. However, the development of multiple hypotheses prior to the research lets us avoid the trap of the ruling hypothesis and thus makes it more likely that our research will lead to meaningful results. Through this approach, all the possible explanations of the phenomenon to be studied can be open-mindedly envisioned, including the possibility that none of the explanations or solutions are viable and the possibility that some new explanation may emerge.

As in the case of the first example, "If it ain't broke, don't fix it!" Chamberlin's observations are quite relevant. Generally, there is a fixation with the existing solution (dare it be said, the *ruling solution*?), or standard way of doing things. This can inhibit the potential for value improvement.

The VM process helps to address this issue, as alternatives are free to be developed that challenge the status quo. The benefits and risks associated with the change are quantified for the decision-makers. Often it is the risk associated with not changing that become the compelling rationale for action.

Temporary Circumstances

Temporary circumstances arise in response to a disruption in the usual flow of work and could manifest in a variety of ways, such as a shortage of a particular material or an unexpected production problem. When these circumstances arise, invariably a solution will be developed as a stop-gap measure. Generally, the work-around is more expensive or time-consuming, and the initial intent is to go back to the old method as soon as the disruption is over. In many circumstances, and especially within larger organizations, there is a tendency to overlook these quick-fixes, and the shift back to normal operations doesn't occur. Value can be diminished in this manner, although rather insidiously.

The communication that occurs during a value study within the multi-disciplined team as they apply the Value Methodology helps to surface these issues and provides a means of correcting the situation.

Honest Wrong Beliefs

These may result from mental conditioning as well as the ready acceptance of opinion, rumor, and speculation without justification or verification. They are often a result of the longtime propagation of many of the other poor reasons for value cited here. There is a certain mythology that has arisen in modern society to which we all have a tendency to subscribe. Many companies and products are unfairly judged by these incorrect beliefs, which results in degradation of product value and corporate image. Some famous examples[12] of this include:

- *"The Chevrolet Nova sold poorly in Spanish-speaking countries because its name translates as 'doesn't go' in Spanish."* This is a classic urban legend that has been repeated in countless marketing textbooks as a cautionary tale for the perils of not understanding a foreign market. The truth is that the Chevrolet Nova's name did not significantly affect its sales; it sold well in both its primary Spanish-language markets, Mexico and Venezuela. In fact, its Venezuelan sales figures actually surpassed GM's expectations!
- *"Dr. Pepper soda is made from prune juice."* The rumor about prune juice being part of the beverage's formula is debunked in a brochure put out by the company. "There are 23 flavors and other ingredients (none of which are

prunes) that produce the inimitable taste of Dr Pepper." I discovered the truth about this one myself after teasing several coworkers about their taste for the soft drink.

- *"NASA spent millions of dollars developing an "astronaut pen" which would work in outer space while the Soviets solved the same problem by simply using pencils."* Most of us have probably heard about the famous "astronaut pen" at some point in our life. The lesson of this anecdote is a valid one, that we sometimes expend a great deal of time, effort, and money to create a "high-tech" solution to a problem, when a perfectly good, cheap, and simple solution is right before our eyes. The anecdote offered above isn't a real example of this syndrome, however. The "astronaut pen" (now known as the famous "Fisher Space Pen") was indeed invented by Paul C. Fisher for use by NASA astronauts in space. However, both American and Soviet space missions initially used pencils. The fact is that NASA did not seek out Fisher and ask him to develop a "space pen"; Fisher did not charge NASA for the cost of developing the pen; and the Fisher pen was eventually used by both American and Soviet astronauts.

The application of the Value Methodology facilitates challenging these beliefs with current facts and helps to dispel them by developing alternatives that would otherwise be dismissed without analysis and quantification of the benefits in the current environment. Through VM's focus on the user, misconceptions, such as those identified above, can be revealed and strategies developed to address them.

Habits and Attitudes

Habits and attitudes are developed by individuals over a lifetime. This ingrained form of behavior can lead to an appalling degree of ignorance with respect to making decisions that will lead to good value. There are a number of layers of habits and attitudes that all of us possess related to our culture, religion, profession, and lifestyle. While many of our habits and attitudes are quite positive, they can also create blind spots with respect to our ability to make value decisions in the workplace. Companies often get into trouble when the motivation profit, which is ingrained in corporate culture, takes control.

Habits and attitudes represent the greatest obstacle in achieving good value. Habitual thinking can be extremely difficult to overcome. If you repeatedly ask somebody the question "Why do you do it that way?" usually by the third time, they will respond "Because that's they way I've always done it!" This type of response is apt to come up even sooner if asked in the workplace. People perform tasks all the time without really thinking about them or knowing why they are doing them. If they stopped to ask things like "Why are we filing these reports?" or "Why do accounting and purchasing both need to approve this requisition?" they might find that the answer is "You don't need to!" What follows are all good examples of habits and attitudes influencing behavior in the workplace:

- We did it that way on our last job.
- It deviates from standard procedures.
- We've never done that before.
- It will set a precedent.
- The boss won't like it.
- It hasn't been tested.
- It doesn't agree with company policy.
- Headquarters will never approve it.

The responses identified above represent obstacles to change based upon habitual ways of doing things. It is important to recognize these for what they are and not to let them get in the way of innovation. Remember, habits are a

FUNDAMENTALS OF VALUE METHODOLOGY

necessary part of our life; however, their very nature is thoughtless. The best way to overcome habitual thinking is to make people aware of what they are saying and then get them to think about it. People are usually not even aware that their habitual responses are rooted so deeply and, once the roots are exposed for what they are, people are more apt to accept changes.

Another aspect of habitual behavior is related to those that are formed by our perceptions. It is important to remember that, to a large degree, the brain functions by interpreting the world around us through the senses. Perhaps the most important of these is vision. Most people depend greatly upon their eyes every single day. Because of this, we are prone to take what we see for granted, and the habits and attitudes that arise from our visual interpretations can inhibit our ability to make good decisions. The following exercises are intended to demonstrate the limitations of our visual senses.

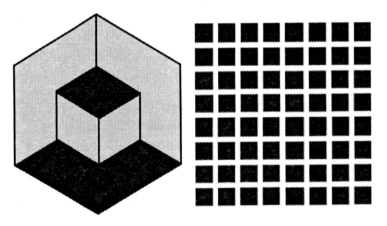

Figure 2-11   *Figure 2-12*

Figure 2-11 appears to be a normal cube with a piece missing from one corner, however, this cube is ambiguous, and may suddenly turn into any of three different aspects. You can empower these transformations by concentrating a little.

Look at the cube, and in your mind's eye, turn the missing corner piece into a solid cube. The small cube will appear to float in space, tilted slightly forward, with a dark top. When this aspect is realized, the cube will take on a completely new three-dimensional appearance. Now try to make the larger cube appear as a *room* with two vertical walls and a darker floor. In this new aspect, the missing corner piece fits snugly into the far corner of the *room*, Remember—*all this is happening inside your head!*

Try turning the cube inside out so that what you are instead looking at a small cube floating in space into a room with two walls and a darker floor. It may take some effort on your part to achieve this transformation. This exercise is useful in demonstrating that it is the brain, and not the eyes, that interpret what we see. Although our eyes see the same image, we can perceive the image in different ways depending on how we choose to think about the visual information.

Our eyes possess millions of specialized light receptors, but only a few of them are active when we look at something. Next to the active receptors are receptors at rest which are recovering from just being used. The image shown in *Figure 2-12* takes advantage of these "sleeping" light receptors.

This figure is known as "Herman's Grid," and is used to demonstrate a visual phenomenon known as lateral inhibition. The fuzzy little black dots in the intersections of the grid are not really there. The rule: white tends to look darker when it is surrounded by black, therefore the intersections appear darker. An active light receptor is an honest light receptor, so the fuzzy dots fade when you look right at them. The fuzzy dots are proof that you can see with nearby, "sleeping" receptors, but you shouldn't always believe them.

To summarize, the old adage "seeing is believing," is simply not true. Our brains and our senses can betray us if we choose to let them by falling into habitual patterns—and habitual thinking can inhibit our ability to make good value decisions.

Attitudes, emotions, and beliefs tend to become habitual. People tend to think, feel, and act the same way whenever they encounter what is interpreted as the same sort of situation that has been previously experienced. As creatures of habit, attitudes support the habits we have acquired. Attitudes can rob us of value. Attitudes support the continuation of existing habits and the acceptance of roadblocks to progress. Attitudes and habits go hand-in-hand. Change one and you will automatically influence the other.

If we approach our projects with a negative attitude and say "we have been doing it this way for a long time, and it works, so why change it," chances are as we examine it we will not find many ways to improve it. However, if we say "this is a good design but we might be able to make it better" chances are that we will find ways to improve it. A quote by the ancient Chinese philosopher Confucius summarizes this discussion rather well:

"It is our habits that take us where we were yesterday, and our attitudes that keep us there."

While there are many reasons poor value exists in the products and services provided today, the systematic approach of the Value Methodology is a proven, effective way to overcome these factors and improve the products and services provided.

SUMMARY

Developing a basic understanding of value is not only essential for the value specialist, but for all individuals and organizations involved in the creation and delivery of products, facilities or services. It is really quite astonishing that so little is understood about the nature of value when so much depends upon ensuring that good value is achieved. Ultimately, it is the customer that will decide value, and not the organization. Those organizations that fail to appreciate this have the unfortunate habit of either undergoing massive overhauls in the form of "corporate reengineering" or, failing that, they become obsolete.

---

1. Project Management Body of Knowledge (2002), Project Management Institute
2. Miles, Lawrence D. (1972) Techniques of Value Analysis and Engineering—2nd Edition, McGraw Hill, New York (pg. 25)
3. Fallon, Carlos (1965) Practical Use of Decision Theory in Value Engineering, (pgs. 45-49, Journal of Value Engineering)
4. Fallon, Carlos (1965) Value and Decision, RCA Monograph
5. De Marle, David (1992) Value—Its Measurement, Design & Management, Wiley, New York (pgs. 16-17)
6. Miles, Lawrence D. (1972) Techniques of Value Analysis and Engineering—2nd Edition, McGraw Hill, New York (pgs. 4-5)
7. De Marle, David (1992) Value—Its Measurement, Design & Management, Wiley, New York (pgs. 3-25)
8. Ibid
9. Data collected from the American Customer Satisfaction Index, 2004
10. Cooper, Robert (1998) "Product Leadership," Perseus Books
11. Chamberlin, T.C., 1890, The method of multiple working hypotheses: *Science* (old series) v. 15, p. 92-96; reprinted 1965, v. 148, p. 754-759.
12. Information regarding urban legends collected from www.snopes.com. Urban Legends Reference Pages © 1995-2004, by Barbara and David P. Mikkelson

Chapter 3—Value Methodology Job Plan

Madame Marie Curie—Chemist

I was taught that the way of progress is neither swift nor easy.
—Marie Curie

In science, we must be interested in things, not in people.
—Marie Curie

I never see what has been done, only what remains to be done.
—Marie Curie

Marie Curie was born Maria Sklodowska in Warsaw, Poland in 1867. She was the fifth and last child of piano player and teacher Bronsilawa Boguska and mathematics and physics professor, Wladyslaw Sklodowski.

In 1891 at the age of 24, Sklodowska went to Paris to study mathematics, physics and chemistry at the Sorbonne. She was consumed by her studies, and subsisted almost entirely on bread, butter and tea. During her years there she changed the spelling of her name to the French version, Marie. She met Pierre Curie in Paris while she studied there, and they soon married in a civil ceremony.

Marie and Pierre Curie devoted themselves to the study of radioactivity, and were among the first to work with radium and polonium. It was Marie Curie who coined the term radioactivity, and she named Polonium after her home country of Poland. Pierre was chiefly concerned with the physical properties of radium and polonium, while Marie worked to isolate radium in its pure state. She and one of Pierre's students, Mr. Debierne, accomplished this, and Marie received her doctorate in 1903 based on her findings. Also in 1903, the Curies won the Nobel Prize for their work along with French physicist, Antoine Henri Bacquerel, who had first discovered natural radioactivity.

She also had to fight the prejudices of her day: hatred of foreigners and sexism which, in 1911, prevented her from entering the Academy of Science. And yet, soon after, she was honored with a Nobel Prize for Chemistry for determining the atomic weight of radium. But her real joy was "easing human suffering". The founding of the Radium Institute by the University of Paris and the Pasteur Institute in 1914 would enable her to fulfill her humanitarian wish.

During the First World War, Marie felt that the use of x-rays would help to locate shrapnel and bullets, and better facilitate surgery. She also realized that it was important not to move the wounded. To address these problems, she created x-ray vans. She later went on to provide x-ray equipment for hospitals and ultimately trained 150 female x-ray operators.

Marie died of leukemia in 1934, exhausted and almost blinded, her fingers burnt and disfigured through her work with radium. Through her dedication and tireless pursuit of science through her methodical approach to problem solving, Marie Curie demonstrates the value of following a proven process. The scientific method, as you will see, shares some parallels with the Value Methodology Job Plan. There are some key differences, however, that this chapter will discuss and explore.

THE VALUE METHODOLOGY JOB PLAN

Within the Value Methodology, there is an organized approach that must be followed if significant results are to be obtained. This organized, multi-phase approach is called the Job Plan. Key to the success of the Value Methodology approach is following these steps in sequence and avoiding the temptation to jump ahead—to try to solve a problem before it has been thoroughly understood and analyzed.

Before introducing the Value Methodology Job Plan, it is useful to first discuss the *scientific method*, which is perhaps the most widely understood and applied approach to problem solving. The original development of the scientific method is largely attributed to Francis Bacon, a persuasive 17th-century English statesman and philosopher (1561-1626) who argued that knowledge was gained only through the gathering of empirical data rigorously and logically refined to a single, essential conclusion. The scientific method *(Fig. 3-1)* consists of four distinct steps:

1. **Observation**—State the problem and research it. Observe a phenomenon or group of phenomena and gather data.
2. **Hypothesis**—Formulate a hypothesis (or multiple working hypotheses) to explain the phenomena. In physics, for example, the hypothesis often takes the form of a causal mechanism or a mathematical relation. In general problem-solving terms, identify a potential solution to the problem. In some cases, predictions are also made as to the expected outcome of the hypothesis or solution.

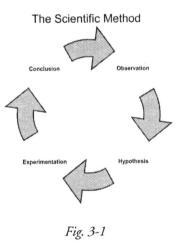

Fig. 3-1

3. **Experimentation**—Perform experiments to test the predictions. In science, the use of several independent experimenters and properly performing experiments is generally required.

4. **Conclusion**—Draw conclusions from the experiments. Summarize the results of the experiments into meaningful conclusions relative to the original hypothesis.

The original Job Plan, as presented by Miles[1], consisted of five steps *(Fig. 3-2)*. These included:

1. **Information Step**—Develop an understanding of the project. Key to this was the process of asking questions of the project development team.
2. **Analysis Step**—Develop an understanding of the project functions. This step was the main point of departure between Value Methodology and other problem solving approaches. Miles created an entirely different way of thinking about problems and systems based on what a thing *"does"* rather than what it *"is."*
3. **Creativity Step**—Identify alternative concepts of achieving the project functions. Although creativity is a fairly routine component of just about every type of problem solving methodology, the creative process in VM focuses on functions rather than objects. This may at first appear to be a rather subtle difference; however, you will come to appreciate the implications are profound.
4. **Judgment Step**—Evaluate the alternative concepts based upon their merits. Miles regarded this as a rather straightforward step, and the assumption was that basic common sense be used to select the best ideas for additional development.
5. **Development Planning Step**—Develop the alternative concepts into detailed recommendations. Also included with this step was the implementation of the alternative concepts into the project.

Miles' VM Job Plan

Fig. 3-2

How does the VM approach to problem solving differ from that of the scientific method? There are several important differences that merit further discussion. These differences are best introduced by quotes attributed to Albert Einstein (1879-1955), one of history's greatest thinkers and scientists.

"The significant problems we have cannot be solved at the same level of thinking with which we created them."

The scientific method first states the problem and then gathers pertinent data. The Job Plan states the problem, gathers data and then defines the *functions*. This is an essential difference in understanding the problem. The process of breaking problems down into functions does this very thing by broadening the level of abstraction involved in order to solve the problem at the most appropriate level.

"Imagination is more important than knowledge . . ."

The scientific method develops a hypothesis (solution), or in some cases multiple working hypotheses. The Job Plan dedicates an entire step to the creation of ideas that will address the *functions*. There is a deliberate separation of creativity (imagination) and judgment (knowledge and experience). This separation is essential if our imagination is to be fully realized.

Since the creation of the original Job Plan, a multitude of variations have been developed to address the specific needs and requirements of individuals and organizations applying VM. This proliferation not withstanding, these five basic steps as conceived by Miles continue to serve as the foundation for all of these, and any Job Plan that does not include them, and in the same relative order, is not properly applying the Value Methodology.

The Job Plan that is being presented in this text consists of eight phases. The phases include the five original steps identified by Miles in the same relative order. Some of these have been divided into sub-phases and most have been renamed to add clarity to the Job Plan. The eight phases of the Job Plan include:

- Preparation
- Information
- Function
- Speculation
- Evaluation
- Development
- Presentation
- Implementation

The Job Plan is graphically illustrated *(Fig. 3-3)*. Typically, the Preparation Phase is performed before the value study, and the Implementation Phase is performed after the value study. A detailed discussion of each of the phases in the Job Plan is provided in the chapters that follow. Provided below is a brief introduction of each phase that includes a description of the objectives sought and considerations relevant to each phase.

PREPARATION

Thorough preparation is critical to the success of any value study. The first part of this preparation is identifying what project is to be studied and when it is to be studied. A variety of techniques may be employed to select the best projects for study and identify the proper timing for the value study with respect to the project's life cycle.

A basic level of understanding is provided by gathering and reviewing the appropriate information before starting a study. Depending upon the type of study, the information required will vary slightly. However, in all studies the project's need and purpose and performance attributes and requirements must be understood, specific goals defined, and current costs gathered and organized.

One of the key steps in meeting these requirements is conducting a pre-study meeting to organize and plan for the value study. This meeting typically includes the value specialist, the project manager, project team, stakeholders, and in some cases the rest of the value team. This meeting will result in a well-defined value study and will identify goals, objectives, assumptions and constraints.

INFORMATION

The primary objective of the Information Phase is to obtain a thorough understanding of the project under study. The information gathered prior to and during the study is reviewed and discussed by the team. Typically, the project team and/or project manager will present the current project status to the value team and answer their questions. Key considerations:

- ♦ The matter of human relations is very important to the success of any value study. "People problems" are usually more difficult to resolve than technical problems. The effectiveness of a value specialist's efforts depends upon the amount of cooperation he or she is able to obtain from the project development team, customers, stakeholders, etc.
- ♦ All pertinent facts concerning the project must be uncovered and drawn together, including customer and owner requirements, the history of the project and its development, cost and performance requirements. All aspects of the project must be questioned and examined: How it is produced, shipped, installed, repaired, maintained, replaced, operated, and what materials are used in its manufacture. It is often helpful if the item can be observed in actual operation. The main considerations are getting all the facts, and getting them from the best sources.

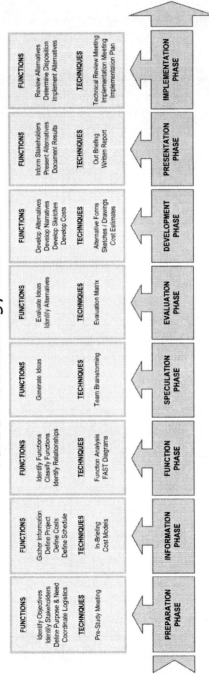

Fig. 3-3

♦ All relevant information is important, regardless of how disorganized or unrelated it may seem when gathered. After gathering all available information, organize the facts. Obtain copies of all important documents. The more information brought to bear on the problem, the more likely the possibility of a successful and productive value study. Lack of total and complete information should not preclude the performance of the VM effort, because more information will become available as the study progresses.

FUNCTION

Function Analysis is the heart of the Value Methodology. The ultimate objective of the Function Phase is to identify functions that are not providing good value and those that are unnecessary. There are three steps in Function Analysis:

♦ Define the functions occurring in the project and categorize the type of functions. All the functions of the project must be determined, and the basic function(s) identified. In order to proceed with the study through the subsequent phases, it is required that the basic function be defined at this time.

♦ Classify the functions into a Function Analysis System Technique (FAST) diagram. The FAST diagram shows how the functions relate to each other and provides the team with a visual image of these function relationships.

♦ Evaluate the functions by developing relationships between cost, performance and function by assigning part or process costs and performance attributes to the various functions. Through this process, the team can analyze which functions have excessive cost and do not provide good value to the customer. An alternative is to estimate worth (lowest cost to perform the function) to each function and analyze the function/worth ratios.

In a typical project, several functions usually stand out as requiring improvement, either from the cost/performance/function relationships that were developed, or through the identification of a function(s) as a root cause of a performance problem.

SPECULATION

In the Speculation Phase of the Job Plan, a creative session is conducted for each function identified as needing improvement during the Function Phase. During these creative sessions, any idea that can be associated with that function is recorded so it may be evaluated later. Typically, brainstorming techniques are used to identify numerous ideas on each function requiring improvement. Generating a large *quantity* of ideas is the goal, rather than the *quality* of the ideas. A large quantity of ideas will lead to a greater number of quality ideas. A key element of creativity is to avoid evaluating the ideas during the creative process.

Speculation should not begin until the problem is thoroughly understood and the specific time for speculation has arrived. Only when the required function has been defined and evaluated should speculation begin. A variety of creative techniques can be employed to stimulate the value team's imagination. Team brainstorming is typically used to initiate the creative process. It is the role of the value specialist to act as coach during the Speculation Phase. All members of the value team must be encouraged to participate. A high level of participation will serve to motivate and energize the creative process. Every attempt should be made during this phase to depart from the "usual" or conventional way of doing things. Experience had shown that it is often the new, fresh and radically different approach that uncovers the best value solution. The focus should first be on the developing ways of performing the function, and second on ways to improve the performance of the function.

EVALUATION

The objective of the Evaluation Phase is to reduce the large quantity of ideas generated in the Speculation Phase to a few high quality ideas through the evaluation process. The value team will discuss and evaluate each idea relative to the project's performance attributes and cost. This process identifies the major advantages and disadvantages of each idea and how it would impact project performance. Once this is done, the team agrees on a rating for the idea. This serves as a filter, and the better ideas are generally taken to the next step and developed further.

Frequently, several ideas or a combination of ideas that compete with one another remain. When this occurs, an evaluation matrix is used that better quantifies the impact of the competing ideas to identify which will best meet the project's need and purpose, performance and cost objectives. Key considerations include:

- Spend project money as you would your own. This is an important rule of thumb when considering the cost of implementing an idea.
- Evaluate the ideas relative to project performance attributes. How will the idea effect project performance relative to need and purpose?
- Compare the advantages and disadvantages of each idea relative to the baseline project.
- Once the three previous steps have been taken in evaluating each idea, rank the ideas based upon their overall merits.

- Refine ideas that may be otherwise rejected. Oftentimes additional team brainstorming can develop a "fix" to a problem that arises during idea evaluation. It is useful to think of the Speculation and Evaluation Phases as cyclical in nature. The surviving alternates are then refined and more cost information is obtained. Detailed estimates are prepared for only the more promising alternates.
- Select ideas for further development. Ideas with the greatest value improvement potential are normally chosen to be developed with further study, testing, refinement and information gathering. If there is more than one idea addressing a specific function that is outstanding, or the differences between two or more ideas are not clear enough to eliminate any of them, then all should be retained and carried over into the next phase.

DEVELOPMENT

Depending upon the type of study, the Development Phase may be completed as part of the study or as follow-up to the study. The objective of this phase is to develop the concepts identified during the Evaluation Phase into specific value alternatives that have been technically validated. The impact of each value alternative should also be quantified as much as possible. Before presenting the recommendations, it is necessary to establish an action plan to organize the team's efforts. Some of the work is performed by individual team members and some by the team as a whole. The action plan should identify the work that needs to be done on each concept to resolve any unanswered questions and confirm that the concept should be formulated into a recommendation. With a good action plan in hand, the team can then finalize and develop each recommendation. Key considerations:

- Are the customer's or user's performance requirements being met?
- Do the cost estimates include all costs of implementation and testing, and are all costs accurate? Are the costs accurate and representative for the project?
- Have schedules for implementation and testing been considered?
- The best ideas in the world will not be accepted unless reasons are provided for accepting them. Prepare all pertinent technical and cost information and list all the advantages and the disadvantages of each alternative concept.
- Provide graphical information relevant to the value alternative if possible. Prepare value alternatives for testing and implementation. Determine what changes will be required in existing schedules, drawings, specifications or contracts. Make sure all the pertinent information is reviewed that might change the value alternative.
- If multiple value alternatives have been developed that address the same issues, the value team should select the one alternative they feel is best for implementation. Others may be prepared in the event the first choice is not accepted by the approval authority.
- Ensure that the value alternative has been fully documented and is presented in a format that will enable decision makers to clearly understand all relevant information. This information should include:

    o   A brief summary of the project and/or project element, including a narrative description of the baseline and alternative concepts.

- Graphical information such as design drawings, diagrams, sketches or process flow charts.
- The estimated cost of the baseline and alternative concepts, including life cycle and implementation costs.
- A description of the impact the value alternative will have on project performance.
- Technical data supporting the value alternative.
- Actions necessary for implementation of the value alternative.
- A suggested implementation schedule.

PRESENTATION

A final report containing the value team's alternatives and a presentation to the project team concludes the value study. The objective is to inform the owner, project team, stakeholders and the customer or user of the value team's findings. This initial presentation should not be advertised as a decision meeting—the decision making process should occur in the following phase, Implementation. The value team typically provides the written report after the presentation.

- ♦ The presentation of the value alternatives, both written and oral, must gain the cooperation of the decision makers and their advisors. It is therefore important that the value alternatives be made in as clear and concise a manner as possible. This will help separate technical objections from emotional ones when it later comes time to make decisions regarding the acceptability of the value alternatives.
- ♦ Use specifics and avoid generalities where possible. If one exception can be found to a generality, this exception can be used to defeat the entire value alternative, even if the exception does not bear directly on the problem. Present facts and be prepared to support them.

- Both the written and oral presentations will draw the attention of people who do not have time to waste. Make sure all the required facts are presented in a concise manner, and then stop.
- Conducting an oral presentation is most helpful when presenting the proposal to the project team. The value team can elaborate on those points which are not clear to the listeners, and questions regarding the value alternatives can be answered on the spot.
- The value team must be diplomatic in the presentation of its alternatives. Often times, members of the project team may feel threatened by the value team's findings. Care must be given to respect the work that has gone before and the constraints under which the project team may have been working. Change is not always easy to accept.

IMPLEMENTATION

The implementation activities are critical to the ultimate success of the Job Plan. During this phase, the project team and the decision makers will review and assimilate the data given to them in the Presentation Phase. An implementation meeting should be conducted once sufficient time has passed to review the value team's findings. The purpose of this meeting is to make a determination regarding the disposition of each of the alternative concepts. Ideally, the value team will be present to provide clarifications and assistance to the decision makers. Alternatives that are accepted will require the development of an implementation plan and schedule for integration into the project. Those alternatives that are rejected should have the reasons for their rejection documented.

Tracking the implementation of value alternatives and auditing the results measures the effectiveness of the VM effort. The project should have some kind of mechanism put in place that will allow the changes to the project's scope, schedule and cost to be managed.

VALUE METRICS

Value Metrics was originally developed as a means to measure the effect of value studies on project performance for the State of California's Department of Transportation, where it was first called the *"Performance Measures Process."* This process was later expanded and refined as a means of measuring value. *Value Metrics* is an extremely useful group of techniques that establish a means for the measurement of a project's cost and performance as it relates to value improvement. *Value Metrics* uses the equation for *functional value,* as discussed in *Chapter 2—Value,* as the basis for measuring value improvement.

As discussed earlier in this chapter, the quantification of cost is relatively straightforward. The quantification of performance is not. There are several reasons for this:

- Performance varies for each product, process and facility
- Performance is often subjective in nature
- Performance standards often do not exist for the project beyond schedule

Value Metrics provides a standardized means of identifying, defining, evaluating, and measuring performance. Once this has been achieved, and the costs for all value alternatives have been developed, it is a relatively simple matter of measuring value.

Value Metrics is a complementary system of concepts and techniques developed to augment the traditional Value Methodology Job Plan. It is not absolutely essential that *Value Metrics* be utilized in order to perform a value study; however, it is well worth the additional effort, as there are a number of significant benefits that it can convey. *Value Metrics* can improve value studies by:

- Building consensus among project stakeholders (especially those holding conflicting views)
- Developing a better understanding of a project's goals and objectives as they relate to Purpose and Need
- Developing a baseline understanding of how the project is meeting performance goals and objectives
- Identifying areas where project performance can be improved through the VM process
- Developing a better understanding of an alternative concept's effect on project performance
- Developing a deeper understanding of the relationship between performance and cost in determining value
- Using value as the basis for selecting the best project or design concept

The concepts and techniques of *Value Metrics* will be introduced in conjunction with each of the subsequent chapters that deal with each specific phase of the Job Plan. The steps include:

- Define performance attributes and requirements—Preparation Phase
- Identify and measure project performance—Information Phase
- Analyze performance—Function Phase
- Stimulate creativity—Speculation Phase
- Enhance evaluation—Evaluation Phase
- Assess performance—Development Phase
- Assess value—Presentation Phase
- Improve decision—Implementation Phase

A summary of each of these complementary steps is provided in *Figure 3-4*, which shows the relation of *Value Metrics* to the traditional Value Methodology Job Plan.

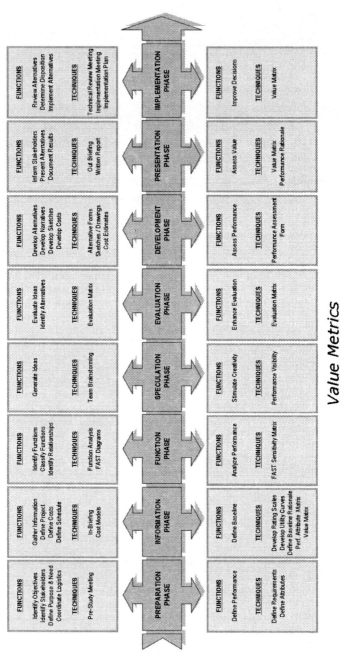

Figure 3-4

SUMMARY

The VM Job Plan provides a vehicle to carry a value study from inception to conclusion. It assures that proper consideration has been given to all necessary facets of the study. The Job Plan divides the study into sets of work elements. The Job Plan requires those performing the value study to clearly define the functions of the project or project element to be studied and provides the value team with a plan for obtaining all the information needed for the study. The Job Plan affords the value team time for creative work and analysis of alternates. This leads the team to the selection of the best value alternatives. The Job Plan concludes with a presentation of specific recommendations to project stakeholders, a proposed implementation schedule, and a summary of benefits.

---

[1] Miles, Lawrence D., (1972) "Techniques of Value Analysis and Engineering," McGraw Hill, New York (pgs. 53-59)

Chapter 4 — Preparation

Vince Lombardi—Professional Football Coach

They call it coaching but it is teaching. You do not just tell them . . . you show them the reasons.

—Vince Lombardi

The harder you work, the harder it is to surrender.

—Vince Lombardi

Vincent Thomas Lombardi was born on June 11, 1913, in Brooklyn, New York. He was the first of Henry and Matilda Lombardi's five children. Vince was raised in the Catholic faith and studied the priesthood for two years before transferring to St. Francis Preparatory High School, where he was a star fullback on the football team. After playing college football at Fordham University, Lombardi took a job as a high school teacher and coach. Later, he returned to his alma mater where he coached the football team. A few years later, he was hired as the defensive line coach at the West Point Military Academy. In 1954, he was hired by the New York Giants as an assistant coach. In three years, he helped bring the Giants from a losing record to become the champions of the National Football League.

In 1958, Lombardi received his first head coach position with the Green Bay Packers. Prior to this time, the Packers had established a reputation as perpetual losers. In 1967, after nine phenomenal winning seasons with the Packers, Lombardi decided to retire as head coach (though he would still act as general manager). The Packers had dominated professional football under his direction, collecting six division titles, five NFL championships, two Super Bowls (I and II) and acquiring a record of 98-30-4. They had become the yardstick against which all other teams were compared.

Compared to offenses in the 21st Century, Lombardi's offense was basic and methodical. Its most famous play is now often referred to as the 'Lombardi sweep' or the 'Packers sweep,' and consisted of the tailback following pulling guards to either side of the field. Lombardi was famous for his pursuit of perfection, often dedicating long hours of film or practice to study just one element of one play.

Lombardi was also known as an innovator. In 1967, at a cost of $80,000, Lombardi had heating coils installed beneath the turf of frigid Green Bay's Lambeau Field in order to keep it from freezing in the winter months. During the 1967 NFL Championship, better known as the 'Ice Bowl' due to the sub-zero temperatures under which the game was played, the system failed. However, some suggest Lombardi actually turned it off intentionally. Regardless, Lombardi's heating grid lasted until 1997, when the Packers replaced it with the current system, which contains more than 30 miles of radiant heating pipe, to maintain a root-zone temperature of 70-plus degrees.

After less than a year after retiring, however, Lombardi realized that he still wanted to coach. He accepted the head coaching position for the Washington Redskins in 1969. During that season, he kept what had become the Lombardi tradition and led the Redskins to their first winning record in 14 years. In January of 1970, his professional coaching record stood at a remarkable 105-35-6, unmarred by a losing season, and the NFL named him their acclaimed "1960s Man of the Decade."

The hallmark of Vince Lombardi's success was his discipline and slavish attention to preparation. The time spent off the field, mentally and physically preparing his team to win, was where he won the game. Vince Lombardi's story is instructive in introducing the first phase of the VM Job Plan, the Preparation Phase.

PREPARATION PHASE

Regardless of whether we are looking at a large, multi-story building or a small manufactured item composed of various parts, the general impression is one of complexity. Humanity has succeeded in creating increasingly complex and complicated structures and products which (it is hoped) will improve the quality of life. Thus, when starting a value study, the value specialist is immediately confronted with the task of separating a distressingly complicated entity into subsystems, selecting certain items for study and ignoring others. Time and labor limitations do not permit everything to be studied; he or she must become skilled in rapidly identifying items that have a high potential for improvement. This chapter provides guidelines on how to select, schedule, and prepare for a value study.

The Preparation Phase includes the following steps:

- Identify projects for value study
- Identify timing of value study
- Conduct pre-study meeting

Each of these steps is detailed further in this chapter and addresses the questions of what project, or parts of a project, will be studied; when in the project's life cycle it will be studied; and how the value study will be organized and executed.

IDENTIFY PROJECTS FOR VALUE STUDY

Identifying the right project or parts of a project (if it is of substantial size, cost or complexity) is the first challenge in preparing for a value study. In most cases, the need for a value study on a specific project will be obvious.

In large organizations where there are either limited funds to conduct value studies or simply too many potential projects to choose from, it may be necessary to give careful consideration in selecting those projects that will offer the greatest return on investment.

In the situations described above, a program to stimulate generation of items for value studies is essential, particularly during the early stages of a VM program. As personnel become more familiar with VM and its benefits it will be found that generation of good study areas becomes automatic, making formal methods of generation less essential. The following techniques may be used:

- *Cost Models*—An excellent source available to owners with continuing requirements for construction is statistical cost analysis. Summaries of construction component cost are developed and continuously updated, based on information obtained on an organization-wide reporting system. Large design organizations also gather and maintain such data, based on a continual review of bid prices and the materials market. An array of these costs provides comparative data in the form of a cost model for each type of facility. The cost model, applied to a meaningful population of comparative costs, will enable management to identify high cost areas. These areas may be earmarked for value study. Cost modeling is discussed in greater detail in *Chapter 5—Information*.
- *Publicizing the Need*—The value manager should explain to the organization what types of studies are wanted and the basis for selection. An invitation to all personnel to submit suggested projects and items to the value manager usually gives good results.
- *Quotas and Project Generation Teams*—Periodically issuing instructions to internal offices to submit a given number of items for study by a specific date can result in a healthy number of projects. The appointment of a

team of about four persons to brainstorm an assigned design for high value study potential usually results in numerous worthwhile items for study.

- *Standing VM Committee*—A committee of top personnel which meets periodically for selection of items or areas will produce a good list of candidate studies. Studies originating from these sources have a better-than-average chance of implementation because they will have been selected by persons who are also the decision makers.
- *Functional Efficiency Summaries*—In this procedure, the primary function of the project is identified. The area devoted to this function is then compared with the total area of the structure. The efficiency of the design is the primary function area divided by the total area.
- *Design-to-Cost Targeting*—A cost model that establishes cost targets for each element of the project will readily show which ones exceed the budget. This information can be determined at any stage of design and can serve as a warning to the value specialist to concentrate his effort on these items.
- *Pareto Analysis*—The Italian economist Vilfredo Pareto (1848-1923), developed the curve known as Pareto's law of distribution. This curve has general application to all areas where a significant number of elements are involved. It points out that, in any area, a small number of elements (20%) contains the greater percentage of costs (80%). Similarly, a small number of elements will contain the greater percentage of unnecessary costs. Thus, if costs of each element are arrayed, with the most costly items at the

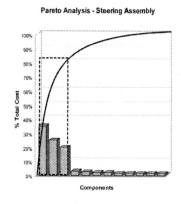

Fig. 4-1

head of the list and the less costly following in order, it will enable the value specialist to concentrate on the relatively few components which contribute most to total cost *(Fig. 4-1)*.

- *FAST Diagrams*—Functional Analysis Systems Technique diagrams give a graphic portrayal of the interrelationship of the functions of any item, assembly or project. On projects that are massive in scale, such as mass transit projects or complex manufactured items such as vehicles, FAST diagrams are useful for revealing key functional areas on which value studies can focus. They permit the analyst to see where simplifications can be achieved. FAST diagrams are covered in detail in *Chapter 6—Function*.
- *Spatial Cost Analysis*—This method assumes that area or volumetric costs (i.e., square feet, cubic meters, etc.) is a direct index of design efficiency. This method is particularly applicable to construction applications. A design having a high cost per square foot would be considered less efficient than one with a lower unit cost. This is not necessarily true and must be applied with caution. For example, a poorly designed building with lots of wasted space might spread the cost of expensive areas such as toilets, kitchens, mechanical, and electrical spaces over a large area, thereby lowering the per square foot cost. On the other hand, in an efficiently planned building with a minimum of wasted space, the cost per square foot will be higher, although the cost will be less. Similarly, the enclosure method of estimating compares the cost per square foot of the original design with unit costs of alternatives on a basis of total surfaces enclosed. "Enclosure," as used here, means any surface such as floors, walls, partitions, roof, columns, piers, stairs, railings and similar items. Thus the cost of the alternative design which has, let us say, 25% less surface area in the form of fewer partitions, etc., would be assumed to cost 25% less. This method can be used to

determine quickly the probable cost of alternatives early in the value process.

Value Indicators

Each system and subsystem must be examined to identify high-cost elements, which then become prime candidates for study. For each such item, the following questions will provide further guidance:

- Is the item expensive? Remember that Pareto's Law states that 80% of the cost of an item is contained in 20% of its components.
- Is it complex?
- Is it a high-volume item? Can a simple change in one item produce large savings in the total project?
- Does it use critical materials?
- Is it difficult to construct?
- Does it have high maintenance and operations costs?
- Does it require specialized skills to create?
- Does it use obsolete materials and methods?
- Are costs simply "out of line"?
- Was the design rushed?
- Have there been problems experienced in the past use of a particular item?
- Is it a state-of-the-art component with low proven acceptance?
- Are life cycle costs unacceptable?
- Does it contain redundant safeguards?
- Does it create an unwanted function of high future cost?
- Does it use traditional design?
- Is the competition producing the item at a lower cost?
- Does top management want improvement?

IDENTIFY TIMING OF VALUE STUDY

It is the responsibility of the project manager or, ideally the value program manager, to ensure that the studies of each project are scheduled at the right time. This requires awareness by all management and project development personnel of the benefits that can be achieved through the VM process and the necessity to incorporate them into all phases of project development. Too often, projects are well advanced before value studies are made. This must not be allowed to happen, and it is the value program manager's responsibility to ensure that all projects are considered for a share of the available VM effort.

When should VM be applied to a project? Theoretically, VM can be applied at any time during a project's life cycle, from conception to completion and eventual replacement. More practically, VM should be applied at specific phases of a project's development in order to achieve maximum results.

Project Planning Phase

The first application of the VM effort should be made during the project planning stage. This is the stage where maximum flexibility exists to make changes without incurring undue expense for redesign. As the project development progresses, the cost to make changes increases until finally a point-of-no-return is reached, where the potential benefits are swallowed up in the cost of redesigning, reordering, and rescheduling.

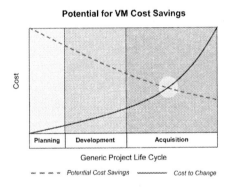

Fig. 4-2

This is shown in (Fig. 4-2). Early in the concept phase a budgetary estimate is produced which defines goals, requirements and applicable criteria. The owner establishes most of this input and makes it available to the project development team. The project development team, in turn, establishes broad objectives and a price framework, which become the budgetary estimate. Studies have shown that it is the project team who has by far the largest impact on the total life cycle cost of a project. The owner, too, has a significant impact on costs by establishing requirements which become the basis for the project development team's efforts. Between them, the owner and the project team will establish roughly 70% of the total life cycle cost of the project by the end of the project planning stage. Thus it is apparent that a VM analysis made during the planning stage has a tremendous potential for improving performance and reducing costs. At this stage of project, the VM effort can assist the owner to establish his true requirements. This requires a complete understanding of the basic function to be performed by the project. Dialogue between the value specialist, the owner, and the project team must be searching and in depth, for VM takes nothing for granted, questions everything, and insists on justification of all requirements. This should be welcomed by the project team, as it assists it in understanding the owner's true requirements and eliminates ambiguities.

Project Development Phases

As project development advances from the conceptual stages through the final development stages, the VM effort should keep pace. Preferably, the value specialist should accompany each project milestone in order to provide continuous guidance to the project team and ensure that value judgments are brought to the attention of the owner for decision. As a minimum, VM analysis should be performed early in the design development stages and accompany the preliminary milestones. At this point, project development decisions have been made which permit a reasonable degree of exactitude in determining cost of systems. Additional VM studies can profitably be performed as late as the final development phase, although the elements that can be changed without inordinate delays and costly redesign expenses will be limited.

Acquisition Phase

The VM effort can also be applied during the acquisition phase (production, construction or implementation) of the product. This arises from two possible situations: When an item has been identified by an earlier VM study, which needs further investigation before a decision is made; and when the contractor, manufacturer or vendor identifies areas which he or she feels can be improved. The first situation may arise when, for example, an item has been identified by the VM effort during the preliminary project development phase, but which requires testing or research prior to decision. Even after the delay inherent in such a process, it may be profitable to pursue it when the potential savings and improvement are of significant magnitude. Value Incentive Clauses provide a means for sharing cost savings between the contractors and owners.

The application of VM during the construction of new facilities is standard practice among major public agencies, including the U.S. Army Corps of Engineers. Contractors are provided incentives to identify and develop proposals to reduce costs and/or improve performance after the construction contract is awarded. This can also be used in manufacturing applications where components of an assembly are sub-contracted out to vendors or other companies for production. In this case, vendors and sub-contractors receive a cash incentive to develop innovations that will reduce cost and/or increase performance.

A great many variations of VM contract provisions are in current use, but there are only two basic types. They are commonly known as the Value Incentive Clause and the Value Program Requirements Clause.

Value Incentive Clause

The method normally used for soliciting the contractor or vendor input is the value incentive clause. This general provision to construction and production contracts solicits the contractor's or vendor's proposals for change through an instrument known as a value change proposal (VCP—traditionally referred to as Value Engineering Change Proposals, or VECPs). It calls for the owner and contractor to share the savings resulting from any approved and implemented VCP. The usual savings sharing rate is 50:50; however, this may be varied in the contract provisions as desired. An acceptable VCP must meet two tests: it must require a change in some contract provision, and it must reduce the contract price. A complete VCP should contain information similar to that of a value alternative, as discussed in *Chapter 9—Development*.

Program Requirements Clause

This type of clause requires the contractor to perform value studies to a specified level, for which he is paid by the owner as a separate item of work under the contract. Clauses with program requirement provisions may also permit incentive sharing for individual proposals, but the contractor's proportion of the savings is considerably smaller than under an incentive provision.

The principle reason for the program requirement approach is to ensure that potential innovations are continuously considered, beginning with the initial project development stages. This type of clause has not been used, at least to any significant degree, in construction contracts. It is more appropriate for research and development and supply contracts, and it has been very successful in these applications. In a comparatively recent construction-related innovation, however, agencies such as the U.S. Army Corps of Engineers, the Environmental Protection Agency, and the General Services

Administration have established modified value program requirements for architect-engineer and construction manager contracts for major facilities.

CONDUCT PRE-STUDY MEETING

Getting off on the right foot on a value study is akin to starting a new job. Laying out the responsibilities of each participant will lead to a well-coordinated effort. This can best be handled in an orientation meeting with the owner, the project team, and the value specialist who will be facilitating the study. At this meeting, the value specialist should outline the entire Value Methodology process. It is important to remember that, in many cases, this will be the project team's and the owner's first exposure to Value Methodology. The project team may be perplexed, realizing that the value specialist is evaluating the project. There will be many underlying fears and questions that should be addressed in this session.

The following is a list of steps that should be included in having a successful pre-study meeting:

- Collect project information
- Identify project scope, schedule and cost
- Identify performance attributes and requirements—*Value Metrics*
- Establish value study objectives and goals
- Define value study scope
- Identify value study participants
- Define value study schedule
- Organize value study logistics

Collect Project Information

It is important to have necessary data available prior to commencement of the value study, in order to conserve time and effort. These data are normally procured by the value specialist and given to the value team members for review prior to the first team meeting. The following are required for a typical value study:

- A clear description of the project's intended purpose and need.
- Project work breakdown structure and scheduling information.
- Up-to-date project scope information (i.e., project reports, design drawings, flow charts, etc.), as it exists at the time the value study is undertaken.
- Specifications, and any applicable codes, regulations, owner guidance, and technical requirements.
- Cost figures, including budgets, unit costs, design-to-cost targets, and latest estimates.
- Special information such as historical data, status of design, schedules, user requirements, etc.
- Persons to be consulted for information, guidance and approval.
- Anticipated volume or repetition of use of the project's output.

Identify Project Scope, Schedule and Cost

The information identified above will provide the value specialist with specific details relevant to the project's scope, schedule and cost. Value Methodology should begin at this fundamental level.

Most projects include a "scope statement" or "need and purpose statement" as a standard element within the project development process. A scope statement should include the following elements:

- **Project Justification or Need**—a narrative describing the need that the project was undertaken to address.
- **Project's Product or Purpose**—a narrative describing the product that the project was undertaken to create.
- **Project Deliverables**—a list and description of the project's outputs (i.e., design drawings, specifications, reports, prototypes, etc.)

- **Project Objectives**—a list and description of quantifiable criteria that must be met for the project to be considered successful. This usually includes cost, schedule and qualitative measures.

A well-written scope statement should serve as the foundation upon which a project is based. Despite their fundamental nature, scope statements are frequently taken for granted and are often poorly prepared. This can lead to serious problems as the project is developed, most of which can be linked to disagreements between stakeholders possessing differing perspectives. The reconciliation of the differences becomes increasingly difficult as the project progresses. The following is an excerpt from a Federal Highway Administration Memorandum concerning this issue.

> *The Project Development Branch (HEV-11) in its review of environmental impact statements has noted a systematic deficiency in the purpose and need section. In our view this deficiency is particularly critical because it helps define what alternatives must be evaluated and, in some cases, selected in order to comply with the myriad of Federal environmental laws, Executive Orders, and regulations.*[1]

The realization of this problem for projects within the sphere of design and construction has been addressed through refinements to the way in which VM is applied. The U.S. Navy's Naval Facilities Engineering Command developed the Function Analysis Concept Design (FACD) as a way to validate project scope through the application of function analysis at the earliest stages of the design process. This specific application of VM will be discussed further in a future text.

The value specialist should begin preparations for a value study with a similar notion of using Function Analysis to validate a project's scope. Function Analysis provides us with a powerful technique for developing a better understanding of wants and needs through the identification, classification and organization of functions. Identifying the project's basic and required secondary functions is really all that is needed at the beginning. Please refer to *Chapter 5—Function,* for a comprehensive discussion of functions.

Define Performance Attributes and Requirements— *Value Metrics*

Once the basic functions and requirements are understood and agreed upon relative to project scope, the next step is to begin the process of defining performance. Performance—or to use project management terminology, project objectives—can be divided into two categories: attributes and requirements. The term "attributes" is used to describe performance characteristics that can possess a range of values, while "requirements" are decidedly absolute in nature. Attributes are flexible; requirements are not. A potential solution that does not satisfy a performance requirement cannot be considered. A performance attribute can be further defined by establishing a range of acceptable parameters. Both performance attributes and requirements should be identified at this early stage of the VM job plan.

The value team will need to have a clear understanding of both the performance attributes and requirements before moving into the subsequent phases of the VM job plan. Performance attributes need to be discretely defined and must not overlap in meaning. Parameters defining the lower and upper range of desired performance should be included as well. Performance requirements should be similarly defined, but more finitely relevant to the actual value of the requirement. The value specialist should lead this discussion with the project's stakeholders during the pre-study meeting, preferably in the presence of the value team members. Only those attributes identified as most critical in meeting the project's purpose and need should be included. For most projects, 4 to 8 performance attributes are usually all that are necessary to do this. The number of performance requirements, however, can vary widely. In the example below, a performance attribute and a performance requirement have been identified (Fig. 4-3).

Performance Attributes vs. Performance Requirements

Performance Attribute	Performance Requirement
Mainline Operations: A measure of the efficiency of traffic operations as they relate directly to the mainline alignment (including on-ramps and off-ramps) based upon a 20-year projected traffic forecast. *Parameters:* Level of Service "A" (Volume/Capacity = 0.0–0.30) to Level of Service "E" (Volume/Capacity = 0.81–0.90) will be considered.	*Seismic Safety:* Any design that does not fully meet current seismic design criteria will not be considered.

Fig. 4-3

Establish Value Study Objectives and Goals

Establishing the goals and objectives of a value study is critical. Value studies may have varying objectives, depending upon the types of issues the project team may be facing. The VM team participants should have a clear understanding of what the study sponsor's VM goals are prior to the commencement of the value study. The goals and objectives could vary dramatically, depending on the state of the project or the reason for performing the value study.

A value study's objectives and goals could be:

- Identify a means to reduce processing time down to 2 weeks.
- Build consensus among stakeholders as to what the project scope should be.
- Improve market share by 5%.
- Get the project back within budget.
- Reduce production costs by 10%.
- Identify methods to reduce litigation risks.
- Reduce manufacturing time by 25%.
- Identify a means to eliminate "poor" customer service ratings.

As these goals and objectives indicate, the Value Methodology can be used in a number of different ways, all of which aim at improving value. The goals and objectives should always relate back to the project's scope, schedule and cost and can be general or specific in nature. Having a clear statement of the value study's goals and objectives will help the value team stay focused on the study sponsor's expectations for the VM effort.

Define Value Study Scope

The scope of the value study should be determined during the Preparation Phase. The value specialist will need to be given guidance from the study sponsor and/or project team. Will the value study consider the entire project or just certain elements? Related to the issue of value study scope is the need to identify the parameters in which the value team can recommend changes to the original project scope. For example, can the value team challenge project objectives, such as design criteria or project delivery milestones? Correctly setting the scope of the value study will help ensure that the value team does not overstep its boundaries or expend valuable time on issues over which they should have no influence.

Projects of all types are generally growing more complex, and time available for development is always limited. Personnel and time available for value studies are also in short supply. In order to maximize benefits of the value study, identified tasks must be matched with available resources (talents, skills, knowledge, and time).

The correlation of resources is often overlooked, yet it is as important as selection of the proper project if maximum return is to be gained. Furthermore, it is not desirable to select items for VM study where it can be anticipated that the net savings will be drastically reduced by the cost of the study itself and the cost of implementation. A yardstick often used is that net savings should be at least $10 for every dollar spent on the VM effort.

Identify Value Study Participants

Once the value specialist has developed a basic understanding of the project, he or she will be in a position to begin identifying the participants for the value study team. Depending upon the value study's budget and the study sponsor's desires, the value team participants may be drawn from a variety of sources:

- Members of the project team
- Project owner or study sponsor's representative
- Customers or users
- External project stakeholders
- Expert technical consultants

Most value study teams include a mix of individuals from these sources. This is desirable because it provides the best cross-section of perspectives on the current project. Members of the project team will be able to contribute their intimate knowledge of the project and its history. Customers or users will be able to provide invaluable information pertaining to how the project's output will be utilized. External project stakeholders can provide important guidance regarding regulatory issues, approval processes and other indirect project impacts that may not otherwise be considered. Expert technical consultants will provide specialized knowledge and will also be able to provide a fresh perspective to the project and its challenges. Although training in Value Methodology is always preferable for value study participants, it is not essential. It will be the job of the value specialist to educate and lead the study team through the VM process.

Another key consideration in selecting value study team members is the technical composition of the team. Ideally, a multi-discipline team will be arrayed, representing expertise from each specialized field of knowledge required to fully develop a project. Selecting a well-balanced technical team will greatly multiply its effectiveness. As the value study team develops alternative concepts, they will need to be able to address technical issues that may arise. Frequently, a new alternative will have unanticipated impacts to other technical areas or even other related projects. Having the right expertise on the team will ensure that these issues can be adequately addressed as they arise. A few examples of value study teams organized for different types of projects are provided on the following page to illustrate the diversity required in achieving the proper balance for value studies *(Fig. 4-4)*.

Examples of Value Study Team Participants

Product Study Fork Lift	Construction Study Highway Improvement Project
❏ Value Specialist (C) ❏ Design Engineer (PDT) ❏ Purchasing Engineer (PDT) ❏ Marketing Representative (PDT) ❏ Accounting Representative (PDT) ❏ Machinist (ES) ❏ Manufacturing Specialist (C) ❏ Vendor Representative (ES) ❏ Retail Sales Representative (U)	❏ Value Specialist (C) ❏ Design Engineer (PDT - State) ❏ Environmental Specialist (PDT - State) ❏ Traffic Engineer (C) ❏ Structural Engineer (C) ❏ Geotechnical Engineer (C) ❏ Construction Specialist (C) ❏ Public Works Engineer (ES - County) ❏ Community Representative (U) ❏ State Police Representative (U)

Process Study City Bulk Mail Handling Procedures	Information Technology Study Applicant Tracking System
❏ Value Specialist (C) ❏ Project Manager (PDT) ❏ HR Dept. Manager (PDT) ❏ Accounting Dept. Manager (PDT) ❏ Contracts Dept. Manager (PDT) ❏ Mail Room Clerk (ES) ❏ Mail Processing Tech. Specialist (C) ❏ U.S. Post Office Representative (U)	❏ Value Specialist (C) ❏ Project Manager (PDT) ❏ Software Developer (PDT) ❏ Systems Analyst (PDT) ❏ Database Administrator (PDT) ❏ Finance Manager (ES) ❏ IT Consultant (C) ❏ Client Representative (U)

(C) – Consultant, (PDT) – Project Development Team, (ES) – External Stakeholder, (U) – User/Customer

Fig. 4-4

Once the participants of the value study team have been identified, the project documents should be given to them for review and study prior to the start of the value study. Each member of the VM team should spend a specified period of time in going through the background information of the project. Usually, 8 to 16 hours per person is allowed for this task, depending on the size and magnitude of the project. Familiarization can be done independently.

Define Value Study Schedule[2]

One of the most important concerns to the design project team will be the schedule for the value study. The value study schedule must fit very closely with the project schedule. Ideally, the value study can be scheduled during a milestone, when the project will be undergoing an interim review or approval period.

Determining the appropriate length for the team portion of the value study should be the first priority in determining the overall value study schedule. For many years there has been a widely perceived notion that a value study should be five days, or 40 hours, long. In fact, the duration of a value study should be based on a number of different factors, including:

- Size and complexity of the project
- Value study goals and objectives
- Value study scope
- Size and expertise of the value team
- Resources available to conduct the study

For a typical five-day value study, the baseline includes time allotments as shown in *Table 4-1*. The shaded area represents those Phases of the Job Plan that occur as a "team" effort.

Five-Day Value Study Model

Job Plan Phase	Number Hours per Study Value Type			
	Construction	Product	Process	Procedure
Preparation	8-24	8-16	20-30	40-60
Information	4-6	2	2	2
Function	4	8-16	8	6
Speculation	4	6	4	4
Evaluation	6-8	16-20	12	8
Development	16	4-8	12	8
Presentation – Oral	4	4	4	4
Presentation – Report	48	80	40	20
Implementation	Times will vary and depend on value study sponsor.			

Table 4-1

Some value practitioners, recognizing the power of the Value Methodology in solving problems, creating new concepts or designs, planning strategies, or streamlining processes or procedures, will require that a longer period of time be devoted to the value study. This may vary from six or eight days to as long as twelve days or more. The longer studies typically require a split schedule and, depending upon the study target, may necessitate a variation in the time allotted to specific VM Job Plan activities.

In some cases, value study sponsors may attempt to limit value studies to three days, or sometimes even shorter periods, without regard for the scope of the study target or the integrity of the Value Methodology Job Plan. Time limitations may result in more enthusiastic participation by the study sponsor's personnel, because they are "losing" less time away from their normal work effort. At the same time, these time constraints require that some portion of the Job Plan be compromised. The Value Methodology Job Plan is often construed to apply only to the formal phases included in the team study: Information, Function, Speculation, Evaluation, Development and Presentation. The Preparation and Implementation Phases, while not always considered formal steps of the VM Job Plan, are integral to the success of any value improvement effort, and are addressed as such in this discussion.

Regardless of the study type, the study target, or the length of the value study, certain pre-study activities must always occur. In addition to project identification, definition of the value study schedule, and team selection, extensive preparation work is required in the form of data collection, cost analysis and models, team information packages, and logistics arrangements. Once the team study is concluded, additional documentation may be required to complete or further refine the developed value alternatives. A complete report is prepared to document the study and results, and implementation actions must occur.

None of the phases and activities associated with the Value Methodology Job Plan (as described in Chapter 3) can be eliminated by reducing the length of a team study; all must occur for every value study, regardless of how long the team sessions last.

Using a construction project as an example, assume the study sponsor has requested a three-day value study. The compressed time is required to maintain the design schedule, the budget to conduct the value study is limited, and the key team members are unable to commit more than three days of time away from their regular responsibilities. *Table 4-2* shows how the hours per phase would differ for a three-day study compared to the 40-Hour Model previously illustrated. The shaded area represents those Phases of the Job Plan that occur as a "team" effort.

There are both advantages and disadvantages associated with the three-day value study approach. While it reduces the value study sponsor's cost for the study, the value team and value specialist are put under tremendous pressure to accomplish a great deal in a short period of time. In order to maintain the integrity of the Job Plan and, at the same time, prevent the activity from being simply a cost reduction exercise, the value specialist's job of keeping the value team focused and on track becomes even more critical than usual. Every phase of the Job Plan is impacted in some way, as listed above. And note that pre-study and post-study time needs to be increased as a result of the compressed team study schedule.

Results of a three-day value study may be limited to mere validation of a project's functional concepts, rather than significant project improvements. Alternatives that are developed are likely to be more conceptual, and less detailed, than value alternatives produced in a longer study and, as a result, may prove more difficult to implement. Most importantly, the results may not be optimized due to the limited time the value team has had to exploit the techniques of the Value Methodology and gain the benefits of team communications and project understanding the techniques offer.

It is possible to have impressive results, which dramatically demonstrate the power of the VM process, even when constrained by a three-day study. However, this scenario represents a double-edged sword, because impressive results only encourage more use of the abbreviated value study approach. Note that a successful value study in a three-day period is highly dependent upon an experienced value specialist and value team.

There are many reasons why a value study might require more than the typical five days. A high profile, controversial project, or multiple funding entities may create specific issues that require more attention by the value team. The project may be over budget, or have other problems associated with its completion. Or it may be a very complex project, which requires a larger team, and has more elements on which to focus.

Three-Day Value Study Model (*Construction Project*)		
Job Plan Phase	Number of Hours	Effect of Reduced Time
Preparation	24-32	More pre-study time required by the value specialist to prepare for the abbreviated value study.
Information	4	Site visit eliminated.
Function	2-3	Less time for team interaction; increased value specialist influence; reduced time for cost/performance/function analysis.
Speculation	2-3	Fewer ides generated; potential loss of significant ideas.
Evaluation	4	Reduced depth of team discussion and analysis of ideas.
Development	8-10	Less detail and potentially less credibility related to value alternatives.
Presentation—Oral	2	Fewer value alternatives to present.
Presentation—Report	64	More time required in report writing to complete development of value alternatives.
Implementation	Times will vary and depend on value study sponsor.	

Table 4-2

So what is to be gained by having more time in which to do a value study? First and foremost, the value team is more intimately involved in the pre-study planning (Preparation Phase), resulting in increased and improved information gathering. Of equal importance, the value team may meet with project stakeholders and decision-makers at the mid-point of the study to validate the direction the team is taking with their value alternative development. And when complex problems are considered, multiple FAST diagrams may be developed.

Obviously a study spanning more than five days requires a split schedule of some sort. There is a significant advantage to having a break of several days between team sessions, as it offers the opportunity for team members to do research and gather additional information needed for development of value alternatives. Too much time between team meetings should be avoided, to reduce the potential for loss of the value team's momentum.

Assuming an eight-day VM Team Study, the breakdown of time spent on each phase of the Job Plan might be as shown in *Table 4-3* below. *Table 4-4* provides an example value study agenda that is six days in length. This example utilizes a schedule split between two weeks.

Disadvantages to the longer study are primarily those associated with time commitments from team members and, depending upon the configuration of the value team, the cost of the value study. It is sometimes more difficult to convince study sponsors that a longer period of time is needed. And as mentioned earlier, too long a break between sessions could negatively affect the value team's momentum.

The true issue is not whether a value study is conducted over three days, or three months. The key is maintaining the integrity of the Value Methodology Job Plan, and making the necessary adjustments in time allotted for all elements of the process, to maximize the results generated. The key is achieving that "fair return" for something exchanged—in this case, time.

Eight-Day Value Study Model *(Construction Project)*		
Job Plan Phase	Number of Hours	Effect of Increased Time
Preparation	32	Includes pre-study meeting
Information	8	Enhanced site visit and discussions with stakeholders.
Function	8	Increased function analysis possible; multiple FAST diagrams can be constructed.
Speculation	4-8	Additional time for creativity; different techniques may be employed.
Evaluation	12-16	Increased evaluation time allows more thoughtful consideration of ideas.
Development	24-28	More credible, well-developed value alternatives.
Presentation—Oral	4	Increased number of value alternatives to present.
Presentation—Report	72	More time required in report writing due to greater number of value alternatives developed.
Implementation	*Times will vary and depend on value study sponsor.*	

Table 4-3

Organize Value Study Logistics

The value specialist should prepare a contact list identifying the roles the various participants will play. This list should include everyone that will be involved in the value effort, including all meeting participants. Names, addresses, phone numbers and e-mail addresses should be included. This list should be distributed to all participants in addition to the value study's objectives, scope and schedule.

Value Study Agenda
Highway Improvement Project

Tuesday, May 18

	Kick-Off Meeting
8:00-8:15	Introductions (All) and Brief Overview of the VM Process (Value Specialist)
8:15-9:30	Project Overview (Project Manager and Project Development Team)
9:30-10:30	Stakeholder Issues, Function Identification, Performance Attribute Identification
	Conclusion of Kick-Off Meeting
10:30-2:00	Site Visit (including 1 hour for lunch)
2:00-3:00	Review/Modification of Cost Estimate
3:00-5:00	Function Analysis/FAST Diagram

Wednesday, May 19

8:00-8:30	Recap of First Day/Additional Information Review
8:30-12:00	Team Brainstorming
12:00-1:00	Lunch
1:00-5:00	Team Brainstorming

Thursday, May 20

8:00-12:00	Evaluation of Ideas
12:00-1:00	Lunch
1:00-4:00	Evaluation of Ideas
4:00-4:30	Assignments of Ideas to Team for Development
4:30-5:00	Review Alternative Development Process

Tuesday, May 25

8:00-9:00	Review/Distribution of Handouts and VM Alternative Forms
9:00-12:00	Alternative Development
12:00-1:00	Lunch
1:00-4:30	Alternative Development

Wednesday, May 26

8:00-12:00	Alternative Development
12:00-1:00	Lunch
1:30-3:30	*Review of VM Alternatives Meeting (Technical Reviewers)*
3:30-4:30	Finalize Team Review of VM Alternatives

Thursday, May 27

8:00-12:00	Group Review and Ranking of VM Alternatives/Sets
8:00-12:00	Presentation Preparation
12:00-1:00	Lunch
1:30-3:30	*Presentation of VM Alternatives Meeting* **(Presentation of VM Study Results to Management and Stakeholders)**

Table 4-4

If a site visit will be included as part of the value study, it will be necessary to coordinate transportation arrangements with the project manager. The value specialist should have the project manager identify key areas to focus on at the site, in order to maximize the time spent out in the field. Ensure that the schedule includes enough time to travel from the location of the value study to the project site and back.

The logistics of a value study should be made with consideration to the overall project. Keep in mind that value studies involve intense effort employing a group of people. Therefore, it is helpful to have the study in a place where interruptions are infrequent and the arrangements are comfortable. Studies are frequently conducted in hotel conference rooms or other conference areas that are isolated from the main working stream. Outside calls coming into the team should be restricted.

Other disturbances should also be kept to a minimum. It is also helpful to have facilities with windows that open to the outside. This helps to provide a good working environment. Reproduction machines and other supplies required for the study should also be available. The location of the study may be in the city where the owner or the project team is located or in the offices of the value specialist. If an existing facility is involved, or where unusual site conditions warrant, the study should take place near the site. This gives the team a chance to visually observe the location and surrounding area of the project. In any event, a site visit by the value specialist and one or more of the other team participants is recommended during the VM effort.

THE VALUE TEAM

Once the participants of the value team have been identified, the next step will be to begin the process of teambuilding. Most of the time, the members of the value team will not be familiar with one another. The value team may consist of people from different departments within an organization or they may be consultants. In any case, it is likely that this will be the first time that many of them will have worked together. The value specialist may want to consider utilizing teambuilding exercises to help develop a strong working relationship and to instill the values identified in *Chapter 1—Introduction*.

Teambuilding Exercises

Successful teams must hold common values as described in the preceding paragraphs. However, before these values can be shared, the team members will need to share something about themselves. The way to accomplish this is by employing simple team building exercises that will help break the ice and introduce the team members to one another. It is always quite surprising how much people have in common with one another regardless of what walk of life they come from.

In some cases, the value specialist may want to also consider including individuals outside of the value team such as members of the project team, project stakeholders, and even the customers or users as participants in these teambuilding exercises. The use of teambuilding exercises will vary greatly, depending upon the size of the group and the amount of time available in the value study. Several teambuilding exercises are described below.

- *Acronym Builder*—The business world is full of acronyms. There are GANTT charts, PERT diagrams and SMART goals. The objective of this exercise is to have everyone develop an acronym that relates to their first name. This exercise includes the following steps:

    1. Each team member is asked to write their name vertically on a flip chart, white board or chalkboard.
    2. A word that somehow describes them should be selected for each initial of their name and written horizontally. It may be a bit of a challenge for some, especially those with long first names!

3. Have each team member tape their acronym poster to the wall *(Fig. 4-5)*.

- *Six Degrees of Separation*—This exercise is based on the concept of the John Guare play and movie adaptation, *Six Degrees of Separation*. The play asserts that we are all connected by six or fewer stages of circumstance or acquaintance. This exercise is both interesting and entertaining, and is useful for showing how we are all connected in some way. The exercise consists of the following steps:

    1. First, arrange the team members into pairs. Have the pairs introduce themselves and make a list of 5-10 things that they have in common with each other (i.e., where they went to school, year they were born, number of years with the organization, likes, dislikes, hobbies, etc.)
    2. Once they everyone has completed their first list, have the team members find someone else in the room that also has one of those 5-10 things in common with them. When they have found that person, have them repeat step one and develop a new list with the new person.
    3. Continue to repeat step two until everyone has met five other people or time is called by the facilitator.
    4. When the team members are done, they should let the facilitator know that they have finished. Optionally, a prize can be given to the first person able to complete the exercise.

- *To Tell the Truth*—This exercise is loosely based upon the old game show of the same name. The participants each relate a story to the rest of the team that is based upon an unusual event that occurred in their life. The rub is that the person relating the story has the option of concocting a phony story instead of recounting a true one. The other team members must determine whether they believe it is true or false. This exercise includes the following steps:

1. Each participant should first secretly determine if they will tell a true story or a false story.
2. The participants should then be divided into pairs. Each person will tell their story and then their partner must then guess if it is or true or false. If both guess correctly, they should find another person to tell their story to. If both guess incorrectly, they should also find another person to tell their story to. If one is correct and one incorrect, the incorrect person is out.

Fig. 4-5

3. Move on and repeat the previous two steps until only one person remains and is declared the winner.

Most of these exercises can be completed in a relatively short time, usually between 15 to 30 minutes. It is easy to dismiss these activities as frivolous; however, the very positive effect they can have in developing a better level of familiarity for the participants should not be underestimated. If team members do not feel comfortable about their environment, they will be less likely to trust others. This can act as a significant impediment in getting everyone to freely contribute to the value effort. Take full advantage of any opportunity to foster teambuilding—it will yield excellent dividends.

SUMMARY

Proper preparation is essential to the success of any undertaking. The value specialist must remember that the results of the value study for a project will be closely scrutinized by the very people who originally developed the project. Establishing a strong, early relationship with the project team, customers and other stakeholders will also help inform and mentally prepare these participants, as well as the value study team members, for the Value Methodology process, and help pave the way for managed change.

---

[1] U.S. Dept. of Transportation, FHWA (1990) Memorandum—Purpose and Need in Environmental Documents

[2] Adams, Ginger R. and Hays, R. Terry (1999) "The Value of Time," SAVE International Conference Paper. The content of this section is condensed from this reference.

Chapter 5 — Information

Steve Jobs—Inventor, Entrepreneur

Sometimes when you innovate, you make mistakes. It is best to admit them quickly, and get on with improving your other innovations.
—Steve Jobs

Expose yourself to the best things humans have done and then try to bring those things into what you are doing.
—Steve Jobs

Steven Paul, was an orphan adopted by Paul and Clara Jobs of Mountain View, California in 1955. Jobs was not happy at school in Mountain View so the family moved to Los Altos, California, where Steven attended Homestead High School. His electronics teacher at Homestead High, Hohn McCollum, recalled he was "something of a loner" and "always had a different way of looking at things."[1]

In 1972 Jobs graduated from high school and registered at Reed College in Portland, Oregon. He dropped out of Reed after one semester, but continued to hang around campus for about a year, taking classes in philosophy and immersing himself in the counterculture of the day. Early in 1974 Jobs took a job as a video game designer at Atari, Inc., a pioneer in electronic video games. After meeting a fellow electronics whiz named Stephen Wozniak, the two decided to create a computer of their own.

Jobs and Wozniak managed to scrape together enough money to start a garage-based computer company that was later to be named Apple. Together, they developed the first personal computer called the Apple I. The Apple I changed people's view on the types of operations a computer could perform and their fledgling company grew rapidly as a result.

The subsequent development of the Macintosh facilitated the reintroduced Xerox's innovative idea of a user-friendly interface system that used pointing device called a "mouse." The Macintosh used a type of interface which contained picture-like icons that represented specific functions or programs to be executed that would later be imitated by software giant Microsoft in the form of a program known as Windows.

In 1985, Jobs left Apple to concentrate on the software side of the industry. After founding a new company called NextStep, Jobs developed a revolutionary programming language called object-oriented programming (OOP), which allowed programmers to write complex software programs in a fraction of the usual time. NeXT Software was sold to Apple Computer in February 1997.

Steve Jobs was later Chairman and CEO of Pixar, the Academy-Award-winning computer animation studios which he co-founded in 1986. Pixar's first feature film, Toy Story, was released by Walt Disney Pictures in November 1995 and became the highest domestic grossing film released that year and the third highest grossing animated film of all time.

Steve Jobs, along with pioneers like Bill Gates, ushered in the "Information Age." He understood the importance of making information accessible, and has played a monumental role in the development of hardware and software designed to manage information on a scale unprecedented in history. Jobs is a fitting front piece for this chapter, which will focus on the Information Phase of the Value Methodology Job Plan.

INFORMATION PHASE

It is said that we live within the "Information Age," which, like all stages of societal evolution, carries with it the inevitable dualities of growth and decay. During the Industrial Age, the world saw unprecedented growth in the efficiency of human effort, especially within the realm of construction, manufacturing and transportation. At the same time, it also witnessed the widespread, and sometimes catastrophic, decay of the environment in terms of pollution, deforestation, and the wholesale extinction of species.

As we have moved from one era to the next, the tendency has been for these unbalanced forces to move back toward equilibrium. The growth we have seen in the past decade in terms of our ability to create information has far exceeded our ability to organize, analyze, and draw meaningful conclusions from it. We are bombarded by words and images watching television, listening to the radio, reading the newspaper or merely walking down the street. Much of the information that is developed in the workplace is equally overwhelming. One need only open their e-mail accounts after a few days away from the office to appreciate this phenomenon. The challenge of the day then, it seems, is to focus on ways to direct our efforts toward the development and organization of data into meaningful forms.

If the success of a project is directly related to the quality and timeliness of the information on which it is based, then this is doubly true for value studies. Most projects, especially during the latter phases of their development, will have generated volumes of information. The project team, which has been responsible for generating, collecting and organizing the data, possesses a level of familiarity with it that the value team will be unable to match. Furthermore, there will be few or even no members of the project team that have a full appreciation and understanding of all aspects of the information used to develop the project.

With respect to project information, the value team will be in an unusual position. On the one hand, they will begin the value study relatively uninformed. On the other, this ignorance does not necessarily bind them to the assumptions and conclusions that have been made by the project team. The goal of the value specialist, as well as the other value team members, in this phase of the job plan will be to first develop a thorough understanding of the project relevant to its scope statement (i.e., need and purpose) which, if properly written, is predicated on the customer's or user's requirements. Once this is accomplished, each member of the value team should focus on their respective areas of expertise in preparation to the development of alternative concepts.

The Information Phase includes the following steps:

- Review and analyze project scope information
- Review and analyze project schedule information
- Review and analyze project cost information

    o   Initial Costs
    o   Life Cycle Costs

- Conduct value study kick-off meeting
- Conduct site visit (if applicable)

In the Preparation Phase, consideration was given to collecting the project information. The focus of the Information Phase is the value study team's review and analysis of this information. It is important to remember that the Information Phase is not a one-way street. In other words, developing a thorough understanding of the project will only occur through the establishment of an active dialogue between the project team, customers, owners, stakeholders, and the value team.

REVIEW AND ANALYZE PROJECT SCOPE AND SCHEDULE INFORMATION

It is critical that the value team have ample opportunity to review all relevant project information prior to the commencement of the value study. It is recommended that at least a week be allotted for value study team members to review the information. Additional time may be warranted for particularly large and complicated projects.

In a perfect world, the different types of project information identified in the previous chapter exist and will be distributed to the value team members in a timely fashion. However, as we all know, we do not live in a perfect world. Invariably, there will be pieces of information that will either not have yet been developed or that are not organized into a format that is immediately useable by the value team. Hopefully, these "information gaps" will have been identified during the Preparation Phase and the project team will be working to develop this information so that it can be made available during the value study. Oftentimes, however, the information will simply not be available in time. This is a rather common phenomenon for value studies, especially those that are performed early in the project life cycle (i.e., at the project initiation or planning stages). When, for whatever reason, this situation occurs, it will be necessary to identify the assumptions that will be used in place of the information. The value specialist should work with the project team in identifying these assumptions and documenting them for inclusion in the report that will summarize the value team's findings.

Value studies conducted for projects that have been developed and managed by a conscientious project team will have a significant advantage, in terms of the completeness and quality of project information, over those that have not. The standards[2] for project management developed over the years by organizations such as the Project Management Institute provide the basis for the sound development and management of projects. Projects that have not taken advantage of these guidelines are generally not as well organized, tend to suffer from poor internal communication, and are more likely to have more information gaps. While value studies conducted for projects that are not well managed tend to be more challenging to conduct, they are also more likely to reap greater benefits. However, this is not to say that well-managed projects will not benefit from the application of the Value Methodology—there is always room for improvement!

As mentioned previously, many times project information will exist; however, it will be in a form that is not readily useable by the value team. This situation is typical for projects that are further along in the project life cycle where large quantities of information have been developed with respect to detailed design aspects. In these instances, it may be beneficial to prepare summaries of this information using tables, charts or matrices to illustrate trends and/or the relationship of this detailed information to the project as a whole. The value specialist should request that team members prepare such informational summaries where appropriate as they review the project information for distribution to the rest of the team.

It is recommended that the value specialist request that the team members prepare a memo detailing questions, issues and concerns they might identify during the course of their review of the project documents. These should be submitted to the value specialist to augment his or her own review of the project. This will help the value specialist in identifying trends within the project (i.e., lack of information, incorrect assumptions, inconsistencies between technical disciplines, etc.) and provide him or her with a better understanding of the project.

Those questions that arise regarding project information that the team feels is critical to address prior to the value study should be directed to the value specialist. It is recommended that a single point of contact be established between the project development and value study teams. Generally, this should be between the value specialist and project manager. Allowing value team members to make direct contact with the project team can lead to communication problems or misunderstandings that may be otherwise avoided. Some of the potential issues include:

- Interrupting or distracting project team members from their work.
- Creating the perception that the value team members are criticizing the work of the project team.
- Developing lines of communication that may contravene internal project communication protocols.
- Accidentally or unintentionally divulging sensitive project information to parties that should not be privy to it.

The project manager will probably have the best overall understanding of the dynamics of the people and issues they are managing and will, therefore, be in the best position to efficiently collect the additional information that value team needs, while minimizing disruptions to the project development process they are charged with managing.

REVIEW AND ANALYZE PROJECT SCHEDULE INFORMATION

A thorough review of a project's schedule information is an important step in the Information Phase. Hopefully, the project will have a well-developed work breakdown structure. For those unfamiliar with this concept, a work breakdown structure (WBS) is a deliverable-oriented grouping of project elements that organizes and defines the total scope of the project. A WBS identifies all activities that occur in delivering the project's output, be it a product, process or facility. The value specialist should be aware that the WBS may exist at several different levels. For instance, one WBS may define the delivery of the design of a facility, while another WBS may define its construction. Depending on the timing and scope of the value study, one or both WBS may be relevant.

From the WBS, a project schedule is generally derived. There exist today numerous project scheduling tools and techniques for project managers. Some of the more prevalent software programs on the market today include Microsoft *Project*® and *SureTrak*® by Primavera. Programs such as these allow detailed schedules to be developed from a WBS. In addition, these programs allow project resources to be linked to activities occurring within the WBS.

There are a number of different ways in which a project schedule can be graphically represented, all of which can be accomplished through the use of project management software. These include:

- Bar charts (also known as Gantt charts)
- Project network diagrams (also known as PERT—Program Evaluation and Review Technique—charts)

Bar charts are useful for showing the relationship of activity start and end dates. These are easy to read and are the standard project schedule representation used for construction and manufacturing projects *(Fig. 5-1)*.

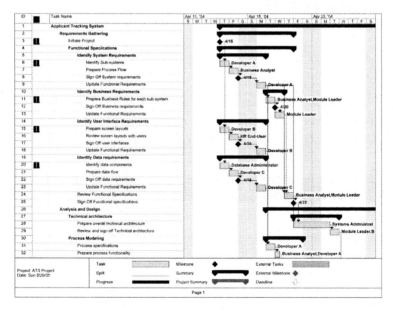

Fig. 5-1

Project network diagrams show logic behind activity sequencing as well as time information. Project network diagrams are extremely useful for developing a deeper understanding of activity/time relationships and are very good for illustrating services and procedures *(Fig. 5-2)*. Chapter 6—*Function*, will further demonstrate the use of project network diagrams in developing an understanding of project functions. Once again, the use of project scheduling software will allow one to easily create both kinds of graphical representations.

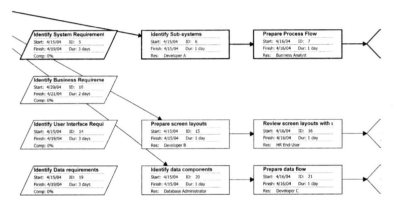

Fig. 5-2

While the use of project scheduling software has become commonplace, the value specialist may encounter projects where it is not being used. It is suggested that the value specialist consider utilizing such software to develop a project schedule, as doing so can be an invaluable aid in identifying potential areas for improvement in project delivery, as well as understanding how the alternatives the value study team will develop later will impact the project schedule. Believe it or not, some project teams do not develop schedules. This is more common for public entities with respect to construction schedules. Some public agencies may be responsible for only developing a design, while construction will be taken care of by a contractor. Therefore, a detailed project schedule for delivery of the design may exist but a construction schedule may not. The argument for the project team not doing this is usually "we aren't responsible for how it will be built or manufactured" or "we don't know how the contractor will bid the work or how manufacturing will assemble it." The value specialist should regard such an attitude as a major opportunity for value improvement.

If this is the case, it is strongly advised that the value specialist work with project team to create a "straw man" construction schedule. If the project team is unable or unwilling to do so, the value team should create one. Similar circumstances may also occur for product and process studies where one entity develops a concept and/or design and another is responsible for its production, implementation or acquisition. Value studies performed on a design should consider the impacts on acquisition.

REVIEW AND ANALYZE PROJECT COST INFORMATION

In the preceding chapter it has already been mentioned that the potential for achieving major savings in any project is greatest during the early phases of the project life cycle. As the project progresses toward completion it becomes increasingly expensive and time-consuming to make changes, regardless of benefits. Finally, a point is reached where the cost to make a change exceeds any potential benefit; it is then simply "too late." Therefore, application of the Value Methodology at an early phase is important

As one writer has put it, "Cost is the principle dimension in value analysis. Without cost for comparison, the analysis of value must necessarily be subjective—and consequently fall short of the full potential."[3] It is necessary to reduce each value alternative to a finite estimate which can be compared to the original project concept. Yet in the early phases of a project, when the potential for savings is a maximum, many areas to be estimated are not clearly defined. Only after the project is well advanced and everything has been fully developed can the task of estimating project costs be made relatively easy and straightforward. But by this time it may be too late to change, and the cost to redesign will be too high and many value alternatives must, regretfully, be dropped by the wayside. It is essential, therefore, to look at methods by which the value specialist can gain an appreciation of costs very early in the project cycle.

Cost is one of the most misunderstood items in business today. The cost of a product under study may vary greatly, depending upon whom you ask and the level of cost they are accustomed to using. Is the cost fully burdened? Does it include profit? Is it just material cost? Construction costs, while detailed parametric information and historical data is often available, are heavily influenced by the availability of skilled labor and vary widely from region to region. Finally, the true cost of procedures and processes within organizations is often unknown.

Cost Visibility

While a prime objective of most value studies is cost reduction, many organizations have their costing systems set up to determine whether or not cost and/or profit targets will be met—not "how much does it cost to produce this product." As mentioned earlier, the cost of management procedures, policies and processes may be unknown. In either case, the use of cost visibility techniques is essential in developing an understanding of project costs.

Cost visibility techniques establish costing ground rules to determine what is included in the product cost. This helps the value study team organize the cost and understand the current cost situation, including the cost-driving elements.

First, determine the appropriate level of cost for the project, depending on the stage of the project's life cycle. For example, a value study focusing on the construction of a new school early in the design process would probably use unit costing (i.e., cost per square meter). A study focusing on an existing product would utilize detailed unit production costs. Once a level of costing has been decided on, it is important to maintain whatever level was chosen throughout the value study in order to maintain consistency and avoid confusion in communicating the cost of alternative concepts.

Listed below are several important items to consider as project cost data is analyzed.

- *Determine Total Cost*—Based on the costing ground rules, determine the total cost for your project. For goods, a product that "sells" to your customer for $18.29 may have a total cost (material, labor and some portion of overhead) of $12.79 for the purposes of the study. For construction projects, the total cost would include all design costs, contractor overhead and profit, design and estimating contingencies, real estate, and mitigation costs. For processes or services, the total cost would include direct and indirect labor costs, as well as any support costs (materials, transportation, office space, etc.)
- *Determine Cost Elements*—Break down the elements of total cost into major areas such as material, labor, and overhead. For construction studies, costs can be broken down by building a system using standard estimating formats such as *Uniformat* and *MasterFormat*.
- *Determine Incremental Unit Costs*—This discipline identifies where costs are being created on a unit basis by component, or elements of a process. This translates into cost per hour, cost per cubic meter, or cost per sub-assembly.
- *Determine Annualized Costs*—To establish a base for determining cost improvements, calculate the

annualized cost of the study item by multiplying the unit cost by the number of pieces produced per year. For product studies, annualized costs will be used at the end of the study to determine annualized savings.
- *Determine Life-Cycle Costs*—Many projects will want to consider the long-term costs associated with the maintenance and operation of products, facilities and processes. These are costs that the customer and/or owner will be very concerned with. Life-cycle costs will be discussed in greater detail later in this chapter.

Cost Models

Upon receipt of the project cost information from the project team, the value specialist should prepare a cost model for the project. The first step in preparation of the cost model is to validate the cost information provided by the project team. The reason for verifying cost information is to ensure that both groups agree on the unit prices, quantity of materials, and/or labor that went into preparation of the cost estimate. If there are discrepancies in the cost, these should be identified early to avoid confusion or misunderstanding during the implementation phase of the project. To construct the cost model, the value specialist and/or the estimator on the value study team distributes cost by process, by trade, by system, and other identifiable areas. This helps the value team at the beginning of the value study to know where the major costs are to be found. Pareto's law of economics indicates that 80 percent of the cost will normally occur in 20 percent of the items being studied.

There are essentially three types of costs models that should be considered. These include:

- *Initial Cost Models*—Initial cost models provide a representation of the acquisition costs of a project. Such a model should include all costs associated with initial production, construction or acquisition. This is the most common and immediately useful form of cost modeling *(Fig. 5-3)*.

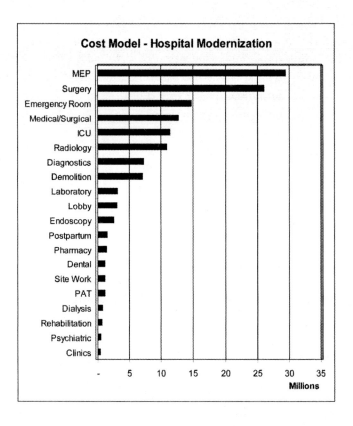

Fig. 5-3

- *Cost-Worth Models*—Based upon a standard initial cost model, a comparison can be made between the cost of any project element and its worth, as evaluated by the value specialist or value study team. As discussed in *Chapter 2—Value*, worth is a subjective, individual assessment of what one is willing to pay for an item. It is usually defined as the least cost means of reliably performing a function. The purpose of a cost-worth model is to identify areas having a cost considerably in excess of the evaluator's opinion of their worth. *(Fig. 5-4)*.

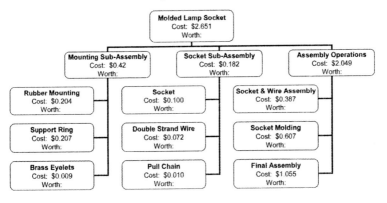

Fig. 5-4

- *Life-Cycle Cost Models*—This type of cost model is useful for illustrating the cost of ownership, especially for facilities and major durable goods. Such a model would include initial project costs, maintenance costs, energy costs, and other factors such as financing, taxes, insurance, etc. *(Fig. 5-5)*.

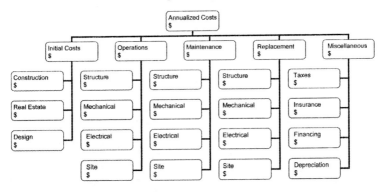

Fig. 5-5

LIFE CYCLE COSTING

There are many definitions of life cycle costing that are in use. The U.S. General Services Administration defines life cycle costing as follows:

> Life cycle costing (LCC) is the development of all the significant costs of acquiring, owning and using an item, system or service over a specified length of time.[4]

Life cycle costing is the total economic cost of owning and operating a facility, manufactured process or product. The life cycle costing analysis reflects present and future costs of the project over its useful life. It allows an assessment of a given solution, and it is a tool for making comparisons. The underriding theme is that life cycle costing is a universal tool to express the multifaceted elements of cost and time in a uniform criterion of equivalent dollars.

The use of the life cycle costing technique has a broad range of applications. In the analysis of facilities, it can be applied during the conceptual, planning, design, construction and operating stages for a facility or product. Its application as an aid for analyzing economic alternatives for purchases at home and in the marketplace has been used by all of us. With the rises in the interest rates and inflation, the use of life cycle costing has been expanded. The impacts are astounding, as will be seen later in this chapter. Before explaining the applications of life cycle costing, facts about its application are addressed.

Every investor or owner wants to know what the total owning and operating costs will be. In both the public and private sectors an increasing

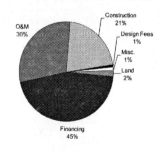

Figure 5-6

interest is being manifested in knowing, to the greatest extent possible, what a project will cost throughout its entire lifetime. This involves both an estimate of construction or production costs and a forecast of the probable costs of energy, maintenance, taxes, and borrowed money. For facilities, the persons involved in life cycle costs are shown in *Figure 5-6*, and it should be noted that the designer has the smallest share of the pie.

Figure 5-7 is a generalized curve which shows whose decisions have the greatest impact on cost. If the area under each segment of the curve represents an impact on cost, it would be seen that the designer or project team has by far the greatest role to play. The initial contractor can only perform within the carefully defined limits of his

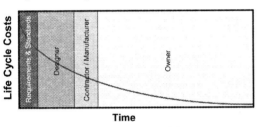

Figure 5-7

contract, and once the design is completed he can have little effect on total costs. The owner has even less influence, although the owner's total expenditures during the life of the facility or product are far greater than money spent on design. This figure illustrates that the best place to save money is in the design or project development phase. In short, good project management and design is worth every cent it costs.

Life cycle analyses are not limited to use only during the planning stage, but can be used at any time during the useful life of the facility. As an example, processing plants that are manufacturing a competitive product must know every element of cost from obtaining and refining the raw products to final transport, marketing, and eventual sale. An owner of a sports complex uses life cycle analysis to account for building amortization, operating and advertising costs, and other expenses to know what he needs to make in order to break even. The use of life cycle analysis affects all facts of our economic livelihood.

While LCC provides an excellent tool for decision making, its application should be understood to avoid possible pitfalls in its use. Fiscal managers especially should appreciate that LCC dollars may not be the same as budget dollars. One of the problems is that cost estimates may not be applicable as budget estimates because they are expressed in constant dollars (excluding inflation) and all cash-flow dollars are converted to equivalent moneys at a common point in time. LCC estimates are not necessarily equivalent to the obligated amounts for each funding year.

While LCC provides an excellent tool to assist in decision making, the analysis of results is based solely on economic factors. The estimates are only as good as the background data forming the basis for costs. Final analysis should account for non-economic criteria that have intrinsic benefits that do not lend themselves to finite cost evaluations. Factors such as safety, reliability, operability, and environmental factors, to name a few, may be more important than monetary savings.

Cost categories to be used in a life cycle cost analysis encompass a broad area. Funds for a project may be spent from the timeframe of years leading up to its completion to the time when the facility, product or process has outlived its usefulness. Following are types of costs that might factor into a total project's life. This is not to say that these are all of the costs involved. However, it serves as a reminder of the major cost factors to look for when performing life cycle comparisons. LCC considerations may include:

- **Investment Costs**—The amount of money expended for assessment of market potential, for time and expenses involved in analyzing site alternatives, and expenses incurred for development of a financial plan. Investment costs may also include expenses for obtaining a line of credit and other financing alternatives. Preparation of stock and bond sales may be another type of investment cost.

- **Land Acquisition Costs**—Costs for realty fees, title searches, legal fees, deed filing fees, insurance, cost of land, and the interest on borrowed money, for the purchase or leasing of land for use for a facility. In addition, the cost of environmental mitigation may need to be considered, depending upon regulatory requirements.

    o   Property Costs
    o   Real Estate Fees
    o   Environmental Mitigation Costs

- **Project Development Costs**—Costs associated with the planning, design, bidding, construction, inspection, and initial start-up of a facility, product or process. Any anticipated future costs for design modifications should also be included.

    o   Project Management
    o   Planning
    o   Design & Engineering
    o   Project Support (i.e., Purchasing, Marketing, Accounting, etc.)
    o   Redesign Costs

- **Construction & Manufacturing Costs**—The cost of constructing, manufacturing or implementing a facility, product or service.
- **Replacement Costs**—Future costs to modify or replace a portion of the project. Usually, specific pieces of

equipment or parts are the major source of replacement costs. Based on the expected life of the components, several replacements may occur during the total project life.

- **Salvage Costs**—The value of the project or product at some future time. Usually salvage value is the amount received from the sale at the end of the life cycle period.
- **Operating Costs**—Costs required to operate a thing. These costs are the day-to-day costs of staffing; energy costs to create and maintain a working environment and to operate equipment; costs of outside services such as waste disposal, water and sewage costs; chemicals and other resources needed to manufacture or to process a product; and the costs of transportation from the source of raw materials to the final delivery point. These costs are often periodic costs falling at scheduled intervals.

  o Staffing
  o Fuel or Energy
  o Chemicals and Supplies
  o Operating Schedule
  o Outside Services
  o Resource Recovery
  o Transportation

- **Maintenance Costs**—Factors included in maintenance costs would include labor, cost of parts, materials, cleaning materials and equipment, and preventive maintenance. Also included are normal maintenance and repair of equipment, painting, etc.

  o Material/Parts/Lubricants
  o Staffing/Labor
  o Preventive Maintenance

FUNDAMENTALS OF VALUE METHODOLOGY

- o Cleaning
- o Durability of Products

- ♦ **Miscellaneous Costs**—Such costs could include insurance policies; federal, state and local taxes; depreciation and the effects of inflation.

  - o Taxes
  - o Insurance
  - o Depreciation
  - o Inflation

- ♦ **Time Value of Money**—Time has a high price tag when evaluating alternatives. The longevity of a project and the lifespan of individual components must be considered in the decision-making process. Cost of money is the interest that is charged on borrowed money for the project.

Elements of cost in a life cycle cost analysis are for the total life of the product. Some costs are one-time expenditures that occur before the project is completed. Others are single expenditures that are amortized for periods up to and beyond its useful life.

The Time Value of Money

As money can produce earnings at a certain rate of interest by being invested for a period of time, it is important to know that one unit of money received at some future date does not produce as much earnings as a unit of money received in the present. This relationship between interest and time forms the basis for the concept of the "time value of money".

Money also has a time value, as the buying power of a dollar varies with time. The relationship between $1 in hand, $1 promised in the future, or a series of payments at the specified times in the future is a difficult concept for many of us to grasp.

During periods of inflation, the quantity of goods and services that can be bought with a certain amount of money decreases as the purchase date moves into the future. Although this change in the buying power of money is important, the concept of the time value of money is even more so, in that it has earning power. It is necessary to know the different methods for computing interest in order to calculate the actual effect of the time value of money in the comparison of alternative solutions.

The following considerations must be kept in mind for application in calculations of investment alternatives:

- Present Value (P) is produced at the beginning of a period, at a time in the present;
- Future Value (F) occurs at the end of the nth period, from a time considered as present (n being the total number of periods—usually expressed in years).
- Annuity Amount (A) is a single payment within a series of equal payments made at the end of each period under consideration.
- Interest Rate (i) is the cost of money established by the organization or lending institution. The federal government's Office of Management and Budget (OMB) frequently updates interest rates per OMB Circular A-94.[5] The interest rate is also referred to as a discount rate.

It is useful to think of the relationship of money at different points in time as a triangle where P equals a single present amount of money; F equals a future single sum of money; and A equals money expressed as a series of equal amounts (like the monthly mortgage payments). *Figure 5-8* illustrates this interrelationship and includes the names of the financial equations involved in calculating the time value of money. These financial equations are provided in *Table 5-1*.

FUNDAMENTALS OF VALUE METHODOLOGY

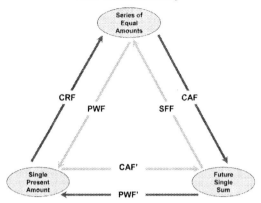

Figure 5-8

Single Payment Compound Amount Factor (CAF')

Given P, find F $\quad F = P \times [(1+i)^n] \quad\quad F = P \times F_{PF,i,n}$

Single Payment Present Worth Factor (PWF')

Given F, find P $\quad P = F \dfrac{1}{(1+i)^n} \quad\quad P = F \times F_{FP,i,n}$

Equal Payment Series Present Worth Factor (PWF)

Given A, find P $\quad P = A \times \dfrac{(1+i)^n - 1}{i \times (1+i)^n} \quad\quad P = A \times F_{AP,i,n}$

Equal Payment Series Capital Recovery Factor (CRF)

Given P, find A $\quad A = P \times \dfrac{i \times (1+i)^n}{(1+i)^n - 1} \quad\quad A = P \times F_{PA,i,n}$

Equal Payment Series Compound Amount Factor (CAF)

Given A, find F $\quad F = A \times \dfrac{(1+i)^n - 1}{i} \quad\quad \begin{array}{l} F = A \times F_{AF,i,n} \\ F = A \times F_{AP,i,n} \times F_{FP,i,n} \end{array}$

Equal Payment Series Sinking Fund Factor: (SFF)

Given F, find A $\quad A = F \times \dfrac{i}{(1+i)^n - 1} \quad\quad \begin{array}{l} A = F \times F_{FA,i,n} \\ A = F \times F_{FP,i,n} \times F_{PA,i,n} \end{array}$

Table 5-1

Differential escalation (i.e., inflation) is taken into account for recurring costs, such as energy, by another formula where "e" equals the escalation rate *(Fig. 5-9)*.

Fig. 5-9
$$P = A \frac{\{(1+e)/(1+i)\}\{(1+e/1+i)^n - 1\}}{\{(1+e)/(1+i)\} - 1}$$

This formula provides us with an escalated Present Worth Factor. Tables to accomplish the same result are contained in various financial references and are much simpler to use.

Life Cycle Costing Methods

Using life cycle costing will aid the decision-making process and increase the sensitivity to cost for operating and maintaining facilities, products and processes. Life cycle costing is actually a series of computations applying economic factors to monetary expenditures as identified in the previous section. The validity of the comparison, like all estimates, is dependent on the quality of the cost estimates used in the analysis. There is no good substitute for sound cost figures. Therefore, before proceeding with a life cycle analysis, be certain of the quantity and the validity of cost parameters to be sure of the accuracy of the results.

- **State Problem.** As life cycle costing can be used as a decision-making tool, its first step involves identification of the problem to be solved. A problem statement will help to focus on the basis of the comparison. A description of the physical facilities and the alternatives to be compared should be defined thoroughly. Before going further into the analysis, check to see if your objectives will be met by the comparisons and the cost parameters in the analysis.
- **Establish Alternatives.** Next the alternative concepts to be analyzed are documented with a listing of background information on physical components of alternatives and the differences. It is essential to establish basic cost and budgeting data of the owner's

program at this time, as the data will form the criteria for life cycle input and guidelines for analysis of results.
- **Establish Parameters.** Life cycle analyses are impacted by *time, cost, and the cost of money*. Time factors include project planning life, sometimes called the useful life of the project; equipment life; the owner's planning schedule; major expansions; and deletions or changes to the total program. Project life estimates, especially for equipment replacement, are hard to predict, as the life of the equipment is dependent on the quality of the equipment and the maintenance performed to keep it in operating condition. The useful life is the time that the facility will be used. Often a facility will have several major renovations during its useful life. Costs for additional renovation expenditures are planned by the owner and are usually included in life cycle comparisons. Cost parameters have been outlined previously. Major impacts are being felt by owners from escalating energy, labor and maintenance costs above the normal inflation rates. These fluctuations in cost are accounted for by use of escalation rates. The cost of money is taken into account by setting interest, inflation, and escalation rates. Monetary loans for financing and tax benefits are part of the analysis.

There are essentially two LCC methods that will be of interest to the value specialist. These include the Present Worth Method and the Annualized Method. Both methods can be set up using spreadsheet software, most of which include macros for all the financial equations identified in Table 5-1. Examples of each have been provided to illustrate this.

- **Present Worth Method**—The Present Worth Method requires that all costs for the life cycle analysis, both present and future expenditures, be brought back to today's baseline costs. Initial costs are already expressed in present worth. Operations and maintenance costs are usually estimates of annual costs, based on stated conditions of use. The interest rate, life cycle period (useful life) should be established by the owner and/or user. This method is illustrated in *Figure 5-10*. This example compares two possible options for a new air conditioning system. Based on input from the project owner, we have been given a life cycle period of 20 years and a discount rate of 10%. The initial costs of both systems are estimated and input into the spreadsheet. Both systems will require the replacement of a major component (in this case chillers) at different periods at different costs. A salvage value at the end of the 20 year life cycle period is also calculated. Note that all replacement and salvage costs, though future expenditures, are based upon present worth dollars. Annual operations and maintenance costs are also converted into present worth dollars. While this method is certainly valid, it does tend to exaggerate costs by converting annuals costs into today's dollars, which makes for some very large sums. There is something misleading in this, especially when applied to facilities, as construction budgets and operating budgets are almost always funded separately.

Life Cycle Cost Analysis - Present Worth Method

Item: Air Conditioning System
Life Cycle Period (n): 20
Interest Rate (i): 10%

		Baseline		Alternative	
	Year	Estimated Cost	Present Worth	Estimated Cost	Present Worth
Initial Costs					
Material		$ 500,000	$ 500,000	$ 700,000	$ 700,000
Labor		$ 40,000	$ 40,000	$ 50,000	$ 50,000
Replacement Costs					
Chiller Replacement	10	$ 100,000	$ 38,550	$ -	$ -
Chiller Replacement	15	$ -	$ -	$ 125,000	$ 29,924
Salvage Costs					
Salvage Value	20	$ (100,000)	$ (14,865)	$ (200,000)	$ (29,730)
Annual Costs					
Maintenance Costs		$ 20,000	$ 170,271	$ 12,000	$ 102,163
Operations Costs		$ 50,000	$ 425,678	$ 21,000	$ 178,785
Total Present Worth Costs			$ 1,159,634		$ 1,031,141
Life Cycle Cost Savings					$ 128,493

Figure 5-10

FUNDAMENTALS OF VALUE METHODOLOGY

- **Annualized Method**—This method is similar to the Present Worth Method but expresses the total cost of ownership as an annual cost. The example *(Fig. 5-11)* uses the same item, costs, life cycle period and discount rate as was used in the previous example. This will allow the reader to compare and contrast how the data is communicated. The primary difference is that all single expenditures, both present and future, are first expressed in present worth dollars, and are then amortized into a series of equal amount along with the annual operations and maintenance costs. Just as most people can relate to making a monthly mortgage or car payment over a period of years, so do most owners better relate to thinking about the costs of ownership as a series of amortized payments. The figures are much smaller and generally easier to comprehend.

Life Cycle Cost Analysis - Annualized Method

Item: Air Conditioning System
Life Cycle Period (n): 20
Interest Rate (i): 10%

		Baseline		Alternative	
	Year	Estimated Cost	Present Worth	Estimated Cost	Present Worth
Initial Costs					
Material		$ 500,000	$ 500,000	$ 700,000	$ 700,000
Labor		$ 40,000	$ 40,000	$ 50,000	$ 50,000
Replacement Costs					
Chiller Replacement	10	$ 100,000	$ 38,550	$ -	$ -
Chiller Replacement	15	$ -	$ -	$ 125,000	$ 29,924
Salvage Costs					
Salvage Value	20	$ (100,000)	$ (14,865)	$ (200,000)	$ (29,730)
		Present Worth	Annual Costs	Present Worth	Annual Costs
Annual Costs					
Initial Costs		$ 540,000	$ 63,428	$ 750,000	$ 88,095
Replacement Costs		$ 38,550	$ 4,522	$ 29,924	$ 3,515
Salvage Costs		$ (14,865)	$ (1,746)	$ (29,730)	$ (3,492)
Maintenance Costs		$ 20,000	$ 20,000	$ 12,000	$ 12,000
Operations Costs		$ 50,000	$ 50,000	$ 21,000	$ 21,000
Total Annual Costs			$ 136,205		$ 121,118
Annual Savings					$ 15,087
Present Worth of Annual Savings					$ 128,442

Fig. 5-11

Whichever method is used, it can be seen from the examples that it is important not to rely solely on initial costs when evaluating options. The alternative air conditioning system, though 40% more expensive to initially install, ended up being the most economical option for the owner when considering the total cost of ownership over the life of the equipment. The value specialist must always consider life cycle costs in the search for improved value.

CONDUCT VALUE STUDY KICK-OFF MEETING

The value study should always begin with a kick-off meeting. The purpose of the kick-off meeting is to introduce the participants to the VM process and the value study schedule and objectives; provide an overview of the current state of the project; provide an opportunity for the value team to receive clarifications from the project team; and to develop an understanding of how the project is performing relative to its scope statement. These steps are bulleted below:

- Introduce value study process, objectives and schedule
- Present project overview
- Identify project constraints and stakeholder issues
- Identify project performance—*Value Metrics*
- Measure project performance

The value study kick-off meeting should be attended by the value team, project team, project owner and/or sponsor, customer representative(s), and any other stakeholders that are not part of the project team but have a vested interest in the project.

Introduce Value Study Process, Objectives and Schedule

It is likely that the majority of those present at the kick-off meeting will be totally unfamiliar with the Value Methodology and may not understand what the value is in conducting a value study! The value specialist must always keep in mind that conducting a value study involves a significant allocation in time, money and resources. There will be some that question the need for conducting the value study in light of the costs. This is why it is important that the value specialist do an excellent job in communicating to the participants the value study process, objectives and schedule. Copies of the value study schedule should be distributed to all participants, and an attendance sheet should be distributed to the group so that names and contact information are documented.

After all the participants have been properly introduced, the value specialist should begin by clearly stating the objectives for the value study, which should have been identified in the pre-study meeting. Following this, the value specialist should refer everyone to the value study schedule and provide a brief overview of each major activity. It is important to stress that the value study will be considering all aspects of value, and not just cost! Cost cutting carries with it many negative connotations, and it is best to avoid dwelling on cost reduction, but rather, emphasize value improvement.

Oftentimes, the value study's sponsor, which may be the project owner, will want to make a few statements regarding the study objectives and current state of the project. The importance of demonstrating the visible involvement of the study sponsor at this early stage of the process cannot be understated. The value specialist should always seek to encourage this, as it sends a very strong message to the participants. Management involvement is much different than management support!

Present Project Overview

An informational overview of the project should be presented by the project team. It is recommended that the project manager initiate this presentation by providing the value team with the project's history and objectives.

Following this introduction, a more detailed presentation of the project should be made by the project team members representing expertise in the various disciplines necessary to develop key project areas. This briefing should focus on a discussion of major project elements rather than finite technical details. For example, a project overview focusing on a new elementary school should include input from the following project team members concerning the following project elements:

- Project Manager—Scope Statement, Project History, Objectives and Budget
- Educational Planner—Educational Specifications, User Requirements
- Architect—Functional Requirements, Building Layout, Exterior and Interior Finishes
- Structural Engineer—Building Structure
- Civil Engineer—Site Work, Vehicular Circulation, Site Utilities
- Mechanical Engineer—HVAC Systems, Plumbing, Fire Protection
- Electrical Engineer—Electrical Distribution, Lighting, Data and Communication Systems

The point here is to acquaint the value team with the "big picture." Hopefully, each member of the value team will have had time to make a more detailed review of the technical documents.

Following this presentation, the value team should be afforded the opportunity to ask questions and receive additional clarifications concerning project information. The value specialist should ensure that the value team members utilize good human relations during this dialogue and that the questions are not phrased in a critical manner. The project team will be the value team's best source of information, and it is critical that a high level of professionalism be maintained in order to foster trust and openness during the VM process.

Identify Project Constraints and Stakeholder Issues

While all of the key participants are present, the value specialist should take the opportunity to ask the project team to identify constraints related to the project. Project constraints typically relate to issues beyond the control of the project team and may include political considerations, funding or revenue

FUNDAMENTALS OF VALUE METHODOLOGY

issues, regulatory requirements, and legal issues. The value team must have a basic understanding of these constraints as they will have an impact on the types of alternatives they will generate later on in the value study process.

In addition to project constraints, there may be other issues that external stakeholders will want the value team to consider. These may include issues related to indirect project impacts to the public. These types of issues are common with construction projects where there may be citizens and businesses that may be directly or indirectly affected by the project. This information should be solicited from the participants and documented.

It is recommended that the value specialist record these on a flip chart or white board, or utilize a multimedia projector so that all participants can be involved in the documentation of these constraints and issues.

Identify and Measure Project Performance—*Value Metrics*

Once the project overview has been completed, the value specialist should review the project's performance objectives with both the value team and the project team. Performance attributes and requirements should be identified and defined prior to the value study, as discussed in *Chapter 4—Preparation*. For example, a project focused on making improvements to a 1.5-ton forklift truck might have identified the following performance attributes and requirements *(Fig. 5-12)*.

1.5-Ton Fork Lift Truck – Performance Attributes & Requirements

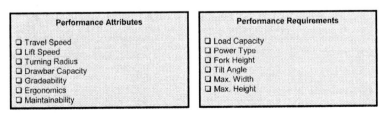

Performance Attributes	Performance Requirements
❏ Travel Speed	❏ Load Capacity
❏ Lift Speed	❏ Power Type
❏ Turning Radius	❏ Fork Height
❏ Drawbar Capacity	❏ Tilt Angle
❏ Gradeability	❏ Max. Width
❏ Ergonomics	❏ Max. Height
❏ Maintainability	

Fig. 5-12

Each of the performance attributes and requirements should also have been defined and documented, so the value specialist should confirm that the project team is still in agreement with them. The value specialist should now ask the project team to describe how the current project is meeting each performance attribute. The rationale provided by the project team should be recorded for each performance attribute, as identified in the example *(Fig. 5-13)*. This information will establish a baseline understanding of how the current project is meeting the project's original scope statement.

1.5-Ton Fork Lift Truck – Baseline Performance

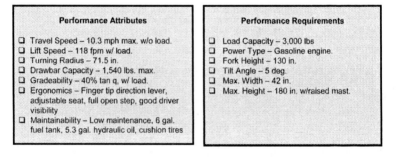

Fig. 5-13

When the project's current performance has been identified, the value specialist should ask the project team to identify specific parameters for each of the performance attributes. It is important to remember that performance requirements do not have parameters, but rather, they establish specific conditions which must be met in order to meet the project's scope statement. A maximum and minimum value should be established for each of the performance attributes. These should reflect the lowest acceptable and highest reasonable performance levels for each attribute and not necessarily the highest and lowest values that are achievable. In the forklift example, the technology exists to create a forklift that can exceed 60 miles per hour; however, such high speeds far exceed the average forklift customer's needs! This is an excellent, if rather obvious, illustration of why parameters must be established using the customer's or user's requirements *(Fig. 5-14)*.

1.5-Ton Fork Lift Truck – Performance Parameters

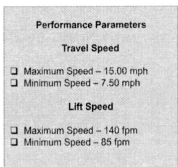

Fig. 5-14

The value team must have a clear understanding of the project's performance attributes and parameters if they are to improve value. The performance must be in line with the customer or user's needs, as unnecessary performance will not contribute to optimum value. The next step in the performance identification step is to begin the process of measuring project performance.

Having established the project's performance attributes and related parameters, the next activity in *Value Metrics* is to set up a system of performance measurement. This is accomplished by developing a rating scale based upon the parameters identified for each of the performance attributes.

For the sake of simplicity, it is recommended that scales based on values ranging from 0 to 10 be utilized. A 0 to 10 scale is something almost everyone can easily relate to. A "0" would represent the lowest acceptable level of performance, while a "10" would define the maximum amount of performance desired relative to fulfilling the project's purpose and need *(Table 5-2)*.

Attribute	Definition	Rating Scale	Unit of Measure/Quantification
Travel Speed	A measure of the travel speed of an unloaded forklift. The speed is measured in miles per hour.	10	15.00 mph
		9	14.25 mph
		8	13.50 mph
		7	12.75 mph
		6	12.00 mph
		5	11.25 mph
		4	10.50 mph
		3	9.75 mph
		2	9.00 mph
		1	8.25 mph
		0	7.50 mph

Table 5-2

The example above assumes that a linear scale is being used, meaning that there is a uniform distribution of measurement between the ratings. However, it may not always be desirable to use a linear scale. For non-linear scales, utility curves should be created for each performance attribute to graphically reinforce the logic of the rating scales. Both Fallon and T. Fowler[6] present good models for developing utility curves for this express purpose. *Figure 5-15* illustrates a non-linear utility curve reflecting customer preference for speeds between 10.5 to 12 mph. Ratings for speeds higher and lower than this range will thus have a smaller incremental effect on performance.

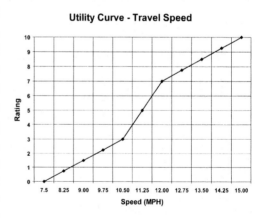

Figure 5-15

FUNDAMENTALS OF VALUE METHODOLOGY

Utility curves provide a graphical means of defining the relationship between the upper and lower parameters of the numeric scale. *Figure 5-16* below shows a range of potential utility curves, and their meanings, for a performance attribute called "travel speed."

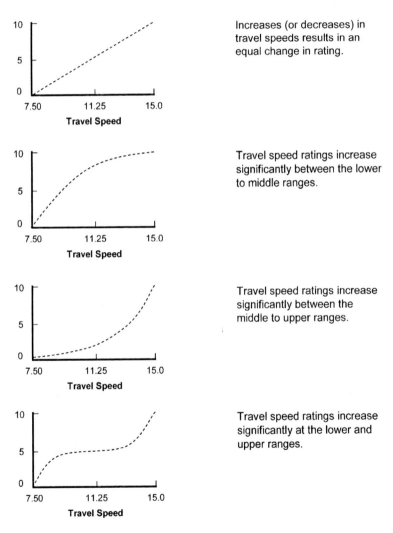

Figure 5-16

There are two possible methods for calibrating the scales—absolute and comparative. The absolute method is quantitative in nature while the comparative method is qualitative. Absolute scales can be used where quantitative data is readily available. The previous examples illustrated for "travel speed" reflect absolute scales. Fractions may also be used for the ratings (i.e., 5.5) if additional sensitivity is needed.

Comparative scales are useful for measuring performance attributes for which hard data does not exist, are subjective in nature, and/or are difficult to quantify within the timeframe of a value study. An example of a comparative scale is shown in *Table 5-3*. This is a useful generic scale that is based in part upon the research conducted by Thomas Saaty in the development of his Analytical Hierarchical Process, or AHP[7]. This scale uses language similar to that used in AHP for eliciting preferences for one alternative as compared to another; however, in this case, the scale is used to compare an alternative concept relative to a baseline concept. This scale uses a linear utility curve.

Attribute	Definition	Rating Scale	Unit of Measure/Quantification
Human Factors	The optimization of the interface between people, technology, and the facility. This attribute considers such issues as: ♦ Ergonomics ♦ Lighting Design ♦ User-Friendliness of Technology	10 9 8 7 6 5 4 3 2 1 0	Alternative Concept is extremely preferred. Alternative Concept is very strongly preferred. Alternative Concept is strongly preferred. Alternative Concept is moderately preferred. Alternative Concept is slightly preferred. Alternative Concept and Baseline Concept are equally preferred. Baseline Concept is slightly preferred. Baseline Concept is moderately preferred. Baseline Concept is strongly preferred. Baseline Concept is very strongly preferred. Baseline Concept is extremely preferred.

Table 5-3

Regardless of which type of scale is selected, it is important to define the performance quantification relative to each of the numerical ratings. This will become apparent later in the process when it comes time to rate alternative concepts.

Individual rating scales will need to be developed for each performance attribute. Once this has been completed, the importance of the various performance attributes relative to the project's purpose and need should next be determined using the *Performance Attribute Matrix*. This matrix utilizes the paired-comparisons method which provides a simple, balanced approach for comparing multiple attributes. It is important to emphasize that these comparisons need to be made within the context of the project's purpose and need statement. Making these distinctions early is important for the value team's understanding of the importance of the performance attributes in meeting the project's purpose and need.

The process for completing the Performance Attribute Matrix involves the following steps:

- **List Performance Attributes**—List all of the performance attributes in the left part of the matrix; assign designators (A, B, C).
- **Discuss Pairs**—Compare attribute A with attribute B asking, "Which of these two performance attributes is more critical in satisfying the project's purpose and need?" Enter "a" in the intersecting box (next to the A designator and above the B designator). Continue for all pairs until the matrix is completed.
- **Total Scores**—Add the number of times each attribute was selected. Half scores (0.5) result from ties, where performance attributes are judged to be of equal importance. In some cases, one of the attributes will receive no points. In this case, one point can be added to each attribute score so that the attribute receiving no points will have at least one point for weighting purposes.
- **Normalize Scores**—Calculate percentages for each attribute, rounding off as needed.
- **Apply Key Performance Attributes**—The highest-ranked performance criteria are used for evaluating ideas during the Speculation Phase. Other performance

attributes are included in the performance assessment of alternatives.

When the Performance Attribute Matrix has been completed, the results should be reviewed with the group to ensure that there is consistency in logic *(Fig. 5-17).*

PERFORMANCE ATTRIBUTE MATRIX
Bridge Replacement Project

Attribute								TOTAL	%
Mainline Operations	A	A	A	A	A	A	A	6.0	29%
Environment - Natural		B	B	B	E	B	B	4.0	19%
Environment - Social			C	C	E	C	C	3.0	14%
Constructibility				D	E	F	D/G	0.5	2%
Maintainability					E	E	E	5.0	24%
Construction Impacts						F	F	2.0	10%
Construction Schedule							G	0.5	2%
								21.0	100%

Fig. 5-17

Alternatively, if greater sensitivity in evaluating the differences between attributes is required, degrees of importance can be added to further stimulate the discussion. The method for doing this is discussed in *Chapter 6— Function,* where the numerical evaluation technique is discussed as applied to determining the relative importance of functions. In addition to this method, the Analytical Hierarchical Process (AHP) method of paired comparisons can also be utilized[8].

The normalized scores that are derived from the Performance Attribute Matrix are utilized as weights in measuring total project performance. All of the information developed on the baseline project's cost and performance at this point can be summarized using the *Value Matrix*.

The Value Matrix permits the comparison of competing sets of value alternatives by organizing the data developed for the performance attributes into a matrix format in order to yield value indices. Value alternatives are compared to the baseline project for the all attributes in order to compare and contrast the potential for value improvement. The matrix is essential for understanding the relationship of cost, performance, and value of the project baseline and VM concepts. Comparing the performance and cost suggests which alternatives are potentially as good, or better than, the project baseline concept in terms of overall value. Comparison at the value index level suggests which alternatives have the best functionality per unit cost, or provides the project with the "best value".

At this stage of the VM job plan, the Value Matrix should be completed for the project baseline. The steps for completing the Value Matrix include:

- **Performance Attributes**—Project-specific performance attributes previously identified and defined during the Preparation Phase.
- **Performance Attribute Weight**—Percentage weights developed on the Performance Attribute Matrix during the Information Phase.
- **Concept**—Project Baseline Concept(s). The design alternative that is used as the "baseline" for the value study is identified as the Baseline Concept. In some cases, other alternative concepts developed by the project team are rated to identify the relative strengths and weaknesses of those alternatives.
- **Performance Rating**—Selected rating on a scale of 0 (low) to 10 (high), based on the measurable scale

developed for each attribute. These were developed previously during the Information Phase.
- **Total Performance**—Arithmetic product of performance attribute weight and performance rating.
- **% Performance**—The difference between the total score for the Baseline Concept(s) and the total score for the value alternatives, expressed as a percentage increase or decrease.
- **Total Initial Project Cost**—Estimated cost of the project with the value alternatives incorporated. The cost should be expressed in a manner consistent with type of project being evaluated. For example, a manufactured item costing $15.36 to produce should be expressed as 15.36 and a transit project costing $350,000,000 would be expressed as 350.00. Life cycle costs should be considered separately, either as a performance attribute or in a separate Value Matrix, in order to avoid confusion.
- **Value Index**—Arithmetic division of total project performance by project cost.
- **Percent Value Improvement**—Net increase (+) or decrease (-) of value index in percent. The value indexes of the alternative concepts are always compared to that of the baseline concept in developing the percent value improvement.

Figure 5-18 provides an example of a completed Value Matrix for the baseline concept.

FUNDAMENTALS OF VALUE METHODOLOGY

VALUE MATRIX
Bridge Replacement Project

Attribute	Attribute Weight	Concept	Performance Rating 1-10	Total Performance
Mainline Operations	29	Baseline Concept	5	145
				0
				0
				0
				0
Environmental - Natural	19	Baseline Concept	5	95
				0
				0
				0
				0
Environmental - Social	14	Baseline Concept	6	84
				0
				0
				0
				0
Constructibility	2	Baseline Concept	5	10
				0
				0
				0
				0
Maintainability	24	Baseline Concept	5	120
				0
				0
				0
				0
Construction Impacts	10	Baseline Concept	5	50
				0
				0
				0
				0
Construction Schedule	2	Baseline Concept	7	14
				0
				0
				0
				0

Overall Performance Alternative	Total Performance	% Performance Improvement	Total Cost ($ millions)	Value Index (P/C)	% Value Improvement
Baseline Concept	518		500.00	1.04	

Fig. 5-18

CONDUCT SITE VIST

Depending on the type of project being studied, conducting a site visit may be scheduled as an important part of the Information Phase. When possible, site visits should always be conducted for projects dealing with facilities. Site visits are also strongly recommended for product studies. An incredible amount of valuable information can be gathered through this firsthand view of the existing site and conditions.

Site visits conducted for construction projects should provide enough time to survey the entire site. Ideally, the project manager or project engineer will lead the site visit and identify the location of key project elements. Existing utilities, site circulation, construction staging, and property issues can be discussed on a firsthand basis. If conducting a site visit is not practical or feasible, consideration should be given to obtaining a video survey of the site, or barring this, aerial photographs of the site.

Site visits for product studies may include a walk-through of the current manufacturing operations. This will help the team gain a better understanding by visualizing the existing process. Many times, the value team members will pick up on small details of manufacturing processes that will open the door to a series of questions. It is surprising how much creativity can be stimulated through this process.

If the study is focusing on an existing product, at least one completely assembled unit should be available for the value team to study. The various parts should also be made available for closer review. It is also useful to see the product itself operate. This is not always possible at the factory location, so consideration should be given to visiting a customer or user site to witness the operation of the product. If the product is large in scale, it is recommended that the value study be physically located near or adjacent to an assembled unit. The ability of the value team to crawl on and inspect the product will again help stimulate creativity and develop a better understanding of the product's functions. If competing products exist, then these should be obtained, or rented in the case of large durable goods, for study and review by the value team.

SUMMARY

During the Information Phase, the value team must gain a sound understanding of the project's scope, schedule and cost. The value team develops an understanding of project scope through a thorough review of project documents, listening to and engaging the project team during the project overview, identifying the constraints and issues of the project stakeholders and conducting a site visit. The application of *Value Metrics* will help the value team develop a much deeper understanding of project performance through the identification of performance attributes and the establishment of a system for measuring performance. The utilization of cost models and the application of life cycle costing methods will allow the value team to develop an understanding of project cost, while the application of project scheduling techniques and software will provide them with a solid grounding with respect to understanding project schedule.

The flow of information requires careful management. The value team must digest an immense quantity of information in a relatively short period. Every effort must be made to make the best use of the information at hand. The techniques and methods discussed in this chapter are presented toward achieving this objective.

---

[1] Halliday, David. 1983. "Steve Paul Jobs". *Current Biography* 5
[2] A Guide to the Project Management Body of Knowledge, 2000, Project Management Institute

[3] O'Brien, J. J (1976) "Value Analysis in Design and Construction," McGraw-Hill, New York

[4] Value Engineering Program Guide for Design & Construction, 1992, General Services Administration, (pg. 7-3)

[5] For the latest information on Nominal Treasury Interest Rates, the Office of Management and Budget maintains a website at www.whitehouse.gov/omb/circulars/index.html

[6] Fowler, Theodore C. (1990) Value Analysis in Design, Nostrand Reinhold, New York

[7] Saaty, T.L. (1980) The Analytical Hierarchical Process, McGraw Hill, New York

[8] Ibid

Chapter 6—Function

Leonardo da Vinci—Artist, Scientist, Inventor

Although nature commences with reason and ends in experience it is necessary for us to do the opposite, which is to commence with experience and from this to proceed to investigate the reason.
—Leonardo da Vinci

The function of muscle is to pull and not to push . . .
—Leonardo da Vinci

The illegitimate son of a 25-year-old notary and a peasant girl, Leonardo was born on April 15, 1452, in Vinci, Italy, just outside Florence. Growing up in his father's Vinci home, Leonardo had access to scholarly texts owned by family and friends. He was also exposed to Vinci's longstanding painting tradition, and when he was about 15 his father apprenticed him to the renowned workshop of Andrea del Verocchio in Florence. Even as an apprentice, Leonardo demonstrated his colossal talent. Indeed, his genius seems to have seeped into a number of pieces produced by the Verrochio's workshop from the period 1470 to 1475. Leonardo stayed in the Verrocchio workshop until 1477 when he set up a shingle for himself.

In 1482 he entered the service of the Duke of Milan. He spent 17 years in Milan, leaving in 1499. It was during these years that Leonardo hit his stride, reaching new heights of scientific and artistic achievement. The Duke kept Leonardo busy painting and sculpting and designing elaborate court festivals, but he also put Leonardo to work designing weapons, buildings and machinery. From 1485 to 1490, Leonardo produced studies on a wide variety of subjects, including nature, flying machines, geometry, mechanics, municipal construction, canals and architecture (designing everything from churches to fortresses). His studies from this period contain designs for advanced weapons, including a tank and other war vehicles, various combat devices, and submarines. Also during this period, Leonardo produced his first anatomical studies. His Milan workshop was a veritable hive of activity, buzzing with apprentices and students.

After leaving the Milan in 1499, Leonardo traveled throughout Italy for a period of about 16 years for a number of employers. In about 1503, Leonardo reportedly began work on the "Mona Lisa." Following the death of his patron Giuliano de' Medici in March of 1516, he was offered the title of "Premier Painter, Engineer and Architect of the King" by Francis I of France. His last and perhaps most generous patron, Francis I provided Leonardo with a cushy job, including a stipend and manor house near the royal chateau at Amboise. Leonardo died on May 2, 1519 in Cloux, France. Legend has it that King Francis was at his side when he died, cradling Leonardo's head in his arms.

Leonardo da Vinci has been dubbed by history as the original "renaissance man" due to his broad range of intellectual and artistic pursuits. In fact, the term *renaissance* refers to the central theme of the period, that of the rebirth and revival of intellectual and artistic achievement and vigor. Central to da Vinci's personal experience was his deep-seated desire to understand the workings, or functions, of things. This included his fantastic inventions, scientific studies, and his detailed analysis and illustrations of human anatomy. Leonardo da Vinci's drive to understand how things function sets the stage for this chapter dedicated to the Function Phase.

FUNCTION PHASE

The functional approach embodies that group of techniques within the Value Methodology which sets it apart from traditional cost reduction and problem solving efforts. The Function Phase consists of three distinct yet interrelated techniques:

- Defining functions
- Classifying functions

    o   Basic vs. secondary functions
    o   Work vs. sell functions

- Evaluating functions

    o   Levels of abstraction
    o   Numerical Evaluation Technique
    o   FAST Diagrams
    o   Relating cost and performance to functions—*Value Metrics*

These techniques are tied together into a system known as function analysis. This system is perhaps the single most important and useful technique in Value Methodology; however, it is the most difficult to explain and also the most difficult to grasp and accept.

DEFINING FUNCTIONS

Function, the specific purpose or intended use for any product, process or facility, is that characteristic which makes it work or sell. In short, it is the reason why the owner, customer, or user needs a product. Function is closely related to use value or the properties and qualities which satisfactorily and reliably accomplish a use.

Preliminary attempts to define the function(s) of a product will usually result in several concepts described in many sentences. While this method could conceivably describe the function(s) satisfactorily, it is neither concise nor workable enough for the functional approach. Value Methodology determines function by consideration of the user's actual need. The traits or performance characteristics that justify a product's existence, in terms of the particular owner, client, or user, are determined.

The first principle in defining a function is that be done so using only two words—a verb and a noun.

The verb answers the question, "What does it do?" This question focuses attention on the function rather than the product or its design and leads right to the heart of the functional approach. This is a radical departure from traditional cost reduction efforts where the question is "What is it?", and which then concentrates on making the same product less expensive by answering the question, "How do we make it cheaper?" Traditional efforts give little thought to functional considerations or the user's needs.

After answering the question, "What does it do?", with a verb that defines the item's required action (it may generate, control, pump, emit, protect, transmit . . .), the second question, "What does it do this to?" must be answered with a noun that tells what it is acted upon, (electricity, temperature, liquids, light, surfaces, sound . . .). This noun must be measurable or at least understood in measurable terms, since a specific measurement must be assigned to it during the later evaluation process which relates cost and performance to function. A measurable noun together with an active verb provides a description of a work function, i.e., INSULATE ENERGY, TRANSMIT LOAD, SUPPORT ROOF, etc. They establish quantitative statements.

Listed below are examples of functions for various types of value studies:

- ♦ In product design studies, electric motors PRODUCE TORQUE, light bulbs GENERATE LIGHT, fuel tanks CONTAIN VOLUME, heating elements PRODUCE HEAT.

- In construction studies, structural columns TRANSFER LOAD, interior walls SEPARATE SPACE, doors CONTROL ACCESS, clerestory windows ADMIT LIGHT, and ceiling tile ATTENUATES SOUND.
- In manufacturing process studies, a machining or casting process is designed to SHAPE MATERIAL, while a material handling procedure is designed to DELIVER MATERIAL, and an inspection process is to VERIFY QUALITY.
- In business process studies, a payroll system is designed to DISTRIBUTE PAYROLL, an inspection report procedure is designed to IDENTIFY STATUS, and a project approval procedure is designed to AUTHORIZE CHANGE.

Simple statements such as these ensure clarity of thought and communicate with little confusion. The selection of the noun is important.

Functional definitions containing a passive verb and a non-measurable noun are classified as sell functions. They establish qualitative statements; i.e., improve appearance, decrease effect, increase convenience, etc. *Tables 6-1* and *6-2* provide lists of verbs and nouns for work and sell functions.

Verbs & Nouns for Work Functions

VERBS		NOUNS	
Actuate	Interrupt	Acceleration	Light
Amplify	Limit	Air	Liquid
Apply	Locate	Circuit	Load
Change	Modulate	Contacts	Noise
Collect	Move	Contamination	Oxidation
Conduct	Prevent	Current	Paint
Contain	Protect	Damage	Panel
Control	Rectify	Data	Protection
Create	Reduce	Density	Radiation
Emit	Repel	Dust	Repair
Establish	Rotate	Energy	Rust
Fasten	Secure	Flow	Speed
Filter	Shield	Fluid	Switch
Ignite	Store	Force	Torque
Impede	Support	Friction	Voltage
Induce	Transfer	Insulation	Volume

Table 6-1

Verbs & Nouns for Sell Functions

VERBS		NOUNS	
Communicate	Facilitate	Aesthetics	Effect
Convey	Improve	Acceptance	Features
Create	Increase	Appearance	Form
Decrease	Maintain	Approval	Identity
Demonstrate	Provide	Beauty	Prestige
Enhance	Reduce	Comfort	Style
Establish	Request	Convenience	Symmetry

Table 6-2

Care must be exercised to provide the correct level of functional definition. For example: The function of a water service line to a building could be defined as PROVIDE SERVICE. "Service," not being readily measurable, does not enable us to seek alternatives intelligently. On the other hand if we define the function of the line as CONDUCT FLUID, the noun in the definition is measurable, and acceptable alternatives, being dependent upon the quantity of water being transported, can be determined. When the noun used is a measurable noun (i.e., the water volume in terms of 'Q' factor in the fluid flow equation), we are a step closer to being able to establish a cost-to-function relationship.

The system of defining a function in two words, a verb and a noun, is known as two-word abridgement. Advantages of this system are that it:

- ♦ Forces conciseness. If you cannot define a function in two words, you do not have enough information about the problem or you are trying to define too large a segment of the problem.
- ♦ Avoids combining functions and defining more than one simple function. By using only two words, you are forced to break the problem into its simple elements.
- ♦ Aids in achieving the broadest level of dissociation from specifics. When only two words are used, the possibility

of faulty communication and misunderstandings is reduced to a minimum.

CLASSIFYING FUNCTIONS

There are several classifications of functions. These include:

- Basic Functions
- Secondary Functions
- Higher Order Functions
- Assumed Functions

Basic Functions

The basic function(s) is the specific purpose(s) for which a product exists. The basic function answers the question, "What must it do?" Basic functions have value (use and functional value). An item may possess more than one basic function. This is determined by considering the customer's needs. A non load-bearing exterior wall might be initially defined by the functional description ENCLOSE SPACE. However, further functional analysis determines that for this particular wall two basic functions more definitive than the above exist; i.e., SECURE AREA and RESTRICT VIEW. Both answer the question, "What must it do?"

There are five rules that govern the selection of basic functions. These include:

- Once defined, a basic function cannot change.
- Basic functions are directly related to the "purpose" element of a project's need and purpose statement.
- The cost contribution of a basic function is usually a fraction of the overall cost of the project.
- Basic functions cannot be sold alone; however, the secondary functions that support the basic function cannot be sold without satisfying the basic function.
- The loss of the basic function(s) will cause a loss in value.

Secondary Functions

Secondary functions answer the question, "What else does it do?" For VM purposes, all secondary functions are considered to have no use value. Secondary functions are support functions and usually result from a particular design configuration. Generally, secondary functions contribute greatly to cost and may or may not be essential to the performance of the basic function. Secondary functions that lead to esteem value (convenience, user satisfaction, and appearance) are permissible only insofar as they are necessary to permit the item to buy or sell. Therefore, while secondary functions have zero use value, they may sometimes play an important part in the marketing and acceptance of a design or product. Value Methodology separates costs required for basic functional performance from those incurred for nonessential secondary functions. Once identified, it becomes easier to reduce the cost of secondary functions, while still providing the appeal necessary to permit the design to sell. Value Methodology attempts to eliminate as many secondary functions as possible.

Higher-Order Functions

Higher-order functions represent the specific need(s) that the basic function(s) exists to satisfy. This function(s) identifies the overall need of the customer and generally relates to the "need" statement of a project's need and purpose. For example, the basic function of a classic mousetrap is to KILL MICE. The higher-order function would be to ELIMINATE MICE.

Assumed Functions

Assumed functions describe functions that lie beyond the scope of the study. They are generally not part of the function analysis process unless the level of abstraction changes the scope of the problem. Levels of abstraction will be discussed in greater detail in this chapter.

Examples of basic and secondary functions include:

- *Overhead Projector*—Its basic function is to PROJECT IMAGES. In addition, the overhead projector has many required secondary functions, such as CONVERT ENERGY, GENERATE LIGHT, FOCUS IMAGE, ENLARGE IMAGE, RECEIVE CURRENT, TRANSMIT CURRENT, SUPPORT WEIGHT, etc. Unwanted functions such as GENERATE HEAT and GENERATE NOISE and the aesthetic function of ENHANCE DECOR also exist.
- *Shopping Center*—Its basic function is to ATTRACT CUSTOMERS. In addition, the shopping center has many secondary functions such as ENCLOSE SPACE, CONDITION ENVIRONMENT, CONTROL ACCESS, PARK VEHICLES, etc. An aesthetic function such as ENHANCE APPEARANCE may also exist.
- *HVAC System*—The basic function of the HVAC System is to CONDITION AIR. The other functions such as HEAT AIR, COOL AIR, MOVE AIR, CONTROL HUMIDITY, DISTRIBUTE AIR, etc., are secondary functions. Unwanted functions such as GENERATE NOISE and the aesthetic function of ENHANCE DECOR also exist.
- *Manufacturing Process*—Its basic function is to PRODUCE PRODUCT. In addition, the manufacturing process has many secondary functions, such as GENERATE SHAPE, MOVE MATERIAL, ATTACH COMPONENTS, INSPECT PRODUCT, etc. GENERATE SCRAP is an unwanted function that plagues most manufacturing processes. Aesthetic functions are generally not found in manufacturing processes.
- *Hiring Procedure*—Its basic function is to FILL VACANCY. In addition, the hiring procedure has many secondary functions, such as CREATE ANNOUNCEMENT, INTERVIEW CANDIDATES, PREPARE REQUISITION, CONDUCT ORIENTATION, EVALUATE APPLICATION, SELECT CANDIDATE, etc. While administrative procedures may have unwanted functions, aesthetic functions are rare.

The value team should first seek to randomly identify project functions. The value specialist should initiate this exercise. Functions should be first written down without respect to classification. It is a good idea to begin by starting at the project's purpose and need and then work downward toward the primary project elements, and then toward specific details as necessary. Once a reasonable list of functions has been prepared, the next step is to begin thinking about function classification. A basic example is provided below *(Fig. 6-1)*. This approach to function classification was the one originally developed by Miles, which he referred to as *random function determination*. What is the basic function of a hammer?

Functions of a Hammer

VERB	NOUN
Drive	Nails
Remove	Nails
Transmit	Force
Apply	Leverage
Provide	Grip
Communicate	Identity

Fig. 6-1

Levels of Abstraction

Determination of the basic function(s) is not always an easy process. For instance, the most offered basic function for a hammer is DRIVE NAILS. This definition, however, immediately stumbles over the obvious question, "What about the other uses of a hammer?" Can't hammers be used for other purposes than driving nails such as those suggested in *Figure 6-2*?

Figure 6-2

The hammer doesn't actually drive the nail; it transmits force from a person's hand and arm to the head of the nail. It doesn't matter to the hammer whether it's a chisel, a cobbler's tack, or a nail. So TRANSMIT FORCE would appear to be a better definition of its basic function. Force can be quantified. But wait! Aren't there still other common uses for hammers as suggested in *Figure 6-3*?

Figure 6-3

A judge's gavel CONVEYS AUTHORITY. A croquet player's mallet MOVES BALL. A doctor's hammer TESTS REFLEXES. Aren't these also basic functions? Well, there is a simple way to check by asking a single question: "If the hammer were unable to transmit force would it still fulfill its reason for being?" For each of the six uses of a hammer identified above, all must transmit force in order to fulfill the associated higher order functions. Here are the answers to the questioned posed above for each use of the hammer.

- A carpenter's hammer must TRANSMIT FORCE to drive a nail into a board.
- A sculptor's hammer must TRANSMIT FORCE to strike the chisel which chips the stone. In this case, the chisel also TRANSMITS FORCE; however, is transmitting force the chisel's basic function?
- A cobbler's hammer must TRANSMIT FORCE to drive the tack into the sole of the shoe.
- A judge's gavel must TRANSMIT FORCE in order to create noise and convey his or her authority to the courtroom.
- A croquet player's mallet must TRANSMIT FORCE to move the ball through the wickets.

- A doctor's hammer must TRANSMIT FORCE to the patient's knee in order to test his or her reflexes.

It appears then that transmit force is indeed the correct basic function. In each case the desired effect is quantifiable. The hammer, depending upon its application, may have a radically different higher order function associated with it. It becomes apparent that a forcing process in either one direction or another in order to develop a multiplicity of two-word abridgements from which one or more levels maybe chosen as the level of the primary function to be studied. This is referred to as the *ladder of abstraction*.

The ladder of abstraction method has been developed as a thought forcing process. To drive one's thinking up the ladder we ask the question, "Why?" To force the thought processes down the level of abstraction, we must ask the question, "How?" *Figure 6-4* illustrates the functions of a pencil using the ladder of abstraction.

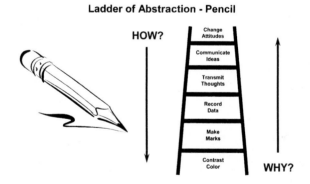

Figure 6-4

Obviously, from the ladder of abstraction, the two-word abridgements at the upper rungs of the ladder are fairly abstract when thinking about the nature of a pencil. The functions on the lower rungs of the ladder, on the other hand, are much more concrete. If MAKE MARKS was the level of abstraction selected for focus during the next step in the VM Job Plan, the Speculation Phase, then the value team might identify other ways of making marks such as ballpoint pens, paintbrushes, chalk, and using chisels on stone tablets. If the team focused on a function higher up on the ladder of abstraction such as COMMUNICATE IDEAS, then the team might identify concepts such as public speech, web-based learning via the internet, billboards and through the publication of periodicals.

The real value of the ladder of abstraction is that more creative ideas can be generated by using more than one definition. It leads to greater fluency (more ideas), greater flexibility (more variety of ideas), and an improved functional understanding of the problem.

This forcing technique can also help team agreement on the level of abstraction or basic function to be analyzed. From this forcing process has evolved the technique known as FAST (Functional Analysis System Technique).

EVALUATING FUNCTIONS

In the previous example, determining which function(s) is the basic function and which are the secondary functions may appear to be obvious. This is not always the case, however, especially when considering complicated and/or very expensive projects. It takes time and experience to train the mind to think using the functional approach, and sometimes the classification of functions requires more careful analysis and evaluation. There are two techniques for the classification in addition to the random function determination process identified above. The two function evaluation techniques are:

- Numerical Evaluation Technique
- Function Analysis System Technique

Numerical Evaluation Technique

For value studies involved with projects where it is not always clear what the basic and required secondary functions are, the value specialist may wish to utilize the numerical evaluation technique. This technique uses a simple matrix to determine the relative importance of functions using a paired comparison method of analysis. The functions are listed vertically and then, using the scaled paired comparison technique, pair-wise comparisons are made by asking the question "which function is more important in meeting the project's need and purpose—*Function A* or *Function B*?" As there are often shades of differences involved in posing such a question, the dominant function in the comparison can be given a weighting of 1, 2 or 3 with respect to the order of magnitude of its importance.

- 1 - Indicates a minor difference in importance. If the decision requires much debate or discussion, then there is probably only a minor difference in importance.
- 2 - Indicates a medium difference of importance. If the decision requires a short period of discussion, then the difference may be moderate in nature.
- 3 - Indicates a major difference of importance. If the decision is made unanimously and instantly, then the difference most likely reflects a major difference in importance.

This pair-wise comparison should be performed for all functions, and is very similar to the process described for determining the importance of performance attributes in *Chapter 5—Information*. The numbered weights (1, 2 or 3) should then be added up for each function. Be sure to add both vertically and horizontally. The function, or functions, with the highest numerical score should provide a pretty strong indication as to what the basic function(s) is. An example of this technique using a simple paired comparison matrix is provided in *Figure 6-5*.

FUNDAMENTALS OF VALUE METHODOLOGY

This example identifies the functions for a fuel storage system. The functions are randomly determined using the basic procedure presented in the preceding paragraphs. Each function is compared to its peers and is evaluated. The results indicate that the function STORE FUEL was by far the most important of the functions—therefore, it can be surmised that it is the basic function of the system.

NUMERICAL EVALUATION MATRIX Fuel Storage System								TOTAL
Store Fuel	A	A-3	A-3	A-3	A-3	A-3		15.0
Resist Corrosion		B	B-3	B-2	B-2	B-3		10.0
Resist Force			C	D-1	E-2	C-2		2.0
Control Flow				D	E-2	D-2		3.0
Direct Flow					E	E-2		6.0
Permit Maintenance						F		0.0
								36.0

Figure 6-5

Once the paired comparison matrix is completed, the functions can be reordered based upon their relative importance. If the functions are plotted on a graph, a basic trend will emerge that is common with all projects (*Fig. 6-6*). Two distinct drops in function scores occur on the graph. The first drop represents delineation between the basic and supporting secondary functions.

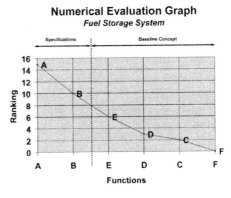

Fig. 6-6

These supporting secondary functions reflect customer requirements. The second drop represents delineation between the supporting secondary functions (customer requirements) and non-essential secondary functions (those that exist by virtue of the design solution chosen to provide the basic function).

The Numerical Evaluation Technique provides a simple way of classifying and evaluating functions; however, it has been largely supplanted by the Function Analysis System Technique.

Function Analysis System Technique[1]

The Function Analysis System Technique, commonly referred to by the acronym FAST, is a powerful diagramming technique for analyzing the relationship of functions. FAST diagrams have the following uses:

- Show the specific relationships of all functions with respect to each other
- Test the validity of the functions under study
- Help identify missing functions
- Broaden the knowledge of all team members with respect to the project.

The Function Analysis System Technique was developed by Charles W. Bytheway of the Sperry Rand Corporation and was first introduced in a paper presented at the 1965 National Conference of the Society of American Value Engineers. Subsequently, FAST has been widely used by governmental agencies, private firms, and value consultants.

FAST was originally used by its inventor as a way to stimulate creativity in order to explore innovative avenues for performing functions. Interestingly, Bytheway claims that he has never completed a FAST diagram. When he found the path he was looking for, he abandoned the diagram. From his perspective, FAST was merely a useful tool for developing the level of understanding of a problem he was looking for—it was not an end in and of itself.

FAST builds on the verb-noun rules described earlier in this chapter. It is an excellent communication technique in that it allows value team members to contribute equally and communicate with one another while addressing the problem objectively without bias or preconceived conclusions. FAST has also proven to be a useful tool for project planning and a good way to present complex concepts to decision makers.

FAST also distinguishes between basic and secondary functions, which make it a natural for classifying functions. However, it does this in a way that provides a means of graphically illustrating the intuitive logic used to determine and test function dependencies through the development of a diagram that, at first glance, appears to resemble a flow chart or network diagram.

The major difference between the Random Function Determination process first described by Miles and the FAST process is in analyzing a system as a complete unit, rather than analyzing the parts of a system. When studying systems it becomes apparent that functions do not operate in a random fashion. A system exists because functions form dependencies with other functions, just as parts form a dependency link with other parts to make the system work.

It is important to understand that there is no "correct" FAST diagram, as in comparing it to an accepted norm, but there is a "valid" FAST model. The degree of validity is directly dependent upon the talents of the value team members. The FAST diagram must be constructed using team consensus, as the discussion the diagram generates is just as important as the diagram itself. A FAST diagram is "complete" only when consensus among its creators is reached.

In the previous section dealing with levels of abstraction, the concept of the "How?" and "Why?" logic was introduced—this intuitive logic forms the basis in constructing FAST diagrams. The directional references of the HOW and WHY questions remain the same. HOW is read from left to right and WHY is read from right to left. Using the examples below, if we were addressing the function TRANSMIT SOUND and asked the question; "How do we transmit sound?" the answer, in the form of a function could be TRANSMIT SIGNAL (Fig. 6-7).

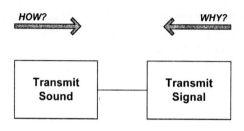

Fig. 6-7

If we continued in the HOW direction and asked, "How do we transmit signal?" the answer could be INPUT DATA (Fig. 6-8).

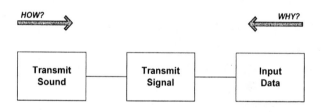

Fig. 6-8

To test the logic of the example above the functions can read in the reverse WHY direction. "Why do we want to input data?" "To TRANSMIT SIGNAL." Why do we want to transmit signal?" "To TRANSMIT SOUND." If the team agrees with the answers we can continue to expand the FAST model, either in the WHY or HOW direction. In the WHY direction we would ask; "Why do we want to transmit sound?" "To COMMUNICATE WORDS"; and "why do we want to communicate words?" "To COMMUNICATE THOUGHTS." Switching to the HOW question we can continue to build in that direction by asking; "How do we input data?" "MANIPULATE BUTTONS." Examining the function inputs thus far, the FAST model would look as follows (Fig. 6-9).

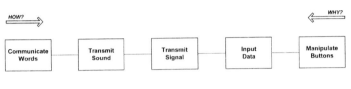

Fig. 6-9

Question: what is the product represented by this FAST model example? If you answered "a cellular phone," consider that the same function model can apply to a walkie talkie, CB radio or standard telephone. This shouldn't be too surprising because all of these products perform the functions described, in the same dependency order. The differences occur when the model is dimensioned in terms of time, legibility, productivity, or other measurements that reflect the problem under study.

Reverse Logic?

Many individuals, when first introduced to FAST diagrams, find it counter-intuitive, especially those accustomed to flow charts and network diagrams. They appear to be backwards! This is one of the most important aspects of FAST and it is what forces those involved in constructing FAST diagrams to think about a project differently. Unlike these more common diagramming techniques, FAST appears to read from finish to start if viewed from left to right. There are a number of reasons for this difference:

♦ The FAST diagram begins with the goal or objective, which focuses our attention where it should be. When beginning any endeavor, we usually know what we want to achieve, so why not begin there? Addressing functions on the FAST diagram with the question WHY, the function to its left expresses the goal of that function. The question HOW, is answered by the function on the right, and describes the approach being utilized to perform the function to the left.

- Changing a function on the HOW-WHY path affects all of the functions to the right of that function. This is a domino effect that only goes one way, from left to right. Starting with any place on the FAST diagram, if a function is changed the goals are still valid (functions to the left) but the method to accomplish that function, and all other functions on the right, are affected. Functions to the right of another function are called "dependent functions," because the way that function performs is dependent on the function to its left.
- Reading the goal, or the left side of the diagram, to the beginning, on the right end (in the HOW direction), goes against our system paradigm. Because it seems "strange," building the model in the HOW direction, or function justification, will focus the team's attention on each function element of the model. Whereas, reversing the FAST model and building it in its system orientation will cause the team to leap over individual functions and focus on the system, leaving function "gaps" in the system.

Another way of thinking about building FAST diagrams is that they are built in the HOW direction and the logic is tested in the WHY direction.

When

The WHEN direction is not part of the intuitive logic process but it supplements intuitive thinking. WHEN is not a time orientation, but indicates cause and effect. Referring to *Figure 6-10,* "when you REVIEW INFORMATION, you should VERIFY AVAILABILITY." VERIFY AVAILABILITY is a supporting secondary function that supplements the function "review information." As a supporting secondary function it can be expanded in the HOW-WHY directions to create a minor logic path and build a subsystem FAST diagram. Since the independent function is not on the major logic path, changing the function would not significantly affect the basic function.

Since functions can be described using a verb and a noun, a general rule to distinguish between the two is to look at the noun. If the noun describes something specific, like a product, it would be considered an activity. Nouns that are general are used to describe independent functions and activities, which are the result of satisfying the WHEN question. Both of these should be placed below the major logic path to indicate their role as supporting functions.

Unwanted secondary functions can optionally be highlighted by using a double, or bold, line around the box.

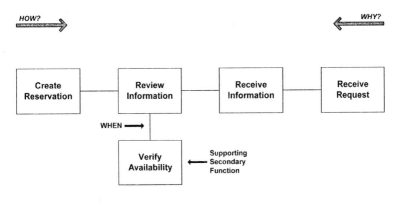

Figure 6-10

Structure of the FAST Diagram

The FAST Diagram is built upon the left-right logic of HOW and WHY and the up-down logic of WHEN. There are several additional elements that are necessary to further communicate the functional relationships. The basic elements of the FAST Diagram are illustrated in *Figure 6-11.*

Scope Lines

Scope lines represent the limits of the value study and are shown as two dashed vertical lines on the FAST diagram. The scope lines demarcate the "scope of the study," or that element of the problem with which the value team is concerned. The basic functions will always be the first function(s) to the immediate right of the left scope line. The function to the immediate left of the left scope line is the higher order function, or output. The right scope line identifies the beginning of the value study and separates the assumed function, or input, from the scope of the study.

Highest Order Function(s)

The objective of the value study is called the "Highest Order Function(s)" and is located to the left of the basic function(s) and outside of the left scope line. Any function to the left of another function is a "higher order function" because reading the FAST model in the WHY direction will lead you to the basic function(s) and the highest order functions (or goals) of the subject under study.

Lower Order or Assumed Function(s)

Functions to the right and outside of the right scope line represent the input side that initiate the subject under study and are known as lower order functions. Functions that lie to the right of the rightmost scope line are also sometimes referred to as "assumed" functions. This is because these functions are generally left up to the customer or user to determine, so an assumption is being made as to what they are.

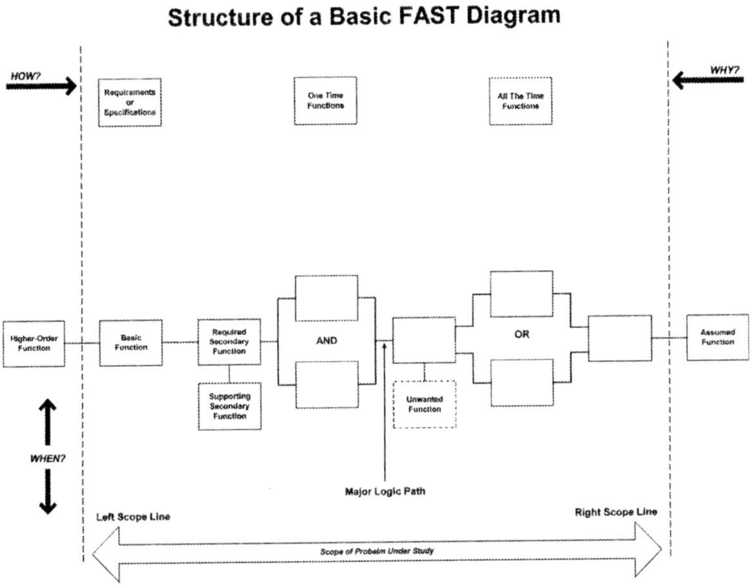

FUNDAMENTALS OF VALUE METHODOLOGY

Structure of a Basic FAST Diagram

Figure 6-11

The terms "higher" or "lower" order functions should not be interpreted as relative importance, but rather as the input and output side of the process. As an example, if we were analyzing a purchase order processing procedure, the function RECEIVE ORDER could be the lowest order function, with the function RECEIVE PRODUCT being the highest order function. How to accomplish the highest order function, RECEIVE PRODUCT, describes the need for the procedure and helps order our thinking to address the purpose of the procedure, or basic function, as "SHIP PRODUCT."

Basic Function(s)

Those function(s) to the immediate right of the leftmost scope line represent the purpose or mission of the product or process under study and are called Basic Function(s). Once determined, the basic function will not change. If the basic function fails, the product or process will lose its market value.

Secondary Functions

All functions to the right of the basic function(s) portray the conceptual approach selected to satisfy the basic function. The concept describes the method being considered, or elected, to achieve the basic function(s). The concept can represent either the current conditions (as is) or proposed approach (to be). Which approach to use (current or proposed) in creating the FAST model is determined by the value team and the definition of the problem under study. Conceptually, all functions to the right of the basic function are treated as "secondary" functions, and are subject to change.

Value studies focused on improving a design or concept that is in progress should first begin by constructing a FAST diagram based on this initial concept. Doing so will reveal potential problems or areas for study. Constructing a FAST diagram based on a design in progress will also be useful for the next step in the functional approach, which involves correlating cost and performance to function. Once this is accomplished, it may be useful, time permitting, to construct a FAST diagram based upon how the value team believes the solution should look. If the value study is focusing on a project that has not begun design or formal planning, then the FAST diagram should be constructed based on what the solution could or should be.

Requirements or Specifications

Requirements and specifications are issues relevant to the project that affect either how it operates or describe qualitative aspects relevant to its design. These items must be achieved to satisfy the highest order function of the project in its normal operations. Although these types of issues may not even be functions, they influence the concept selected to best achieve the basic function(s), and satisfy the customer's or user's expectations. These types of issues are generally included as

FUNDAMENTALS OF VALUE METHODOLOGY

part of the FAST diagram and are displayed above the diagram and are not connected directly to the main body of the diagram. It is suggested that these special issues are labeled as such or a graphic key (i.e., dashed box, shadow box, etc.) be used to distinguish them from the other functions that are part of the FAST diagram.

Logic Path Functions

Any function on the HOW or WHY logic path is a logic path function. If the functions along the WHY direction enter the basic function(s), it is a major logic path. If the WHY path does not lead directly to the basic function, it is a minor logic path. Changing a function on the major logic path will alter or destroy the way the basic function is performed. Changing a function on a minor logic path will disturb an independent (supporting) function that enhances the basic function.

Dependent Functions

As discussed previously, starting with the first function to the right of the basic function, each successive function is "dependent" upon the one to its immediate left (or higher order function) for its existence. That dependency becomes more evident when the HOW question and direction is followed. If any function on a minor or major logic path is changed, it will affect all the functions to the right of the changed function. Therefore, those functions affected are dependent functions, because their existence depends on the functions to their left.

Independent Functions

Independent functions generally represent an augmentation to the function they are connected to on the logic path. They are said to be "independent" because they do not depend on other functions for their performance. Independent functions may be located above or below the logic path and are always considered to be secondary in nature.

AND / OR Lines

In some cases, it may be desirable to differentiate how functions may be connected. One way to do this is through the AND / OR lines. The AND connection is represented by showing a split or fork between functions *(Fig. 6-12)* and indicates that both paths must be followed. AND lines can also indicate that the connecting functions are of equal or lesser importance, depending on how they are drawn.

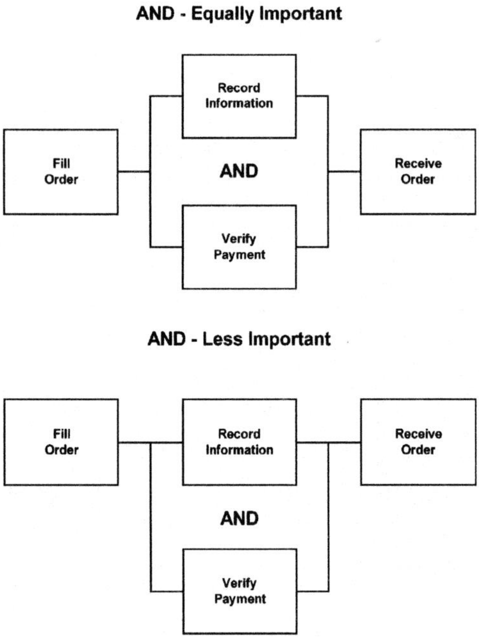

AND - Equally Important

AND - Less Important

Fig. 6-12

The OR connection is represented by lines emanating from the root function at different locations *(Fig. 6-13)* and indicate a choice in the function path. OR lines may also indicate function paths equal or lesser importance similar to AND lines. AND / OR lines may also be drawn in the vertical, or WHEN direction.

OR - Equally Important

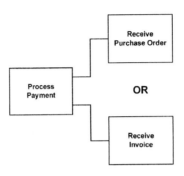

OR - Less Important

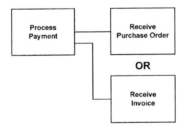

Fig. 6-13

Examples of FAST Diagrams

Examples of FAST diagrams for projects in design and construction, manufacturing, and management have been included on the following pages for reference. It is important to emphasize that there are many ways to construct a FAST diagram; however, they must all follow the same structural rules. The differences usually relate to the verbs and nouns used to define the functions and differences in the degrees of abstraction used.

Six examples of FAST diagrams are provided. These include:

- *Bridge Replacement Project*—The purpose of this project is to replace an existing bridge across a lake and improve the existing roadway geometry of two curves immediately south of the structure. The existing bridge is at the end of its useful life and the structural integrity of the superstructure is such that retrofitting is not economically feasible. An additional lane will added in the southbound direction to lengthen a truck-climbing lane immediately to the south of the structure. The substructure will also be designed to accommodate future widening. This FAST diagram represents the baseline design concept for the replacement project (Fig. 6-14).
- *Disposable Lighter*—This FAST diagram represents the functions of a standard disposable butane lighter that one might purchase at a convenience store. Despite the simplicity of the FAST diagram, you may be surprised by the functional complexity of such a simple item. Note that there are 16 secondary functions that support but one basic function *(Fig. 6-15)*.
- *Hiring Procedure*—This FAST diagram represents the existing hiring procedures of a company. The assumed function, or input, to the procedure begins with an analysis of the company's workforce. The higher order function, or intended output, is that the newly hired employee will be assigned to staff a new project. Note the large number of functions arrayed in the WHEN direction. This is a common phenomenon of FAST diagrams related to procedures, where many activities may occur in parallel *(Fig. 6-16)*.
- *Recycled Water System*—This project involves the design and construction of a citywide recycled water system which will supply recycled water to several landscape

irrigation users and groundwater recharge facilities. This system will reduce overall water demands by utilizing treated effluent that would otherwise be discharged into a local river. The project includes an extensive pipeline, reservoirs and modifications to an existing water pollution control plant. This FAST diagram represents the baseline design concept for the new system *(Fig. 6-17)*.

- *Manufacturing Process*—This FAST diagram illustrates the functions involved in the assembly of an automotive component. The input to the study scope begins with the delivery of the required materials to the factory and concludes with the shipping of the completed component to the manufacturer that will incorporate the part into the production of a new automobile. Although this is a relatively simple diagram, the value of the FAST diagram will become obvious when labor and material costs, as well as performance attributes, are referenced to the functions, revealing activities yielding poor value *(Fig. 6-18)*.
- *Medical Records Management System*—In this example, we have a FAST diagram that illustrates an existing medical records management system that deals with sensitive patient health history information. In this example, one of the functions has been identified as an "unwanted" secondary function, DISCARD RECORDS. The value team would obviously want to focus on generating ideas that would eliminate the presence of this function from the system *(Fig 6-19)*.

FAST Diagrams VS. Flow Charts[2]

Many value practitioners who frequently perform value studies of processes and procedures believe that the development of a FAST diagram is unnecessary because a flow chart essentially represents the same thing. The fact is, there a number of critical differences between FAST diagrams and flow charts (or network diagrams, if you prefer).

One might interpret that the *functions* of a process or procedure represent the purpose(s) for which the functions are intended, whereas the *activities* are the physical acts of performing those functions. A FAST diagram arranges functions in a logical manner to answer questions like "How?" and "Why?" in order to define the *purposes* for which the process or procedure is in place. The process flow chart, on the other hand, specifies what *actions* occur by people and/or equipment to accomplish the intended functions.

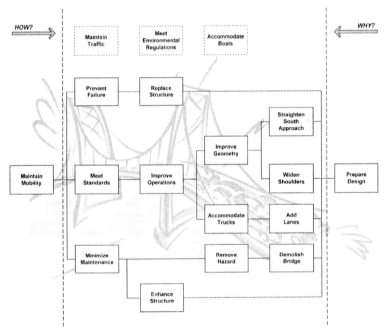

Fig. 6-14

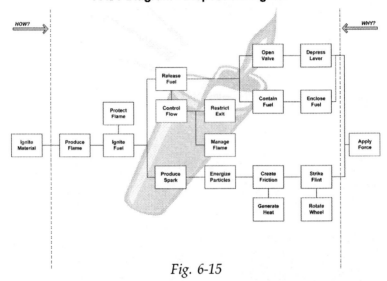

Fig. 6-15

FUNDAMENTALS OF VALUE METHODOLOGY 193

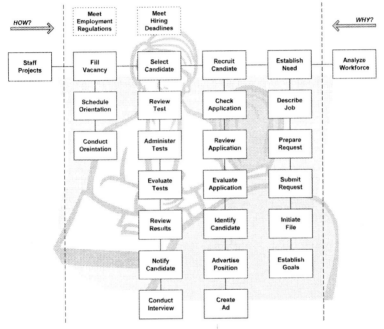

Fig. 6-16

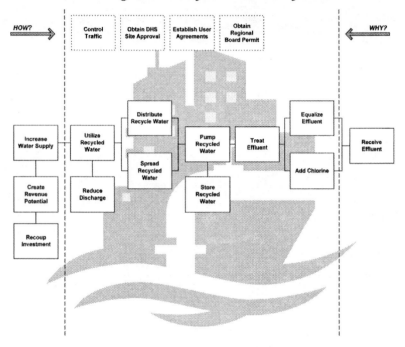

Fig. 6-17

FAST Diagram - Manufacturing Process

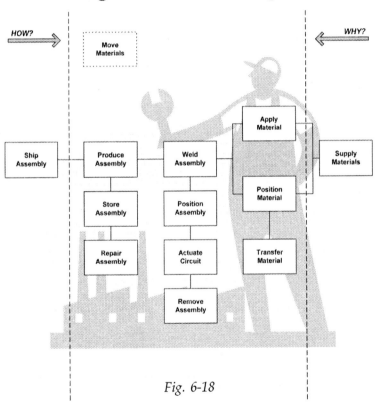

Fig. 6-18

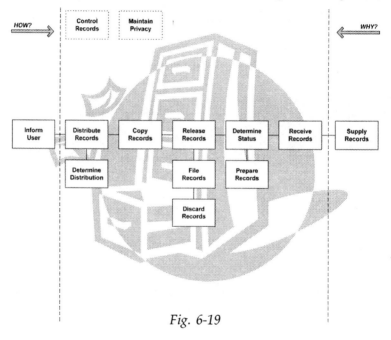

Fig. 6-19

Referring to the Merriam-Webster dictionary, consider that the definition of "analysis"—which is performed as part of the Function *Analysis* System Technique diagram—is defined as "an examination of a complex, its elements, and their *relations*." Kaneo Akiyama, in his book titled Function Analysis[3], states "Things that are static, fixed, and apparent can be defined in terms of shapes and colors. This is not the case with functions, which are dynamic, *relative*, and process-oriented." In terms of a value study, FAST diagrams are used to break down a process or procedure into its individual elements, and graphically represent how they *relate* to one another. A flow chart, on the other hand, is defined as "a diagram that shows step-by-step progression through a procedure or system.". The flow chart is the graphic representation of activities which considers the before and after implications, i.e., the sequence of events.

To further illustrate these differences using an example, a FAST diagram developed by a team involved in decertifying State property for use by other individuals or organizations was developed by a value team in order to validate why it takes twenty months to complete the decertification process (Fig. 6-20).

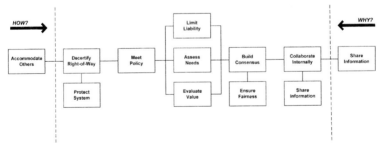

Fig. 6-20

The value team was charged with finding ways to reduce the timeline for decertification, and defining roles and responsibilities. The baseline process utilized a flow chart more than a decade old combined with input from management and value team members during the value study kick-off meeting. After refining the flow chart to represent the existing process, the team developed the FAST diagram.

Relating the functions above to activities on the flow chart enabled team members to eliminate, modify, or add activities, as appropriate. For example, the activities shown on *Figure 6-21* (excerpted from the flow chart) are actions taken to COLLABORATE INTERNALLY and BUILD CONSENSUS.

A quick comparison of the original flow chart and the FAST diagram will reveal the fundamental differences between the two techniques. The baseline flow chart activities supporting two of the functions, COLLABORATE INTERNALLY and BUILD CONSENSUS, included a lengthy checking and rechecking process, which took an elapsed time of approximately 11½ weeks. Because the team was focused on the two *functions* mentioned above, they were able to modify the activities to accomplish those functions in 7½ weeks. They focused on functions rather than on activities and came up with alternative ways, i.e., fewer activities, to accomplish the required functions.

FUNDAMENTALS OF VALUE METHODOLOGY

Flow Chart - Decertification Process

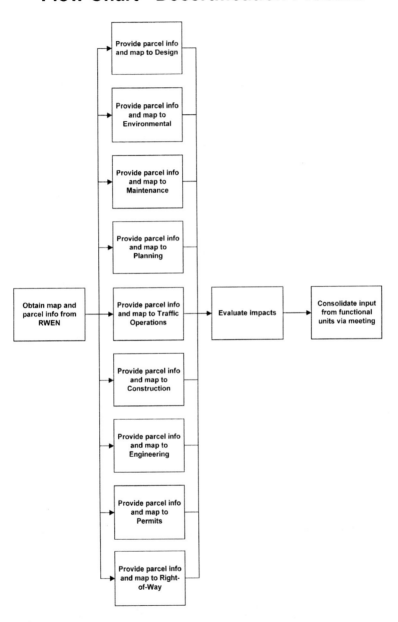

Figure 6-21

Function Analysis System Technique could be described as the system, and the flowchart as the process required to implement the system. FAST is also a good method for identifying flaws in the system, in that it enables the team to determine where unneeded or unwanted functions are included, and/or needed or wanted functions are missing.

Charles Bytheway, the originator of the FAST method, used the system to stimulate creativity. He emphasized use of what he called "thought-provoking questions" as opposed to focusing on completion of the FAST diagram, believing that success was defined by developing creative alternatives (solutions) based on the functions derived from answering the provocative questions. This approach brings up a very big difference between a FAST diagram and a flow chart: although it is not imperative for the FAST diagram to be complete, a flow chart must be completed to represent the entire process being defined.

FAST diagramming is one of, if not the, most powerful communications tools used in the Value Methodology, and it is extremely effective for getting a multi-disciplined team to reach consensus on the scope of the process or project being analyzed. At the same time, a FAST diagram must not be misinterpreted to represent activities on a flow chart. FAST reflects the divergent opinions and feelings of people. It is a subjective, albeit collective, representation of a process scope. The flow chart, on the other hand, is the objective representation of what actually happens to accomplish the required functions.

Relating Cost and Performance to Function—*Value Metrics*

The team is now ready to consider a key aspect of Function Analysis, which is the determination of the relationship of cost and performance to function. These relationships direct the value team to the areas of greatest opportunity within a project by identifying those functions indicating performance and cost mismatches. Relating cost to function has been a standard VM practice. Function Analysis can be further augmented by also relating performance to function.

Although not essential, it is recommended that a FAST diagram be constructed first before analyzing cost-function and performance-function relationships. The reason for this is that the value team may find through the application of FAST that they missed functions that were overlooked during the random function identification process. Once a proper FAST diagram has been completed, and all of the functions have been identified, the value team can begin by first analyzing cost-function relationships by using a simple cost-function matrix.

The functions within scope are listed across the top of the matrix. Then the major cost groups are listed down the left-hand side of the form with the associated incremental costs in the total cost column. The value team will need to use their best judgment in splitting up the cost of a single element or component among multiple functions. Costs should be extracted from existing project data where available, such as a construction cost estimate, bills of material, or labor/time estimates. Next the function(s) impacted by each project element is identified. Once this is done, the team must estimate how much of the cost of each element belongs to each function. This need not be a precise estimate. Finally, all columns are added vertically to determine how much cost is allocated to each function. Typically, three or four functions will be responsible for 60 to 80 percent of the total cost. *Figure 6-22* shows an example of a cost-function matrix.

Once the cost-function matrix has been completed, the costs can be assigned directly to the functions on the FAST diagram.

COST-FUNCTION MATRIX — STEERING GEAR

Item	Total Cost	Transmit Force	Convert Energy	Transmit Torque	Direct Fluid	Receive Torque	Contain Pressure	Restrict Travel	Dampen Shock	Adjust Length	Allow Attach	Shield Contam.	Receive Fluid
Valve Assembly	23.53		5.25	3.75	4.88	1.65	4.50				3.50		
Housing Assembly	35.86	20.45			11.85			1.80			0.80	0.10	0.86
Tie Rod Assembly	27.49	20.39						0.60		3.00	3.50		
Tube Assembly	7.26	2.90	2.56								0.60	1.20	
Rack	14.78	5.33	9.45										
Bellows	1.90											1.90	
Rod Bushing	3.21		2.90									0.31	
Rack Guide	3.59	2.75						0.70	0.14				
Housing Cover	1.19											1.19	
Final Assembly	8.82	1.75	2.20		1.37	1.80	0.20	0.20		0.25		0.15	0.90
Scrap	3.44	0.15	1.93	0.75	0.05		0.18			0.30			0.08
TOTAL	131.07	53.72	24.29	4.50	18.15	3.45	4.88	3.30	0.14	3.55	8.40	4.85	1.84
%	100.0%	41.0%	18.5%	3.4%	13.8%	2.6%	3.7%	2.5%	0.1%	2.7%	6.4%	3.7%	1.4%

Figure 6-22

Expanding on this basic cost-function matrix, the value team should next consider the relative influence that the functions have on performance. The performance-function matrix is used to explore relationships between functions and their contribution to project performance. As with the cost-function matrix, there can be multiple functions that contribute to project performance. This can simply be expressed in terms of a gross percentage. This data can then be plotted on a performance-function matrix *(Fig. 6-23)*.

PERFORMANCE-FUNCTION MATRIX — STEERING GEAR

Performance Attribute	Transmit Force	Convert Energy	Transmit Torque	Direct Fluid	Receive Torque	Contain Pressure	Restrict Travel	Dampen Shock	Adjust Length	Allow Attach	Shield Contam.	Receive Fluid	Total %
Responsiveness	60%	30%	5%		5%								100%
Ergonomics							20%	20%	60%				100%
Maintainability	20%	10%	5%	20%	5%	20%		10%			10%		100%
Reliability	15%	10%	5%	5%	5%	5%		20%	5%		20%	10%	100%

Fig. 6-23

As with the cost data, the performance data should then be applied directly to the FAST diagram. Cost data is recorded in the upper right corner of the function. The percent total cost for the basic functions is indicated to show the major cost trends. A sensitivity matrix located below the FAST diagram relates functions and performance. Each column of functions

FUNDAMENTALS OF VALUE METHODOLOGY

is designated a number in the upper left hand corner. The sensitivity matrix cross-indexes the performance attributes with the function numbers. Different colored or shaded marks express the order of magnitude of the function in terms of contributing to total project performance *(Fig. 6-24)*. In this example, a black dot represents a function having a "major" performance contribution (assume a 30% or greater contribution) while a white dot represents a function having a "minor" performance contribution (assume less than 30% contribution).

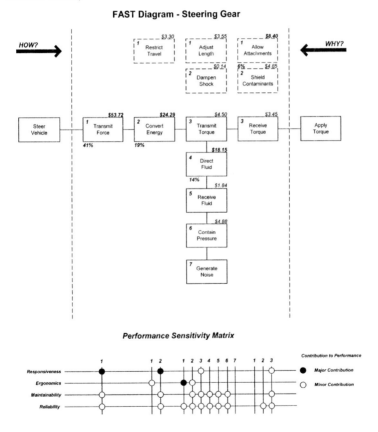

Fig. 6-24

In this example, several functions indicating a potential for poor value include DIRECT FLUID, which has a relatively high cost with a low contribution to total performance, and ADJUST LENGTH, which has a relatively low cost but high contribution to total performance. It is important to remember that a function indicating a high contribution to performance does not necessarily mean that the function is performing well. These cost-performance mismatches should lead the value team to focus further on these functions during the Speculation Phase.

This method provides a highly effective tool for considering the relationship of function, cost and performance. Value team members will be able to see not only high cost functions, but also performance critical functions. It is at this point that the direct consideration of performance can begin focusing a value team's efforts on performance improvement and, ultimately, total value improvement.

SUMMARY

The Function Phase is what gives Value Methodology the unique perspective in understanding problems. As has been stated elsewhere in this text, understanding the problem is at least half the battle in coming up with solutions that will ultimately contribute to improved value.

Developing a mastery of the functional approach takes practice. A solid comfort level will be developed only through repeated application. All value practitioners must strive to develop these skills, especially the powerful technique of FAST diagramming.

Anyone who professes to employ the Value Methodology should be asked if they utilize Function Analysis and, if so, how they apply it. This is the primary test in determining whether VM is truly being applied. If the concepts and techniques of function analysis are neither or understood or employed properly, then it can be said with absolute certainty that whatever process it is claimed is being used, it is not Value Methodology.

---

[1] Kaufman, J.J. (1994) "The Principles and Applications of Function Analysis System Technique." J.J. Kaufman & Associates. This section draws upon the research of Jerry Kaufman's in the construction and application of FAST diagrams.

[2] Adams, Virginia, (2004) "FAST Doesn't Flow." This section is condensed from a technical paper presented at the 2004 SAVE International Conference in Montreal, Quebec.

[3] Akiyama, Kaneo (1991) "Function Analysis: Systematic Improvement of Quality and Performance," Productivity Press.

Chapter 7 — Speculation

Albert Einstein—Physicist

Imagination is more important than knowledge.
—Albert Einstein

Common sense is the collection of prejudices acquired by age eighteen.
—Albert Einstein

Albert Einstein was born on March 14, 1879, in what is Ulm, Germany. His father was a manufacturer of electrical equipment. There were no early indications of Einstein's intellectual capabilities; in fact, there was even some concern on the part of his parents when he was a small child that he might be somewhat challenged. During his school years he showed no special aptitude because of his dislike for rigid methods of instruction, and he was cited by school officials as being disruptive. Einstein was fascinated by mathematics and science, subjects that he studied on his own. He became a high school dropout when he left school to join his family in Milan.

In 1896 he was able to enroll at the Swiss Federal Institute of Technology in Zurich after making up a number of subject deficiencies. At the institute the academic fare did not suit him either; he managed, however, to pass the required examinations for his degree. In the two years following his graduation in 1900, he subsisted on odd teaching jobs. By 1902 he had secured a position as patent examiner at the Swiss patent office in Bern, where he worked for the next seven years.

The year 1905 was a momentous year for science, for without any academic connections, Einstein published, at the age of 26, four papers in the journal Annalen der Physik—papers that were to alter the course of 20th Century physics. The first dealt with the random thermal motions of molecules in colloidal solutions, called Brownian motion, first noted in 1827 by the English botanist Robert Brown. Einstein's second paper reinforced the quantum theory of light developed by Max Planck in 1900. In it Einstein established the photon nature of light by accounting for the photoelectric phenomenon discovered in 1902. For this contribution, Einstein was awarded the Nobel Prize in physics in 1921. The third and most famous of Einstein's 1905 papers dealt with the special theory of relativity: "Zur Electrodynamik bewegter Korper" ("On the Electrodynamics of Moving Bodies"). And the final paper of that year introduced the now famous equivalence between mass and energy in the equation $E=mc^2$. Because of this work, Einstein received his first academic post in 1908 at the University of Bern, which was followed by several others in Europe before he settled at the Institute for Advanced Study in Princeton in 1933.

Einstein thought of himself more as philosopher than as scientist, and in many ways he was from the same mold as the Greek natural philosophers, such as Plato and Aristotle, in trying to understand the natural world through mental concepts instead of experimentation. His success did draw on the insights of predecessors and the powerful analytical tools of mathematics, but most of all it was the result of an unerring intuition, the likes of which have been equaled by very few.

Albert Einstein embodies the concept of creativity and imagination through his ability to release himself from the constraints of conventional ways of thinking. His life and times serve as an excellent lead into this chapter's discussion of the Speculation Phase.

SPECULATION PHASE

The purpose of the Speculation Phase is to produce new ways to perform project functions. In other words, it is all about creativity. In this chapter, the concept of creativity will be explored and techniques for fostering creativity will be presented.

CREATIVITY

What is creativity? The American Heritage Dictionary defines the word "creative" as:

1. Having the ability or power to create: *Human beings are creative animals.*
2. Productive; creating.
3. Characterized by originality and expressiveness; imaginative: *creative writing.*

This is a pretty simple definition, though rather uncreative! If you asked this question to some very creative people, you might be surprised by what they have to say about the subject:

> *"I am enough of an artist to draw freely upon my imagination. Imagination is more important than knowledge. Knowledge is limited. Imagination encircles the world."*—Albert Einstein, Physicist

> *"Sometimes I think the human mind is like a compost pile. It contains a variety of ingredients all stewing together toward the ultimate end of producing something useful. Some ingredients aid the process, some hinder it, and others are inert."*—Roger von Oech, Ph.D., Creativity Consultant

> *"All children are artists. The problem is how to remain an artist once he grows up."*—Pablo Picasso, Artist

> "When I am working on a problem I never think about beauty. I only think about how to solve the problem. But when I have finished, if the solution is not beautiful, I know it is wrong."—Buckminster Fuller, Architect

> "The best way to have a good idea is to have lots of ideas."—Linus Pauling, Chemist

> "Creativity takes courage."—Henri Matisse, Artist

Much has been written concerning creativity by history's greatest artists, scientists, architects and inventors. Hundreds of quotes could easily be added to those listed above; however, what is interesting about these perspectives on creativity is that they all follow a number of basic themes. These themes include:

- *Problem Sensitivity*—Being aware that a problem exists, combined with the ability to state the problem so that it does not limit or confine thinking. The ability to make keen observations, be inquisitive, maintain healthy skepticism, and appreciate the contributions of others.
- *Idea Fluency*—Being able to produce ideas in copious quantities, closely coupled with the ability to restrain judicial thinking.
- *Flexibility*—Effecting quick and frequent reorientation of approaches. The ability to toy with elements and concepts, formulate wild hypotheses, and express the ridiculous.
- *Originality*—The ability to associate unrelated ideas and things and synthesize them into new solutions to a problem.
- *Constructive Discontent*—To be dissatisfied with existing conditions and possessing an attitude of mind that seeks to improve conditions.

- *Imagination*—The ability to confront and deal with reality by using the creative power of the mind. There are two general categories—controllable and uncontrollable. Creative ability is a product of the controllable category.
- *Innovation*—The ability to build on or improve the ideas of others.
- *Fundamental Knowledge*—Being well grounded in basic laws and concepts, well read, and conversant with many fields of thought. Knowledge provides a foundation from which creativity can draw upon.
- *Curiosity*—Possessing a wide range of interests. To be curious to know how things work and to be fearless in asking "why?"
- *Self-Confidence*—Developing the proper frame of mind toward creativity and to be sure of one's own ability to find new and better solutions and having the courage to present new ideas to others.
- *Motivation*—Possessing a strong inner drive to work toward a problem solution. Constructive motivation is considered a key to basic creative performance.
- *Permissive Environment*—It is always easier to work in an environment which encourages new ideas. The characteristics of a permissive environment include:

    o   Freedom of expression
    o   Job satisfaction
    o   Effective communications
    o   Mutual respect and encouragement

- *Emotional Balance*—The creative process is fraught with generalization, freewheeling, ambiguities, and disorder that are often frightening and uncomfortable. A high level of tolerance during the creative phase is absolutely essential in maintaining a team's enthusiasm and performance.

ROADBLOCKS TO CREATIVITY

In his groundbreaking book on creativity, *A Whack on the Side of the Head*[1], Roger von Oech identified a number of "mental locks" that inhibit creativity. These mental locks exist for one of two reasons. The first is that we usually don't need to be creative for most of the things we do. This is where our habits and routines come into play. Thus, most of the time there is really no incentive to be creative. The second reason is that when we really do need to be creative, the very habits, routines, and attitudes that we rely upon to get us through our typically mundane lives literally lock down our creative side. The ten mental locks identified by von Oech include:

- "The right answer."
- "That's not logical."
- "Follow the rules."
- "Be practical."
- "Avoid ambiguity."
- "To err is wrong."
- "Play is frivolous."
- "That's not my area."
- "Don't be foolish."
- "I'm not creative."

These mental locks, or *roadblocks*, will stifle creativity unless they are recognized and overcome. The value specialist must take the lead in doing this. A discussion of each of these roadblocks is provided below as well as some strategies that can be applied to counteract them, regardless of what creativity approach is being used.

"The Right Answer" and "Follow the Rules."

It could be argued that we are most creative the day we are born. As infants, we have absolutely no knowledge of the world. Therefore, we do not know what is possible or impossible. We have not yet formed any habits, routines, or attitudes—nor do we have any concept of what these things are! We are purely creatures of imagination.

As we mature, and begin to develop the ability of our minds to think critically, the first limits to our creativity are set, much like fence posts. Eventually, we hear the word "No!" directed at us for the first time by a concerned parent. Over a period of time, and a constant litany of "No's!"

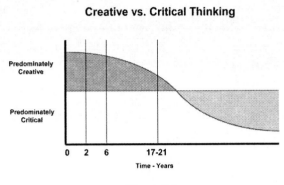

Figure 7-1

we begin to develop an understanding of right and wrong, good and bad, yes and no. Slowly, and insidiously, this assault on our creative thinking increases as we learn the rules. If the change in our preference for creative vs. critical thinking were plotted on a graph, it might look something like the one shown in *Figure 7-1*.

In Vincent Ruggiero's *Becoming a Critical Thinker*[2], he distinguishes the functions of creative and critical thinking:

> *"Thinking is sometimes regarded as two harmonious processes. One process is the production of ideas (creative thinking), accomplished by widening your focus and looking at many possibilities. The key to this process is to resist the temptation to settle for a few familiar ideas. The other process is the evaluation of ideas (critical thinking), accomplished by narrowing your focus, sorting out the ideas you've generated, and identifying the most reasonable ones."*

Larry Miles recognized this phenomenon, and his understanding of critical vs. creative thinking led him to separate these two types of thinking by doing them at different times in the job plan, which is why the Speculation and Evaluation Phases are separate, distinct steps.

By the time we have completed our primary education, we have been taught that there is generally only one right answer to any given problem, and that the right answer is the one that is commonly accepted. This emphasis on critical thinking dominates our educational system. We are only given fleeting opportunities to exercise creative thinking during our education and most of these are limited to art, music, and writing classes.

In any event, regardless of whether we are developing our creative or critical thinking skills, we are taught to do so within the context of school, which is in turn governed by countless rules, regulations, and expectations of behavior. By the time we have established our professional careers, we have established a lifetime of mental conditioning from which it is very difficult to escape.

In beginning a creativity session, the value specialist should do two things in addressing these roadblocks. These are:

- *There are no "right" answers!*—First, communicate to the value team that the first goal in the Speculation Phase is to generate as many different ideas as possible. In order to do this, no criticism will be allowed! The ideas will be evaluated in the following phase, so everyone will have an opportunity to voice their opinions about the ideas later.
- *There are no rules!*—Secondly, as long as the ideas are focused on addressing the function or functions that the value team identified for value improvement during the Function Phase, and the first condition above is met, there are no other rules.

"That's Not Logical," "Avoid Ambiguity" and "Be Practical."

The emphasis of our educational system on critical thinking places greater value on thinking that is "logical," "orderly" and "practical" than thinking that is "ambiguous," "chaotic" and "abstract." This "right brain" or "hard" method of thinking tends to subordinate our "left brain" or "soft" thinking, and as a result, our creativity tends to suffer.

Individuals involved in professions such as marketing, advertising, and design are generally more adept at left-brain or soft thinking because they are more concerned with developing concepts and ideas. On the other hand, individuals engaged in technical disciplines such as engineers, programmers, and analysts are particularly predisposed to right brain or hard thinking because they are more concerned with turning concepts into concrete reality.

Obviously, we need to use both the left and right parts of our brain to be successful; however, during a creativity session it is the left side that needs the extra stimulation! The value specialist should consider the following in breaking through these roadblocks:

- *Use metaphors to soften up thinking!*—The use of metaphor is one of our greatest creative gifts and is used extensively by artists, musicians, writers and poets. Try using metaphors to change your perspective on things. Try asking questions like "How is our product like an onion?" "How is this review process like going to the movies?" You may gain valuable insight on the problem as well as spark your creativity.
- *Encourage "what-iffing!"*—Simply asking the question "what if?" can give creativity a jump start. What-iffing is a great way to change paradigms. "What if we didn't have that funding deadline to meet?" "What if we could make it out of plastic?" "What if the customer didn't care how the thing looked?" "What if we didn't need management approval?"
- *Think ambiguously!*—The VM process provides an excellent means to utilize the concept of ambiguity through the functional approach. A simple way to

expand our creativity is to simply focus on ways of accomplishing the higher-order function (i.e., the function immediately to the left of the one on which we are focusing our creativity). Increasing the level of abstraction is a surefire way to do this. Instead of "How else do we control access?" we might ask "How do we enforce security?" Instead of asking "How do we transmit force?" try asking "How do we drive nails?"

"To Err is Wrong," "Play is Frivolous," and "Don't be Foolish."

Creativity takes courage, as pointed out by the famed painter Henri Matisse, who is credited with fathering the Fauvist movement around 1900. The reason creativity takes courage is that there is the possibility that any new or original idea may result in failure. It is important to recognize that failure, in and of itself, is not necessarily a bad thing. It is not the fear of failure, but rather the fear of embarrassment that is at the root of this particular roadblock. Mistakes are a natural part of the learning process and are an essential part of the creative process.

The value specialist will at some point be faced with a group of participants during a creativity session where nobody will have the guts to suggest anything. This may be happening for a number or reasons. It may be that a manager or "boss" is in the room and that there is a general fear among subordinates of contradicting or embarrassing themselves in front of a superior. It may be that some of the participants are shy or introverted by nature. It may be that some are genuinely bored or disinterested. Whatever the case, one of the best things the value specialist can do is to lighten up the group's mood. Humor can work wonders, especially when people feel they can laugh at themselves. Humor, in and of itself, requires creativity and is an excellent means of stimulating the imagination. You do not need to be a trained comedian to instill a sense of levity. A few tips for breaking through these roadblocks include:

- *Don't be afraid to laugh!*—The value specialist can get the ball rolling by throwing out a few goofy ideas to loosen the participants up a bit. Self-deprecation is an excellent way to demonstrate a willingness to laugh at one's self. If the value specialist can show everyone that he or she is not afraid of embarrassment, it will go a long ways in making the others in the group feel safe in sharing their ideas.
- *Failure is an option!*—The value specialist should ensure that criticism will be dealt with harshly at this point in the job plan. It is surprisingly difficult for most to keep their mouths shut when they have a reason for why something won't work. Don't give in to this temptation. There are a number of clever, and amusing, tactics that can be applied to this end. I have a colleague that once brought in a foam stick to a creativity session that she would use to whack over the heads of those that couldn't keep from making critical remarks. Another method is to have anyone who makes a critical remark contribute a quarter to the kitty.
- *Avoid "groupthink!"*—There will usually be many "sacred cows" for most projects. These often prove to be particularly troublesome areas to get people's creative input on. There is a tendency for people to conform to the standard way of thinking in these situations. The value specialist should take this as an excellent opportunity to play the fool and shake things up a bit. Challenge the group's established notions of thinking: "So what if the bridge falls down!" "Who cares about profit, lets just give 'em away!" "Who needs emergency lighting? Just give everyone flashlights!" I guarantee you will get a response.

"That's Not My Area" and "I'm Not Creative."

The value team will most likely include individuals representing a variety of disciplines and have expertise in specific areas. Although specialized knowledge is essential for the success of most projects, it can also create mental roadblocks by limiting thinking to known solutions. In fact, some of the best ideas and solutions are conceived by others in the group that come from an entirely different area of expertise than that of the area being focused on. Oftentimes this is because these individuals do not know any better!

Another interesting fact is that creative people think they are creative, while people who are not creative think they aren't! This phenomenon is known as the Self-fulfilling Prophecy, or Pygmalion Effect. In 1971, Robert Rosenthal, a professor of social psychology at Harvard, described an experiment in which he told a group of students that he had developed a strain of super-intelligent rats that could run mazes quickly[3]. He then passed out perfectly normal rats at random, telling half of the students that they had new "maze-bright" rats and the other half that they got "maze-dull" rats.

The rats believed to be bright improved daily in running the maze—they ran faster and more accurately. The "dull" rats refused to budge from the starting point 29% of the time, while the "bright" rats refused only 11% of the time. Rosenthal concluded that this boost in performance was attributed to the fact that the students with the "smart" rats treated the animals more gently, showed greater enthusiasm for the experiments, and were more relaxed. Those with the "dumb" rats essentially communicated feelings that were the opposite of these. In essence, the Pygmalion Effect is an actual phenomenon where our perceptions about our performance have a direct impact on the outcome of our performance.

- *I'm not a doctor but I play one on TV!*—One technique that seems to always produce results is to give a team member a pen and ask them to go up to the whiteboard and draw a sketch of a solution. An accountant may draw a very interesting sketch for a carburetor because she isn't an automotive engineer. A construction engineer may sketch a revolutionary flow chart for a change order administrative process. Anyone who has played the game *"Pictionary"* will appreciate how a little left-brained thinking can bring out the artist in all of us!

♦ *Try hitchhiking!*—Einstein was once quoted as unabashedly saying: "The secret to creativity is knowing how to hide your sources." What he meant was that most ideas are built upon the ideas of others. Despite not being an expert in a given field, don't be afraid to throw out an idea. Your idea might provide the creative spark that the "expert" needs to break through those mental roadblocks.

♦ *Believe in yourself!*—As corny as it may sound, how you, and others, feel about yourself does indeed influence your outcome. The value specialist should encourage others throughout the creativity session by instilling confidence in themselves and their team. You've got to believe the worth of ideas and have faith in the creative process. Pessimism is not going to get he job done!

CREATIVITY TECHNIQUES

There are literally hundreds of creative techniques that have been developed, most of which have sprung up during the past 50 years. Regardless of the technique chosen, it is recommended that the value specialist begin by focusing on those key functions that were identified as having a good opportunity for value improvement. This will help keep the value team's creative thinking focused on areas that will yield the best return on their efforts.

This text will introduce only those creative techniques that the authors have had direct experience with and have proved to be particularly compatible with the VM process. These techniques include:

- Classic Brainstorming
- Brain Writing
- Brain Sketching
- Morphological Analysis
- Creativity Checklists

Classic Brainstorming

This technique is probably the most widely used creative technique, as it is relatively simple and takes advantage of the group's creative synergism. It works best with smaller groups (typically 4 to 10 people, which is the size of most value teams). Here is how it is done:

- Write the function to be brainstormed on a flip chart, whiteboard or other system where everyone can see it. Make sure that everyone understands the problem or issue
- Review the ground rules with the group:

    o   Avoid criticizing ideas / suspend judgment. All ideas are as valid as each other.
    o   The emphasis should be on the quantity of ideas— a large number of ideas is the aim. If you limit the number of ideas, people will start to judge the ideas and only put in their "best" or more often than not, the least radical and new.
    o   Freewheeling. Don't censor any ideas, keep the meeting flow going.
    o   Listen to other ideas, and try to piggyback on them to other ideas.

o   Avoid any discussion of ideas or questions, as these stop the flow of ideas.

- The value specialist should enforce these few rules and write down all the ideas as they occur.
- Clarify and conclude the session. Ideas that are identical can be combined, all others should be kept. When finished with one function, move on to the next!

Brain Writing

Brain Writing (also called Trigger Sessions) is a good way of getting lots of ideas down from untrained, or reluctant, participants. Here is how it works:

- Identify the function to be focused on.
- Each member of the group writes down his or her ideas using brief statements (5 minutes only).
- One member reads out his or her list—others silently cross out ideas that have been read out loud and write down "hitchhiked" ideas.
- The second member reads out his or her list of ideas not already covered, and this process is repeated until everyone has shared their list.
- The last member reads out his original list and his or her "hitchhiked" list, and the procedure is repeated in the opposite direction.

A good group will be able to manage at least a half-dozen passes. Everyone's paper is then collected and can be combined into a single list of ideas—all duplicates should have been crossed out during the session. The value specialist may want to write down the "surviving" ideas on a flip chart or whiteboard as the process evolves.

A variation on this technique has everyone, using Post-it notes or small cards, write down their ideas, and place them in the center of the table. Everyone is then free to pull out one or more of these ideas for inspiration. Team members can create new ideas, variations, or piggyback on existing ideas.

Brain Sketching

This technique is related to Brain Writing, but utilizes evolving sketches rather than written lists of ideas. As usual with most Brain Writing techniques, only limited facilitation skill is needed.

- A group of 4-10 people sit around a table, or in a circle of chairs. They need to be far enough apart to have some privacy. The function to be focused on is identified.
- Each team member privately draws one or more sketches (each on a separate sheet of paper) of how the function might be solved, passing each sketch on to the person on their right when it is finished. The sketches should not take more than five minutes or so to draw.
- Participants take the sketches passed on to them and either modify or annotate the existing one, or use it to stimulate a new sketch of their own. The amended original and/or any new sketches are then passed on to the person on their right when ready.
- After the process has been running for a suitable period and/or the energy is running lower, the sketches are collected by the facilitator.
- It will probably help to display all the sketches and to discuss them in turn for clarification and comment.

Brain sketching can be a very effective approach when dealing with designs, whether it is for a product or a facility of some kind. This method allows people to think visually, which is often more effective for design related projects.

Morphological Analysis

Morphological Analysis is a structured comprehensive system for methodically relating problem elements to develop new solutions. The steps in morphological analysis are:

- Define the problem in terms of its attributes. For instance, the attributes of a pen might include size, shape, color, line quality, etc.
- Develop a model which makes it possible to visualize every possible solution. If a problem has only two attributes, the model takes the form of a large rectangle divided into a series of small squares. The horizontal axis represents one variable and is subdivided into the different forms of this variable. The vertical axis represents the other variable and is similarly subdivided. Each small square represents a combination of two versions of the variables. If the problem had three variables the model would take the form of a cube. More than three variables can be used, but the technique usually becomes unmanageable by usual paper and pencil techniques.

The technique can be illustrated by approaching the problem of analyzing the possible combinations controlling an industrial process. The three variables might be mechanical drive mechanism, material, and manufacturing process. One axis of the cube lists all the different drive mechanisms that might be considered. Another axis is subordinated into types of material from which the gears, links, etc. are to be manufactured. The third axis lists the various manufacturing processes to be used. *Figure 7-2* illustrates the resulting structure, which offers up to 125 possible combinations. Each of these possible combinations could be considered in turn. Through computer-aided analysis, the ability to analyze the permutations for items with large numbers of attribute combinations is virtually unlimited. Morphological Analysis is an especially good system for exploring new products with various combinations of attributes.

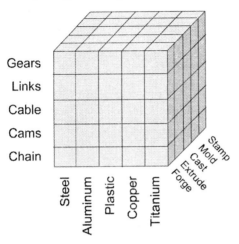

Figure 7-2

Creativity Checklists

To stimulate thinking along creative lines, the following questions, and related examples, may prove helpful. In every case, the intent is to force the value team to take a new look at the item, system, component, or action that is being studied. Einstein is quoted as saying *"The important thing is to not stop questioning."*

Put it to other uses

- Are there new ways to use it as it is?—Using helicopters to patrol high-tension transmission lines over mountains.
- What other ways could it be modified?—Fishing rods made of fiberglass imbedded in plastic.
- What could be made from this?—Wallboard manufacturer who added a line of jigsaw puzzles.

- How about salvaging?—Rubber maker who found that wasted strips of surgical tubing could be sold as rubber bands.
- What other uses could be added?—Telephone companies installing transcribed records to furnish the latest weather reports.
- Could the width be increased?—Center strip on new throughways.
- Could new ingredients be added?—Chlorophyll in toothpaste.

Make it smaller

- What if it was lower?—Trend in automobiles a few years ago.
- What if it was narrower?—Reduce the width of a forklift so it can get down narrower isles.
- What if it was lighter?"—Railroad cars that weigh no more than trailers.
- What if it were more streamlined?—Tank-type vacuum cleaners.
- What if it were condensed?—Full-size umbrellas can fit into a purse.
- What if part of it was eliminated?—Tubeless tires.

Make substitutions

- Could other parts be used?—Fluid drive instead of gears on cars.
- Could other materials be used?—Argon instead of vacuum in electric light bulbs.
- Could we produce it using a different process?—Stamping instead of casting.
- Could a different power source be used?—Electricity instead of vacuum to run windshield wipers.
- Is there another way?—Air lift that saved Berlin.

Rearrange it

- Could the pattern be changed?—One-way streets.
- Could the layout be revised?—New wrinkles in supermarkets.
- Could the sequence be altered?—Flashbacks in movies.
- Could the cause and effect be transposed?—Medical diagnosis technique.
- Could it be repackaged?—Microwave popcorn that comes in its own popping bag.
- Could it be reorganized or regrouped?"—New defense systems in football.

Imitate and adapt

- What else is like this?—Studies of birds made by the aircraft pioneers.
- What parallel does the past provide?—What modern dress designers do in devising new creations from ancient art.
- Could other processes be copied?—The cultured pearl industry, whereby nature is imitated by sticking beads into oysters so as to produce pearls.
- What other ideas might be adaptable?—Rudolf Diesel got his engine ideas from a cigar lighter.

Modify it

- What other shape could be used?—A buggy-maker tapered the roller bearing which Leonardo da Vinci had invented 400 years before.
- What other form could be used?—Detergent powders instead of bars of soap, or liquid soap instead of either.
- Could we change the style or look?—Higher (or lower) skirts.
- What other color could be used?—What the television industry did to develop color TV.

- Could we make it move differently?—Christmas tree lights that bubble.

Make it bigger

- Could we make it take longer?—The baker who featured slow-baked bread.
- Could the frequency be increased?—The doctor who originated the idea of lighter but more frequent meals for ulcer patients.
- Could we increase its strength?—Reinforced heels and toes in hosiery.
- Could we increase its height?"—Circus clown on clear plastic stilts.
- Could we make it go down instead of up?—Furrier who attaches his label upside down, so it can be read when the coat is over a chair.
- Could its usual roles be switched?—Have the welders review and modify the design and engineers assemble the parts.
- Could we make it go up instead of down?—Dining room light which throws a beam upward from the floor to a reflector on the ceiling.
- Could it be done the opposite way?—Elias Howe perfected his sewing machine by designing a needle eye at the bottom instead of at the top.

Combine it

- What about using alloys?—Newest mixtures of synthetic fibers.
- What old ideas could be merged?—Window washers which combine a brush with a built-in hose.
- What about considering ensembles?—Shirts with neckties and handkerchiefs to match.

- Can different products be marketed together?—Drugstores sell blades to those who ask for shaving cream and vice versa.
- Can different purposes be combined?—To avoid changing from one pair of glasses to another, Ben Franklin cut the lenses in two and stuck them together, with the reading halves below. Thus he invented bifocals.

Stimulate Creativity—*Value Metrics*

One of the many benefits of *Value Metrics* is that it provides a natural means of stimulating creativity by placing greater emphasis on project performance. In the Function Phase of the Value Methodology job plan, the relationship between cost, performance, and function was discussed through the use of FAST diagramming.

Typically, high-cost functions are selected as targets for team brainstorming during this phase. The work done in the Function Phase with respect to performance should have highlighted the performance critical functions, which deserve every bit of attention that is given to high-cost functions.

The performance attributes themselves can also serve as creativity stimulators by incorporating them into questions directed at the value team, similar to the questions presented above in conjunction with creativity checklists. For example, one might ask:

- "How could we improve maintainability?"
- "How might we reduce construction impacts?"
- "How could we improve lift speed?"
- "How could we reduce delivery time?"

In either example, the important thing is that the consideration of performance figures into the creative process as a means of augmenting the generation of ideas.

SUMMARY

In this chapter we have discussed creativity. Creative thinking, particularly in the area of idea generation, should be used in all phases of a project's development. Brainstorming, as a problem solver, is used extensively in value studies and other problem areas. In VM a number of techniques are used which assist in the identification of problems, the generation of ideas which suggest solutions, the analysis of these for feasibility, and finally the development of practical solutions. There is no specific combination of these techniques that is prescribed for all VM efforts, nor is there a predetermined degree to which they should be utilized. The selection of specific techniques and the depth to which they are utilized is primarily a matter of judgment and varies according to the complexity of the subject under study.

A multitude of opportunities will develop by applying creativity to a problem. Creative sessions will be more fruitful if a multi-disciplinary team is able to participate in an environment free from distractions and judgment. The quality ideas will occur as a by-product of the quantity of ideas generated. By following the guidelines for creativity provided in this chapter, there should be no problem developing the quantity of ideas necessary to achieve the quality ideas ultimately desired. Creativity techniques are used to break loose from the mental roadblocks that restrict people's creative thinking. Exercise the imagination, have the will to succeed, and who knows—ideas may be developed that will revolutionize the project.

---

[1] Von Oech, Roger,(1983) A Whack on the Side of the Head: How to Unlock Your Mind for Innovation, Warner Books Edition, New York

2. Ruggiero, Vincent Ryan (2002) Becoming a Critical Thinker, Houghton Mifflin Company, New York
3. Rosenthal, Robert and Jacobson, Lenore. Pygmalion in the Classroom: Teacher Expectation and Pupils' Intellectual Development. Irvington Publishers: New York, 1992.

Chapter 8—Evaluation

Aristotle—Philosopher, Mathematician

Some men are just as sure of the truth of their opinions as are others of what they know.
—Aristotle

It is the mark of an educated mind to be able to entertain a thought without accepting it.
—Aristotle

Aristotle was born in 384 B.C. at Stagyra, a Greek colony and seaport on the coast of Thrace. His father Nichomachus was court physician to King Amyntas of Macedonia, and from this began Aristotle's long association with the Macedonian Court, which considerably influenced his life.

In his 18th year he left Stagyra for Athens, then the intellectual center of Greece and of the civilized world. Here he became the pupil of Plato, but soon made his master aware of the remarkable penetration and reach of his intellect, for we are told that Plato spoke of Aristotle as the "Intellect of the School." He remained at Athens twenty years, during which the only facts recorded, in addition to his studying with Plato, are that he set up a class in rhetoric, and that in so doing, he became the rival of the celebrated orator and rhetorical reader, Socrates. Following the death of his mentor Plato in 347 B.C., Aristotle soon found himself employed by King Philip of Macedon as the tutor of his young son, Alexander.

The writings of Aristotle may be said to have embraced the whole circle of knowledge of his time. Many of them are lost; of those that remain the most important are the "Organon," or "Logic," "Rhetoric," "Poetics" and "Meteorology." His Organon is his complete development of formal reasoning, and is the basis and nearly the whole substance of syllogistic or scholastic logic. This science he almost entirely created and he may also be said to have created the basis for the natural sciences. In his great work on animals he amassed a stock of genuine observations, and introduced a method of classification, which continues to this day. His treatises on Rhetoric and Poetics were the earliest development of the Philosophy of Criticism, and still continue to be studied. The same remark is applicable to his elaborate work on Ethics.

Aristotle's convictions were so strong that they later led to oppose some of Plato's teachings. The philosophy of Aristotle differed from that of Plato on many points, especially in the fundamental doctrine termed the Theory of Ideas. The Platonic "ideas" or "forms," were conceived as real existences. Aristotle was opposed to this doctrine; his whole method was in marked contrast to that of Plato, and was based on the principle that all philosophy must be founded on the observation of facts.

Aristotle serves as the archetype for critical thinking. No other philosopher can be named whose influence has been so far-reaching and so long continued. This chapter focuses on critical thinking as applied to the evaluation of ideas and some of the techniques, and unique challenges, of the Evaluation Phase.

EVALUATION PHASE

The purpose of the Evaluation Phase is to systematically reduce the large number of ideas generated during the Speculation Phase to a number of concepts that appear the most promising in meeting the project's objectives. The proper evaluation of the ideas requires the use of a methodical approach that will organize the critical thinking of the value team and minimize the tendency to evaluate by emotions and assumptions rather than facts. The key steps in the Evaluation Phase include:

- Evaluation techniques
  - Enhance Evaluation—*Value Metrics*
- Selecting ideas for development

Before discussing these steps in detail, however, it is first worth exploring the concepts involved in the evaluation process itself.

THE EVALUATION PROCESS

The Evaluation Phase is often neglected by value practitioners because it is viewed as a rather straightforward, obvious exercise in critical thinking. Based on the discussion from the previous chapter with respect to our inherent bias toward the use of critical thinking over creative thinking, one might be led to believe this.

In Miles' classic text on value analysis he wrote a mere two paragraphs on the "Judgment Step." What he basically says is that the step should be "... *performed by one person, consulting with others as required.*"[1] Other noted practitioners and writers, such as Art Mudge, provide only limited guidance in the evaluation of ideas, primarily through the use evaluation by comparison of advantages and disadvantages[2].

The fact is that the evaluation of large groups of ideas is not always such an easy task, or at least it shouldn't be! Hopefully, the value team will have invested a lot of hard work in generating ideas during the Speculation Phase and have withheld judgment until now. Many participants will be chomping at the bit to let everyone know what they really think about many of the ideas, especially those that deal with their area of expertise! It is very easy to dismiss ideas based on a single reason. It is much more difficult to give ideas the thorough evaluation that they might otherwise deserve. All the creativity in the world will be useless unless the value team is willing to perform due diligence in evaluating ideas.

There are a number of factors worth discussing that may prevent the value team from performing a good, thorough evaluation of the ideas, most of which have to do with the innate biases of the participants. These factors are based upon basic rules of thumb, or heuristics, that allow us to make quick decisions by simplifying the decision-making process. While these heuristics are often very helpful in making decisions, they can also create mental roadblocks that prevent objective decisions. These include:

- The Anchoring Heuristic
- The Availability Heuristic
- The Confirmation Heuristic
- The Representativeness Heuristic

The Anchoring Heuristic

The *anchoring heuristic* describes the tendency for people to explain or describe an event by fixating on the first number or evidence they hear. Based on research conducted on this behavioral phenomenon, the anchoring heuristic demonstrates that in areas of ambiguity or uncertainty people often latch onto random flashes of certainty or confidence. With respect to the evaluation of ideas, this heuristic describes the tendency for people to favor an initially chosen hypothesis or solution that we are later not easily able to shift away from when considering alternative ideas and concepts. The anchoring heuristic is related to the ruling theory phenomenon identified by Chamberlin in *Chapter 2—Value*.

Perhaps the best example of the anchoring heuristic is within the field of judicial decisions. The interpretation of laws is generally anchored by past judicial decisions that are deemed to be similar and/or relevant to present cases. While past legal precedence is certainly an important consideration in making judicial decisions, it can create a significant bias that may overshadow facts and circumstances that might otherwise contradict legal precedence.

The anchoring heuristic can be minimized by utilizing group evaluation techniques rather than relying on individual evaluation methods. Drawing upon the experiences and perspectives of people representing different disciplines and philosophies will help expand the discussion and keep this heuristic from eclipsing ideas that deserve further consideration.

The Availability Heuristic

The *availability heuristic* occurs when people estimate the probability of an outcome based on how easy that outcome is to imagine. Therefore, vividly described, emotionally-charged possibilities will tend to be perceived as being more likely than those that are more difficult to visualize or are difficult to understand, resulting in a corresponding cognitive bias.

An important corollary finding to the availability heuristic is that people asked to imagine an outcome immediately perecive it as more likely than those that were not. And, that which was vividly described is viewed as more likely than that which was provided a dull decription. This tendency seems to be commonplace in mainstream media. An excellent example of this was the hype surrounding the much ballyhooed Y2K crisis in which it was widely reported that technology would fail, and modern society along with it. The following are quotes from various sources prior to the new millenium:

> "You wouldn't want to be in an airplane, you wouldn't want to be in an elevator, and you wouldn't want to be in a hospital . . . (government and business leaders) are not thinking about the contingency plans that they ought to be thinking about today, not waiting a year from now . . . (these) need to be put into place to minimize the harm from widespread failures."
>
> —Sen. Chris Dodd, Year 2000 Tech Committee Senate Hearings into Y2K, June 12, 1998

In the most dramatic warning yet of impending computer crisis in the government, a congressional panel said Wednesday that 37 percent of the most critical computers used by the federal agencies will not be updated in time to handle dates in 2000 and will be subject to widespread failure. The new estimate calls into question assurances by the Clinton administration that it is moving quickly enough to avert serious outages.

—The Wilmington (Delaware) News Journal, March 5, 1998

Y2K issues could place workers, communities and the environment at risk, the EPA said. How can a computer problem wreak havoc with chemicals? The so-called millennium bug, in which computers may mistake the year 2000 for 1900, is hard-wired into a small, but significant, percentage of computerized equipment used by chemical handlers. Confused by the date, errant chips could trigger failures in process controllers, air monitors, security systems, laboratory instruments, safety-shutdown equipment and explosion-suppression systems, among others. The problem is that no one—not the government, the public or even the industries themselves—knows for sure how many companies are vulnerable to Y2K problems....

—The Oregonian, November 11, 1999

These articles conjure up images of massive power outages, the collapse of government and the release of toxic chemicals into the environment. Of course, the Y2K crisis did not materialize as described in the statements above, but the imagery assoicated with it generated a great deal of fear and left little to the imagination.

An opposite effect of this phenomenon, called denial, occurs when a potential outcome is so disturbing that the very act of contemplating it leads to an increased refusal to believe it might happen. In this case, people that were asked to imagine a disagreeable outcome actually made them view it as less likely.

The value specialist should try to develop a basic understanding of this facet of human behavior, as it is probably the single strongest influence in our decision-making psychology. Provided below are a number of questions. Think about each one for a moment. The answers are provided on the following page.

Questions:

1) Which is a more likely cause of death in the United States: being killed by falling airplane parts or being killed by a shark?
2) Do more Americans die from homicide and car accidents, or diabetes and stomach cancer?
3) Which claims more lives in the United States: lightning or tornadoes?

Answers:

1) In the United States, the chance of dying from falling airplane parts is 30 times greater than dying from a shark attack. Because shark attacks receive more publicity and because they are easier to imagine (after seeing the film Jaws, for example), most people rate shark attacks as the more probable cause of death. Since information about shark attacks is more readily available, the availability heuristic helps explain why people overestimate the chances of dying in this unusual way.
2) More Americans die from diabetes and stomach cancer than from homicide and car accidents, by a ratio of nearly 2:1. Many people guess homicide and car accidents, largely due to the publicity they receive and in turn, their availability in the mind.
3) More Americans are killed annually by lightning than by tornadoes. Because tornadoes are often preceded by warnings, drills, and other kinds of publicity, the most common answer is tornadoes. The large amount of information about tornadoes, coupled with the

availability heuristic, leads to the misconception that tornadoes are a more frequent cause of death.[3]

Utilize examples, such as the ones provided above, to illustrate the bias created by this heuristic when it arises. Safety is often an important performance attribute for many types of projects. It is also probably the most obvious trigger for the availability heuristic because a product, process or facility that is perceived as "unsafe" conjures up vivid images of the consequences.

The value specialist needs to help the value team place performance attributes such as safety into proper perspective. One technique to do this is to make statements that will appeal to the participants' logic rather than their emotions. Provided below are some examples using this technique:

- "If we want this highway project to be completely safe we should limit the speed to 5 mph or, better still, shut it down altogether." Obviously, shutting down the highway would make it safe; however, the other performance requirements would not be met. The point here is that safety is indeed an important consideration; however, it is but one aspect of performance.
- "If we want to eliminate any possibility for product liability, then we should send out a company representative to demonstrate to the consumer how to operate their new ladder." While this idea might, in concept, eliminate all potential consumer lawsuits, it would no doubt bankrupt the company offering such a service.

Confirmation Heuristic

The *confirmation heuristic* (also referred to as confirmation bias) describes the tendency for people to seek evidence that confirms rather than challenges their current beliefs. Confirmation bias occurs when people selectively notice or focus upon evidence which tends to support the things they already believe or want to be true while ignoring that evidence which would serve to disconfirm those beliefs or ideas. Confirmation bias plays a stronger role when it comes to those beliefs which are based upon prejudice, faith, or tradition rather than on empirical evidence.

For example, if we already believe or want to believe that someone can speak to our deceased relatives, then we will notice when they say things which are accurate or pleasant but forget how often that person says things which are simply incorrect. Another good example would be how people notice when they get a phone call from a person they were just thinking about but don't remember how often they didn't get such a call when thinking about a person.

Similarly, studies have shown that people will often "read over" a section in a newspaper or magazine article that is in conflict with their beliefs, without being aware that they are doing it. One of the problems with the confirmation bias is that people become so dogmatic and rigid in their viewpoint that they aren't open to competing explanations or to adapting their position in light of new facts or interpretations.

The confirmation bias is best addressed by thoroughly, and objectively, evaluating an idea or concept that might otherwise be dismissed out of hand. Seek to invite the opinions of individuals that hold differing views. It's not unusual for participants on a value team, especially those that might already be involved on the project team, to try and look for reasons why a new way of doing something won't work. This is a perfect example of why it is wise to include team members that do not have a personal interest in the baseline concept to help provide balance in evaluating new ideas.

The Representativeness Heuristic

The *representativeness heuristic* describes the tendency of people to judge the probability of an event by finding a 'comparable known' event and assuming that the probabilities will be similar. As a part of creating meaning from what is experienced, people need to classify things. If something does not fit exactly into a known category, the tendency is for people to approximate with the nearest class available. Overall, the primary fallacy is in assuming that similarity in one aspect leads to similarity in other aspects.

A prime example of the representativeness heuristic is called the *gambler's fallacy*, in which people place belief in runs of good and bad luck. This heuristic also describes the tendency to ignore base rates (the relative frequency with which an event occurs) as well as regression towards the mean (where an extreme value is likely to be followed by one which is much closer to the mean).

The use of this heuristic can, however, can systematically lead one to make poor judgments in some circumstances. For example:

- It might be assumed that someone with a laid-back attitude and long hair is from California, while someone who is very polite but rigid might be assumed to be from England.
- People will often assume that a random sequence in a lottery is more likely than an arithmetic sequence of numbers.
- If two salespeople from a large company both displayed aggressive behavior, the assumption may be that the company has established a policy of aggressive selling, and that most other salespeople from that firm will also engage in aggressive techniques.

The value specialist should seek to develop an understanding of these heuristics and biases and try to recognize them when they occur, as they can quickly, and unfairly, abort ideas that may otherwise prove to have merit. The representativeness heuristic is oftentimes the worst, and most unfair, of the four heuristics discussed in this chapter. In its most destructive form, this heuristic is really nothing more than prejudice based upon broad stereotypes. The value specialist must be use tact in disarming this behavior. One technique might be to state an obviously absurd stereotype in which the offender could be classified. For example, if it was an architect, one could say that "Architects don't care about what buildings cost—only what they look like." Such a statement is likely to get the individual's attention and may help instill greater sensitivity before making similar statements in the future. Steer clear of racial, religious or gender based statements, as these are likely to cause more harm than good!

EVALUATION TECHNIQUES

There are a number of evaluation techniques that can be employed by the value specialist to evaluate the ideas generated during the Speculation Phase. The techniques that will be presented in this chapter include:

- Evaluation by Simple Rating
- Evaluation by Comparison
- Nominal Group Technique
- Evaluation Matrix—*Value Metrics*

Evaluation by Simple Rating

A relatively quick way to evaluate ideas that is commonly used by value practitioners is to identify a set of evaluative criteria, discuss the merits of the idea relative to the evaluative criteria, and then assign the idea a rating based on how well it addresses the evaluative criteria.

For example, an information technology project that is addressing the development of a new database management software program might identify the following evaluative criteria:

- User Friendliness
- Flexibility
- Cost

Each idea should then be discussed relative to these evaluative criteria and then a numerical rating be assigned using any scale (1 to 3, 1 to 5, or 1 to 10 are most common). The scale should reflect overall acceptability of the idea, and each number on the scale should be defined. For example, a 1 to 3 scale might consist of:

1) Idea is unacceptable. Drop from further consideration.
2) Idea has potential. Consider only after all 3's have been developed.
3) Idea is acceptable. Develop idea into a value alternative.

The ideas are placed on a list and rated according to the scales. This method is fairly fast but tends not to be as thorough as the techniques described below.

Evaluation by Comparison

This approach simply identifies and compares the advantages and disadvantages of an idea relative to the project's baseline concept. The value specialist should facilitate the discussion of each idea and record the advantages and disadvantages. Based on this discussion, the value team should be able to make conclusions as to which ideas merit further exploration in the Development Phase, and which ideas should be eliminated from further consideration *(Table 8-1)*.

Evaluation by Comparison

Idea	Advantages	Disadvantages
Improve sight distance at Smith Lake Rd. and Highway 7 by removing vegetation east of Smith Lake Rd.	• Improves sight distances • Reduces accident rate potential at this intersection • Addresses major traffic congestion problem at this intersection	• Increases cost • Increases right-of-way requirements • Significant impact to orchard • Does not provide any assurance that traffic from Smith Lake Rd. will have better access to highway

Table 8-1

Nominal Group Technique

The nominal group technique was originally developed as an organizational planning method by Delbecq, Van de Ven and Gustafson in 1971. This technique, with a few minor modifications, provides an effective means of prioritizing ideas through a consensus-driven process. This process includes the following steps:

- After the ideas have been captured following a creativity session, the value specialist will ask each participant to read, and elaborate on, their ideas to ensure everyone understands the concept. Duplicate ideas can be crossed out and the remaining ideas are numbered or assigned some type of code.
- The value specialist asks each person to write down, in a few minutes, the idea numbers or codes that seem especially important. Some people may feel only a few items are important; others may feel all items are important. The value specialist then goes down the list and records the number of people who consider each item a priority.
- Session participants are then asked to choose up to 10 ideas that they feel are the most important and rank them according to their relative importance. The idea they felt was most important should get at "10" down to their least important which would get a "1." These rankings are collected from all participants, and aggregated *(Table 8-2)*.

Sometimes these results are given back to the participants in order to stimulate further discussion, and perhaps a readjustment in the overall rankings assigned to the various responses. This is done only when group consensus regarding the prioritization of issues is important to the overall research or planning project. As its name suggests, the nominal group technique is only "nominally" a group, since the rankings are provided on an individual basis.

Nominal Group Technique

Idea Code	Participant 1	Participant 2	Participant 3	Ranking
A	8	10	10	1 = 28 votes
B	5	4	6	6 = 15 votes
C	2	1	3	9 = 6 votes
D	9	8	7	3 = 24 votes
E	10	7	9	2 = 26 votes
F	3	3	2	8 = 8 votes
G	6	9	8	4 = 23 votes
H	1	2	1	10 = 4 votes
I	7	6	5	5 = 18 votes
J	4	5	4	7 = 13 votes

Table 8-2

One interesting variation of this technique involves posting the idea lists on large sheets of paper on the wall so everyone can see the ideas. Once the ideas have been discussed, the value specialist hands out colored stickers (3 to 10 colored dots, depending on the number of ideas) to the participants and asks them to place the stickers next to the ideas they feel strongest about. Assuming each participant has a different color assigned to them, when the ranking is complete, it will be easy to determine which ideas are worth pursuing further into the Development Phase. The beauty of this technique is that also helps in assigning the ideas for development to those team members that felt strongest about them.

Enhance Evaluation—*Value Metrics*

The Evaluation Phase of the Value Methodology Job Plan is often first to be cut when time constraints arise, when a thorough, deliberative process is often what is most needed. The consideration of performance attributes is paramount during this phase in order to ensure that alternatives that may improve performance are thoroughly evaluated.

The evaluation process should consider each idea with respect to the performance attributes. Discussion should focus on the aspects of how the idea would improve or degrade performance relative to the baseline concept. During this discussion, the rationale for each idea relative to performance is documented. This documentation can be very valuable to project stakeholders, even for those ideas which are ultimately rejected, as they provide a very thorough discussion of project issues. Many times, project stakeholders will want to know why an idea was not further developed into an alternative. This conscientious approach should satisfy this requirement.

Many ideas are typically discarded based on unfounded statements with respect to only one aspect of performance. The process described above forces participants to articulate their criticism in an organized way that addresses all aspects of performance, not just those that immediately come to mind. Additional in-depth discussion is often required before potential performance-related benefits are revealed.

The *Value Metrics* approach to evaluation considers performance first, followed by cost. When both performance and cost have been considered, a final rating is assigned to the idea. Those ideas offering both cost and performance benefits are ranked most highly, followed by those that improve only one or the other. The "+/-" notation provides a simple means of expressing the degree of improvement (+1 or +2) or degradation (-1 or -2) of the idea relative to the baseline concept. This notation is also applied to cost. These numerical expressions are used solely to assist the value team in focusing the discussion and identifying advantages and disadvantages. The Evaluation Matrix is shown in *Table 8-3*. The following steps are required to complete the Evaluation Matrix:

- **Idea Evaluation.** The example Idea Evaluation records the results of the evaluation discussion. The performance attributes are coded (MO, EN, ES, C, M, CI, PS) to facilitate discussion and recording of ratings.

- **Performance Attribute.** The VA team, as a group, judges the ideas relative to performance of the functions required. Ideas are rated on a five-point system, with a maximum possible rating of a plus two (+2) points, and a minimum of negative two (-2) points:

    o   +2 Greatly improved
    o   +1 Some improvement
    o   0 No significant change
    o   -1 Slight degradation
    o   -2 Significant degradation

- **Advantages/Disadvantages.** Notations on the pros and cons of the idea are made. Complete documentation is essential, both as a record of the team evaluation and as a guide to the future development of the alternatives. *Advantages and disadvantages should describe the reason for a ± change in the rating.*
- **Cost:** Once the idea has been evaluated against the performance measures, the value team should make a cursory assessment of the idea's potential cost impacts using the same ranking system identified above for performance criteria.
- **Rank.** Once each idea is fully evaluated, it is given a ranking number, based on a scale of 1 to 5:

    5   Significant Value Improvement—Develop as a value alternative
    4   Good Value Improvement—Develop as a value alternative
    3   Minor Value Improvement—Develop as time permits
    2   Minor Value Degradation—Do not develop further
    1   Significant Value Degradation—Do not develop further

IDEA EVALUATION
Bridge Replacement Project

Ideas		Performance Attributes							Advantages	Disadvantages	$	Rank
#	Span River	MO	EN	ES	C	M	CI	PS				
1 Construct trestle adjacent to east side of existing bridge and shift alignment of the new bridge adjacent to trestle		-1	0	1	2	0	0	0	• Reduces costs • Reduces visual impacts • Reduces bridge length • Eliminates one trestle	• Requires additional test borings—this may require new or amended permits • Geometry not as desirable	2	4
2 Shift the east alignment option so that it is directly adjacent to the existing bridge and construct one trestle on the east side of the new bridge		1	0	1	2	0	0	-1	• Reduces costs • Improves geometry • Reduces visual impacts • Reduces bridge length • Eliminates one trestle	• Requires additional test borings—this may require new or amended permits	2	5
3 Utilize pre-cast segmental construction		0	0	0	-1	0	0	0		• Concerns about transporting pre-cast segments • Limited contractor experience in pre-cast	-1	2

Ranking Scale: 5 = Major Cost/Performance Improvement   4 = Moderate Cost/Performance Improvement   3 = Minor Improvement
2 = Cost and/or Performance Reduction   1 = Does Not Meet Project Need and Purpose

Performance Attributes: *Significant Improvement +2, +1, 0, -1, -2 Significant Degradation*
MO — Mainline Operations   EN — Environmental-Natural   ES — Environmental-Social   C — Constructibility
M — Maintainability   CI — Construction Impacts   PS — Project Schedule

Table 8-3

ELECTING IDEAS FOR DEVELOPMENT

Regardless of the technique employed to evaluate the ides, the evaluation process should have narrowed down the list of ideas considerably. The remaining ideas identified by the team for further investigation in the Development Phase should be listed by priority, based upon the outcome of the evaluation.

In some cases further evaluation may be necessary, especially if it appears that the list of surviving ideas appears to be larger than there will be time for the value team to adequately develop. In cases such as this, it may be advisable to attempt to make a quick estimate of costs in order to develop a better understanding of the magnitude of savings (or cost increase) involved. Alternatively, the nominal group technique can be employed to help rank the remaining alternatives in order of importance.

Once the ideas have been listed according to their priority, they will need to be assigned to the value team members for development. It is important to emphasize that the entire team may be involved in the development of an idea into an alternative; however, it is best to assign one individual on the team to bear the responsibility that the idea is fully developed and does not fall through the cracks. This speaks to the old adage: "If it's everybody's job, than it's nobody's responsibility!"

It is recommended that the value specialist request that team members select those ideas that they are most interested in developing. If there appears to be a general reluctance for team members to select ideas, than the value specialist should assign them to team members, based upon the relevance of the ideas to their respective disciplines. Once the ideas have been assigned, the value team will be ready to move into the Development Phase.

SUMMARY

The evaluation of ideas requires the value team to think critically, rationally and objectively. Developing an understanding of the many heuristics that are involved in the evaluation process is the first part in achieving this goal. The second step is selecting an evaluation technique that is most suitable based upon the time constraints, the ability and personality of the value team, and the capacity of the value specialist to keep the team focused on providing a balanced and objective assessment of the ideas.

---

[1] Miles, Lawrence D. (1972) *Techniques of Value Analysis and Engineering*, McGraw Hill, New York (pg. 58).
[2] Mudge, Arthur E. (1989) *Value Engineering: A Systematic Approach*, J. Pohl Associates, Pittsburgh, PA
[3] Plous, Scott (1993) *The Psychology of Judgment and Decision Making*, McGraw-Hill Higher Education,

Chapter 9 — Development

Thomas Edison—Inventor

Opportunity is missed by most people because it is dressed in overalls and looks like work.
—Thomas Edison

Genius is 1% inspiration and 99% perspiration.
—Thomas Edison

Thomas Alva Edison (1847-1931) was born in Milan, Ohio where he was the youngest in a family of seven. As a youth, he was employed as a telegraph operator where he began his affinity for electricity.

In 1868 Edison patented his first invention and also learned a tough lesson. He took his electric vote-recording machine to Washington for a demonstration. He was later told that his machine was too efficient and did not allow sufficient time for negotiation and maneuvers. The lesson to be learned is that inventions are only good when they are needed. Edison would not make the same mistake again.

Three years later he devised an improved version of the stock ticker. Offering it for sale to Gold and Stock Telegraph Company, he was reluctant to ask for the $50,000 he wanted for it, so he asked what it was worth to them. They offered him $40,000, which provided the capital for an engineering firm in Newark, New Jersey. He was only twenty-three years old at the time. During the next six years he developed the mimeograph and improved upon the telegraph and the typewriter. He also invented wax paper.

Around 1876 he wanted to expand further and create an invention factory. Edison said he wanted to turn out an invention every ten days. What seemed like a grandiose plan proved to be achievable, and often a patent was obtained every five days. He had a committed staff that helped produce many significant inventions. One of these was the carbon telephone transmitter; this device greatly improved the sound clarity of the telephone. One of Edison's favorites was the phonograph. The invention was a sensation and firmly placed him as a major inventor.

Edison is most famous for the electric light bulb. Though not an original Edison invention, it was he who made it practical. The problem had been the inability to make it work for long periods of time. Edison rectified this by using scorched cotton thread as a filament. It sustained light for forty straight hours. More importantly, he helped devise a system whereby homes and businesses could be supplied with electricity.

Edison was known as the "Wizard of Menlo Park." He attributes much of his "genius" to hard work. Edison had many notable failures, but through perseverance and great effort, he was able to develop a prolific number of ideas into reality. Edison's life illustrates the importance of the Development Phase as part of the VM Job Plan.

DEVELOPMENT PHASE

The core of a Value Management Study includes the Function Analysis, Speculation, and Evaluation Phases of the job plan. At the completion of the Evaluation Phase, the value team will have identified a number of concepts that will need to be developed into finite recommendations.

The team members are responsible for preparing these recommendations, which are based upon a comparison to the project baseline concept. All recommendations are ultimately documented with written descriptions, narratives providing its justification, sketches, performance assessments, calculations, and cost comparisons (both initial and possibly life cycle). These recommendations are referred to as value alternatives.

There are two steps in the Development Phase. These include:

- Develop value alternatives
- Review value alternatives

DEVELOP VALUE ALTERNATIVES

Those concepts that were short-listed during the Evaluation Phase will be developed into value alternatives. The information that will be developed for the value alternatives must be organized in a way that will allow the project team and decision makers to easily understand the concepts involved, their justification, and their effect on cost and performance.

The value alternatives should be organized using a standardized format. Value programs and practitioners utilize a wide variety of formats for value alternatives that are based upon the type of information that is required by the decision makers of an organization to determine its acceptability. The value specialist should, therefore, ensure that whatever format will be used will contain all of the information that will be needed by the project team and/or decision makers and adjust the format of the value alternatives accordingly.

Regardless of the project type, there are certain pieces of information that any decision maker will need to have. A complete set of forms containing this basic information *(Fig. 9-1)* should include:

- Descriptions of baseline and alternative concepts
- Discussion and justification of the alternative concept

- Financial information (initial cost and life cycle costs, as applicable)
- Performance assessment (impacts to project scope and schedule)
- Graphical information (flow charts, diagrams, sketches, etc.)

In addition to this basic information, there may be a number of additional pieces information that may include:

- Project management considerations
- Redesign and/or implementation costs
- Technical reviewer or stakeholder comments
- Value team member review comments

FUNDAMENTALS OF VALUE METHODOLOGY

Value Alternative Forms

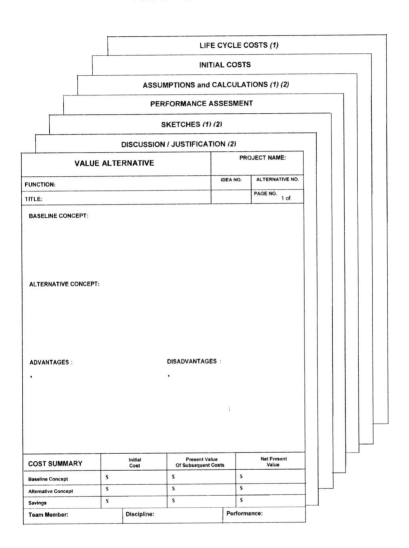

Notes: (1) Optional, depending on needs of the alternative
(2) Additional back-up sheets may support calculations and costs

Figure 9-1

The forms presented in Figure 9-1 will be discussed in further detail, relevant to the following steps in the development of value alternatives:

- Verify technical validity
- Determine costs
- Assess performance—*Value Metrics*
- Develop narratives

If the procedures identified in this chapter are followed, the value team should be successful in developing value alternatives that will do a thorough job in communicating the concepts to the project team and decision makers. Hopefully, this information will be presented clearly and concisely enough by the value team to make the decision-making process an easy one. An example of each of the forms used to capture this information is provided at this end of this section. A complete list of generic value alternative forms is provided in Appendix C of this text.

Verify Technical Validity

Assuming that all of the short-listed ideas were assigned at the end of the Evaluation Phase, the value team members will be ready to begin documenting the information they will be developing for each value alternative. The first step in this process is to verify the technical validity of the value alternative. In other words, will it work?

Depending on the nature of the concept, technical viability may or may not be obvious. If it is not, the value team must consider this first, before expending any additional time on the concept. Verifying technical validity may involve different activities, for example:

- A concept involving an alternative highway alignment may require that the value team's highway design

engineer lay out the geometry on a topographic map in order to ensure that the horizontal and vertical sight distances can be achieved. Will there be additional right-of-way needed? Will additional earthwork be needed? Will the alignment alter the environmental footprint? The value team will need to address all of these issues before proceeding with further development of the alternative.
- A concept involving modifications to a latch spring assembly for a screen door should involve a physical mock-up to test its performance. Will the new latch keep the screen closed while the equipment on which it is mounted is in operation? Will the latch stick? Can the new latch be produced using existing materials or will new material stock be required? The value team will need to ensure that questions such as these are answered before moving on.
- A concept involving the development of a standardized form to be used by six different city agencies to track funding requests should include a meeting with budget personnel from each agency to identify the necessary information required to process the request. Does each agency use the same terminology? If not, can a standardized language be developed? Does each agency require the same number of approval signatures? If not, can these be consolidated and standardized? In this case, the value team will need to work directly with stakeholders to actually develop a standardized form before completing other alternative development activities.

It is important to note that the value team need only develop the concept, at most, to the level of the baseline concept. In some cases, especially for projects involving facilities, it may only be necessary to develop the concept at a preliminary level to ensure that it is fundamentally sound. In other words, it is not necessary to develop the design in AutoCAD, as this is an activity that may take far more time than is available to the value team. Both the value team and project team must keep in mind that any value alternative that is ultimately accepted will need to be integrated into the project by the project team.

As the value team verifies the alternative's technical feasibility, any technical calculations or assumptions should be documented. These, along with any sketches, diagrams or other graphical information will be included as part of value alternative's documentation. If it turns out that the concept is not technically viable, then the reason(s) why it will not work should be documented and then dropped from further consideration.

Determine Costs

Once the value team feels confident that the concept will actually work, the next step will be to assess its financial impacts. Hopefully, the value team will have been provided with the project baseline's cost data prior to the value study. This cost data should serve as the basis for developing the costs for the value alternative. In some cases, the concept behind a value alternative may so radically differ from the baseline concept that it will be necessary to develop a completely new cost estimate from scratch. In such cases, the value team must be careful to document where they are obtaining cost information to support the alternative. Any assumptions should be well documented and justified.

If life cycle costs will be affected by the value alternative, a life cycle analysis should be included as part of the value alternative documentation. Information pertaining to life cycle periods and discount rates should be obtained from the project team or project sponsor.

In performing cost estimates, it is always advisable that a side-by-side comparison of the baseline and alternative costs be made in order to show which areas differ in cost. In developing the costs of the alternative concept, it is not always necessary to provide an estimate of the complete project—it is usually only necessary to include project costs that will change as a result of the implementation of the value alternative.

Assess Performance—*Value Metrics*

Once the technical feasibility and costs have been identified, the value team should have a fairly good idea that the value alternative will indeed provide an improvement in value. The next step is to assess the impacts that the value alternative will have on project performance.

Each of the performance attributes originally identified, defined, and benchmarked during the Information Phase should be reviewed with respect to the value alternative. A statement of performance should be made for each attribute. Each performance attribute should be considered and the rationale for the change (or no change) relative to the baseline should be noted.

A standard form can be used which includes the baseline concept's performance score and attribute weight, as well as a space to record the alternative concept's performance score. The change in performance, if any, must be assessed using the scales and parameters originally established and must be relative to the effect of the change on the entire project. An alternative may provide a dramatic improvement relative to the project element being considered; however, the overall effect upon the total project may be relatively minor or even insignificant. The rationale should relate to both; however, the performance rating must relate to the total project. This is important to understand, as the objective of the value study is to improve the total value of the project as a whole. The cumulative or synergistic effect of multiple alternative concepts on performance is discussed in *Chapter 10—Presentation*. The net change in performance for the alternative concept is expressed in a percent format.

Develop Narratives

The last step in finalizing the documentation for a value alternative is preparing the narratives and any additional graphical information such as sketches or diagrams. Having developed the technical concept, identified costs and assessed performance, the value team members should now have a thorough understanding of the alternative concept. This information should now be summarized by developing a thorough narrative of the value alternative, which should include:

- A brief description of the baseline concept
- A brief description of the alternative concept
- A list of advantages and disadvantages of the alternative concept as compared to the baseline concept
- A discussion of the alternative, including a thorough description of the technical details and any further language that will provide the rationale for why the change is justified.
- A summary of the alternative's financial impacts.

This information should be documented on a series of forms that will allow the project team and decision makers to review it in an organized fashion.

The writing should be prepared so as to allow management personnel, who may be of a non-technical background, to understand the basic concepts involved in the value alternative. Detailed technical information should be included to supplement this discussion so that the project team can review and verify the technical details of the value alternative.

A complete example of a value alternative, with all the forms listed in the final order in which they will appear in the written value study report, is provided on the following pages (*Figs. 9-2 to 9-7*). These forms should be modified to suit the needs of the project under study.

REVIEW VALUE ALTERNATIVES

When all of the value alternatives have been completed, they should be reviewed by the value specialist and each of the value team members. This internal review is very important, as it will allow each team member to check for errors and ensure that narratives are complete and that the performance has been assessed properly, especially with respect to their respective disciplines.

The value team should identify any errors and/or note any suggested revisions based on their review. These edits should be incorporated into the written report when the value alternatives are eventually submitted for review.

When assessing performance for each alternative, it is often a good idea for the value specialist to conduct this as a group activity. Alternately, the value team member responsible for developing the alternative can take the first cut at it, so long as the entire value team reviews these initial ratings and has the opportunity to comment. In any event, the performance assessments should be the result of the consensus of the value team.

It is also advisable to have members of the project team, or other designated technical reviewers, to review the value alternatives midway through the Development Phase. This will allow the opportunity for a "reality check" to ensure that the value team's assumptions are correct and that there are no fatal flaws based on a cursory review.

VALUE ALTERNATIVE			
Bridge Replacement			
FUNCTION: Improve Geometry		**IDEA NO.** IG-1	**NUMBER** 1.1
TITLE: Modify Highway Alignment			**PAGE NO.** 1 of 6

BASELINE CONCEPT:
The baseline concept utilizes a relatively straight alignment, which provides for a straight bridge and eliminates the reversing curves on the southern end of the project limits. The geometry of the baseline concept features a 600 meter radii curve on both the southern and northern conforms, and a straight bridge. A viaduct-type structure or embankment must be constructed for the bridge approach at the south end of the bridge due to the steep down slope on the east side of the roadway. This area has several small streams that would be affected by the construction. The desired design speed is 110 kph (68 mph). One of the alternatives considered by the Project Team was an easterly alignment, which was based on a curved structure similar to what is proposed in this alternative, but did not include significant earthwork, and thus could only provide a 400 meter curve at the southern end which did not meet the desired design speed.

ALTERNATIVE CONCEPT:
This alternative concept would modify the easterly alignment described above between Sta. 104 and Sta. 110 by shifting the roadway west into the hillside at the southern project limits. The geometry of the alternative would feature a 600 meter curve on the roadway at the southern end of the project limits, a 900 meter curve on the bridge, followed by a 720 meter curve back into the existing roadway on the northern end of the project limits. This improvement of curve radius at the southern project limits would meet the desired design speed.

ADVANTAGES:
- Significant construction cost savings
- Improves north side tie-in geometry
- Improves south side geometry by eliminating reversing curves
- Large radius curves fit better with canyon theme
- Reduces impact to forest for preliminary foundation studies/drilling
- Reduces impacts to drainage and to lake
- Supports selection of the shortest length bridge
- Keeps impacts to forest to existing highway alignment
- Eliminates need for approach viaduct or embankment/retaining wall at southern tie-in required for straight alignment

DISADVANTAGES:
- Increases cut slope area
- May require a spoils disposal site
- Crosses existing alignment
- Requires revegetation of cuts
- Requires a superelevation on bridge due to need for curved structure
- Curved structure may complicate structure construction
- Curve and superelevation on bridge will complicate structures maintenance
- Curve will reduce sight distance making maintenance more hazardous

COST SUMMARY	Initial Cost	Present Value Subsequent Cost	Net Present Value
Baseline Concept	$ 87,743,000	$ 0	$ 87,743,000
Alternative Concept	$ 75,314,000	$ 0	$ 75,314,000
Savings	$ 12,429,000	$ 0	$ 12,429,000
Team Member: John Smith	Discipline: Design	PERFORMANCE:	+12%

Figure 9-2

VALUE ALTERNATIVE		
Bridge Replacement		
TITLE: Modify Highway Alignment	NUMBER 1.1	PAGE NO. 2 of 6

DISCUSSION / JUSTIFICATION:

This alternative captures the benefits of both the "East" and "Straight" alignments options:

- The shorter structure and north tie-in benefits of the "East" alignment and the elimination of the reversing curves in the "Straight" option.

- The "East" alignment would accommodate a bridge approx. 584 m (1916 ft) in length, while the "Straight" alignment requires a bridge approx. 674 m (2211 ft) in length. (The East alignment structure is approx. 90 m (295 ft) shorter in length). This presents opportunity for cost savings.

- The impacts of the cut slope work are offset by avoiding the embankment/retaining wall work required at the southern project limits for the "Straight" alignment.

The right-of-way impacted by this alternative is under Forest Service control. With better topographic information there are many refinements that can be made to this concept.

Figure 9-3

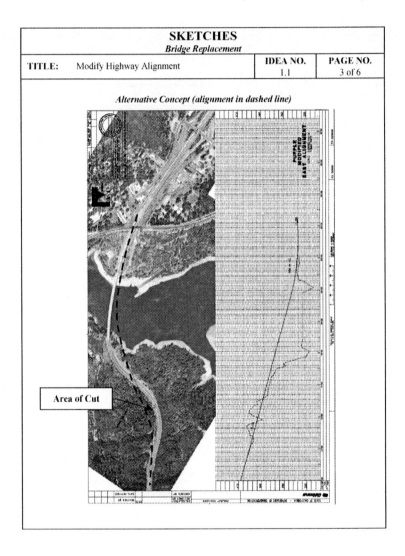

Figure 9-4

PERFORMANCE ASSESSMENT
Bridge Replacement

TITLE: Modify Highway Alignment	NUMBER 1.1	PAGE NO. 4 of 6	
CRITERIA and RATING RATIONALE for ALTERNATIVE	Performance	Baseline	Alternative
MAINLINE OPERATIONS Both the baseline and alternative concepts meet the desired design speed, however, this alternative provides for a larger radius curve at the north tie-in and the southern tie-in. The long, straight, downgrade at 6.0% in the baseline option may invite higher speeds that would be greater than the design speed. Thus, the larger radius curve option provides for a more forgiving transition into the existing alignment.	Rating	5	6
	Weight	29	29
	Contribution	145	174
CONSTRUCTION SCHEDULE The bridge would be about 90 meters shorter for this alternative, however, there would be more earthwork and an additional conflict with existing traffic – consider it be a push in terms of overall schedule.	Rating	5	5
	Weight	7	7
	Contribution	35	35
MAINTAINABILITY Bridge maintenance will be slightly more complicated due to curved and super-elevated structure.	Rating	5	4
	Weight	19	19
	Contribution	95	76
CONSTRUCTION IMPACTS The alternative avoids large fills and retaining walls on the southern end of the alignment. Cut material can be used for any necessary fills on northern end (lessens need for any needed import).	Rating	5	6
	Weight	7	7
	Contribution	35	42
CONSTRUCTIBILITY This alternative trades off additional earthwork for a reduction in embankment and retaining walls.	Rating	5	5
	Weight	5	5
	Contribution	25	25
ENVIRONMENTAL IMPACTS – NATURAL The alternative locates the alignment further away from nesting eagles and avoids filling in a deep drainage ravine on the south side.	Rating	4	6
	Weight	10	10
	Contribution	40	60
ENVIRONMENTAL IMPACTS-RECREATIONAL This alternative is more favorable because it places the new bridge further away from an existing boat ramp.	Rating	5	6
	Weight	24	24
	Contribution	120	144
		495	556
Net Change in Performance:			+12%

Figure 9-5

ASSUMPTIONS and CALCULATIONS			
\multicolumn{4}{c}{*Bridge Replacement*}			
TITLE:	Modify Highway Alignment	NUMBER 1.1	PAGE NO. 5 of 6

Cost Estimating Assumptions:

Roadway:

- Length of road construction difference is assumed to be insignificant.
- Disposal/embankment waste sites can be obtained.
- Earthwork/Disposal – Quantities developed by John Smith using CAICE
- Baseline Cut: 39,000 m3, Fill: 61,000 m3
- Alternative Cut: 142,000 m3, Fill: 71,000 m3

Structure:

- Reduced structure length: 91 m x 31.5 m = 2,866 m2. Unit costs based on Project Report.
- Approach structure is eliminated for a savings of $3,600,000 based on Project Report.

Figure 9-6

CONSTRUCTION ELEMENT		BASELINE CONCEPT			ALTERNATIVE CONCEPT		
Description	Unit	Quantity	Cost/Unit	Total	Quantity	Cost/Unit	Total
ROADWAY ITEMS							
Earthwork	m3	100,000	20	2,000,000	213,000	20	4,260,000
Reduction in structure length	m2	21,231	3,869	82,142,739	18,365	3,869	71,054,185
Viaduct structure	ls	1	3,600,000	3,600,000	-	-	-
TOTAL				$ 87,742,739			$ 75,314,185
TOTAL (Rounded)				$ 87,743,000			$ 75,314,000
						SAVINGS	$ 12,429,000

INITIAL COST ESTIMATE
Bridge Replacement

TITLE: Modify Highway Alignment
NUMBER: 1.1
PAGE NO.: 6 of 6

Figure 9-7

Providing the opportunity for this mid-point review will help to provide stakeholder "buy in" prior to the exit briefing that will be held the final day of the value study. It will also reduce the potential of developing value alternatives that are technically flawed or otherwise unacceptable, thereby minimizing wasted effort and maximizing the value team's credibility.

The value specialist must be careful to avoid the temptation to throw out valid alternatives simply because they may be unpopular. The reviewers must present a credible reason for excluding a value alternative at this stage in the process. Additionally, the value specialist should seek to invite the reviewers in on a staggered basis, thereby minimizing disruptions to the value team, who will usually be pressed for time. This review should be more of an "over the shoulder" review rather than a formal meeting.

If reviewers are present, their comments should be documented and included as part of the value alternative in the written report. This feedback will be valuable and will help with the future implementation of the concept should it be accepted during the Implementation Phase.

Also during the review process, the value team should consider a number of additional strategies that will facilitate the acceptance of proposed changes within an organization:

- Develop an implementation overview plan to identify key individuals or groups involved in the implementation effort.
- Review specific proposals with key managers of effected departments and solicit their support.
- Seek input regarding implementation tasks and estimated timetables.
- Highlight the overall advantages of the proposed changes to various levels of supervision *before* final recommendations are presented to the executive group.

- Identify risks and concerns so they can be included in the final presentation to the executive group.
- Above all, be patient and thorough in your discussions, giving consideration to the fact that the proposed changes will, in some cases, cause additional effort to achieve implementation.

SUMMARY

The success of the Development Phase will depend greatly upon the technical knowledge and experience of the value team members and the degree of effort they apply in developing the documentation for the value alternatives. The value specialist will have to facilitate and manage the efforts of the value team members to ensure that all of the ideas selected for development in the Evaluation Phase are fully considered and/or developed.

Above all else it is important that the value team fully take ownership of the concepts they will be presenting to the project team and decision makers. This requires that all of the value team members review and contribute to the development of all alternatives. Through teamwork and diligence, the value team, and ultimately the project, will be rewarded many times over.

Chapter 10—Presentation

Gabrielle "Coco" Chanel—Fashion Designer

A fashion that does not reach the streets is not a fashion.
—Coco Chanel

Fashion is not something that exists in dresses only. Fashion is in the sky, in the street; fashion has to do with ideas, the way we live, what is happening.
—Coco Chanel

The genius behind the Fashion Empire of House Chanel was Gabrielle Bonheur Chanel, born in 1883. Coco Chanel did not always dream of becoming a famous fashion designer. She danced, attempted to be an actress, sold hosiery, rode horses, dispensed mineral water, and worked as a cabaret singer. Coco Chanel opened her first millinery store in 1909 in Paris. This says quite a lot about Chanel in that she was able to turn a small boutique that employed two teenage girls into one of the most profitable fashion houses of all time.

Soon she was expanding to couture, working in jersey, a first in the French fashion world. By the 1920s, her fashion house had expanded considerably, and her chemise set a fashion trend with its "little boy" look. Her relaxed fashions, short skirts, and casual look were in sharp contrast to the corset fashions popular in the previous decades. Chanel herself dressed in clothes having a masculine aesthetic, and adapted these more comfortable fashions which other women also found liberating. Coco Chanel introduced her signature cardigan jacket in 1925 and the famous "little black dress" in 1926. Her fashions had a timelessness sense of style to them and proved to have tremendous staying power. They didn't change much from year to year—or even generation to generation.

Probably the single element that would ensure Chanel's legacy was not a piece of clothing, but rather, a perfume named after her called Chanel No. 5. It was first launched in its art deco bottle in 1923 and holds the distinction of being the first perfume to bear a designer's name.

Her fashion empire at her death brought in over $160 million dollars a year. The noted German Designer Karl Lagerfeld has assumed the artistic directorship of the House of Chanel since 1954. Certainly it can be said that Chanel did an incredible amount for the development of fashion. By maintaining her incredible business sense, and her uniqueness, Chanel helped create what modern fashion is considered today.

Coco Chanel was an entrepreneur who was determined to break old formulas and invent new ways of expressing herself. She serves as an archetype for the importance of selling change. Nearly single-handedly, she redefined the role that women would play by redefining their image and successfully selling it to modern society. By her death in 1971, the French couturier had long since established herself as the 20th Century's single-most important arbiter of fashion. Coco Chanel illustrates the value of selling change and serves as a segue into the discussion of the Presentation Phase.

PRESENTATION PHASE

In the Presentation Phase, the value team presents specific recommendations to the project team and decision makers, in the form of value alternatives, which are intended to improve project. Those that will be receiving the recommendations should have the authority to make the necessary decisions. There are two steps that are included as part of this phase. These include:

- Assess value—*Value Metrics*
- Conduct exit briefing
- Prepare and submit written report

It must be emphasized that the objective is not merely to present the value team's findings, but to *sell* the ideas to the project team and decision makers.

SELLING CHANGE

The best ideas in the world will remain unrealized unless they can be communicated clearly and convincingly to those in a position to act on them. Those with experience in marketing, sales and advertising no doubt understand the importance of selling new ideas and concepts. Those that are employed in technical positions, or even those in project management, may not understand the value of selling change.

Most engineers, designers, programmers and other technical specialists will usually cringe when the subject of "selling" is brought up. Why is this? Clearly, this aversion to sales is rooted in the professional culture of dealing in facts and absolutes. In my experience, the perception that most technical people conjure up when the topic of sales is discussed is that of the dreaded used car salesman. In their minds, selling is typically fraught with "dishonesty," "misrepresentation of the truth," "exaggeration" and even outright fraud. These mental images and emotions are further reinforced by the availability and representativeness heuristics discussed in *Chapter 8—Evaluation*.

The value specialist will probably need to help some members of the value team overcome these mental roadblocks to selling change. Provided below are a number of strategies that can be employed to sell change:

- **Share the Credit**—Oftentimes, the project team will have vested an enormous amount of effort in developing the project's baseline concept. The important thing to recognize is that not only has time and effort been invested, but also pride. Pride can be a major obstacle in overcoming change. If the value team has developed a concept that is particularly strong, it may be wise to demonstrate how the stakeholders and/or project team members have contributed to the development of the value alternative. If others outside the value team can feel some pride in ownership of a new concept, they will be less apt to resist it.
- **Find Champions of Change**—There will most likely be members within the sponsoring organization that will be advocates of change. Hopefully, these individuals will have been identified early on in the process by the value specialist. The value team must seek to include these individuals in group meetings and seek their input, especially in the exit briefing, as they can provide valuable leverage in motivating change within an organization.
- **Sell the Concept of Change Early**—The earlier people can get involved with the value process, the more time there will be to prepare them for change. The value specialist should work with the study sponsor and project team in preparing everyone for change. Everyone involved needs to understand that the value team is simply an extension of the project team. They are there to help the project team develop a better project, not to embarrass or criticize anyone. The decision makers must understand this as well, especially that the value team will have the advantage of hindsight that the project team did not have.

- **Use Language to Communicate Ideas with Enthusiasm**— The value team should consider brainstorming ways of selling their most important, and potentially valuable, concepts. Developing key catch phrases and sound bites can really help sell big ideas by creating links between words and concepts. The objective of selling an idea is to persuade others that it is a good idea. This does not mean lying or misrepresenting the truth. The use of a few choice words can help make ideas stick in the minds of decision makers.
- **Sell Value Improvement**—Keep in mind that the objective of the Value Methodology is to improve total project value, not just reduce costs. This means communicating to the project team and decision makers that the value team has been focusing on all aspects of the value equation which include scope, schedule, and cost. Assuming the *Value Metrics* approach has been utilized as part of the VM process, the value team will be able to show in detail how project performance will be affected by the alternatives they have developed. Selling value improvement will be much easier then merely selling cost reductions.
- **Be Prepared**—All of the blood, sweat and tears that went into developing the technical aspects of the value alternatives will pay off when the value team is hit with the tough-minded technical questions from the project team. One of the best ways to sell ideas to technical reviewers is to have developed all the facts. If a question arises concerning an issue that the value team has not addressed during the Development Phase, let everyone know that the value team will research the question and find the answer. In the zeal to sell ideas, don't be tempted to gloss over disadvantages or potential problems. The project team and decision makers will appreciate the forthrightness and honesty, which will in turn only foster trust and respect.

- **Create Excitement**—Visible enthusiasm on the part of the value team will in and of itself help sell its ideas. If the value team is obviously indifferent about its work, than you can bet that everyone else will be too. An enthusiastic and ebullient attitude is infectious and will be difficult to resist if it is genuine.
- **Use Graphics to Convey Ideas**—The use of graphic images is one of the best ways to sell ideas. Sometimes, even a simple sketch or diagram can sell a concept in ways a report full of words could never achieve. When using graphics, less is more. Seek to communicate ideas visually as simply and clearly as possible.
- **Recognize Others for their Efforts**—Recognition can be more important than pay for many. The value specialist should take time to recognize the project team and other contributors for their efforts. The exit briefing provides an excellent opportunity to do this directly. Conveying a sense of graciousness will demonstrate respect for the hard work of others. This will not go unnoticed.
- **Communicate Concisely**—Time is a valuable commodity, especially for executive level management. Avoid getting into minutiae when presenting value alternatives during the exit briefing. Focus on the facts and present the concepts as concisely as possible. When presenting value alternatives using software such as Microsoft PowerPoint, seek to limit alternatives to one slide of no more than five or six bullets. The idea is to communicate the key concepts—the technical details will be provided in the written report.

ASSESS VALUE—*VALUE METRICS*

Following the development of the alternative concepts, the value team must next consider how they could be applied to the project in concert with one another. Typically, the value team should develop a number of potential implementation strategies that might be considered by the decision makers. It isn't essential to consider every possible permutation at this point, just a few that seem to be the most logical. Once an implementation strategy(s) has been identified, the value team should review each of the alternatives that are a part of that strategy with respect to its impact on performance. It may be that the cumulative effect of several minor performance improvements offered by various alternatives equate to a larger combined performance improvement. The total effect should be recorded on the performance rating matrix based on the revised rating. This approach generally improves the thoroughness of the documentation of the alternative concepts and provides better information for the decision makers. While this information should be included in the discussion of the alternative concept, this process helps to ensure that the relative performance information is captured.

Once aggregate performance ratings have been developed for each implementation strategy, cost, performance, and value should be summarized in a manner similar to that described previously for the baseline concept *(Fig. 10-1)*.

This example provides a cross-section of concepts possessing widely differing costs and performance ratings. It is worth noting that in this example, the alternative concept with a minor cost increase and significant performance improvements appears to provide the best overall value solution.

CONDUCT EXIT BRIEFING

Conducting an exit briefing at the conclusion of a value study is always advisable. The exit briefing provides an opportunity for the value team to directly present the value alternatives it has developed to the project team, stakeholders, and decision makers. This face-to-face meeting may be the best opportunity for the value team to sell its ideas.

The purpose of the exit briefing is purely for informational purposes. It is not, and should not be, a decision-making meeting. The value team may need additional time to further solidify the value alternatives following the conclusion of the value study and, in any case, the value study report will need to be written, edited and finalized. Those that will be reviewing the value team's efforts must have ample time to properly review the documentation prior to making any kind of decision regarding the acceptability of the value alternatives. This decision-making meeting will take place during the Implementation Phase, which is discussed in the following chapter.

The exit briefing should be conducted within a relatively brief timeframe—60 to 90 minutes is generally a good rule of thumb. The exit briefing may be conducted using a multimedia presentation or a simple oral presentation, depending upon the resources available. A list of the value alternatives, including titles, cost and performance impacts should be handed out to the meeting participants. It is generally a good idea to avoid handing out draft copies of the value alternatives, as this will distract meeting attendees from focusing on the value team's presentation, which is more about selling the alternatives then reviewing them for technical content.

When preparing for the presentation, it is important to provide a clear and concise picture of the value alternatives by addressing such questions as why they should be implemented, who should be involved in their implementation, and the timing required. The value team must structure their presentation ahead of time if they are going to keep to the schedule. A presentation should be structured into three sections: the introduction, body and conclusion. Provided below is a simple outline for an exit briefing.

VALUE MATRIX
Bridge Replacement Project

Attribute	Attribute Weight	Concept	Performance Rating 1	2	3	4	5	6	7	8	9	10	Total Performance
Mainline Operations	29	Baseline Concept					5						145
		Value Strategy 1				4							116
		Value Strategy 2						6					174
		Value Strategy 3					5						145
		Value Strategy 4					5						145
Environmental - Natural	19	Baseline Concept					5						95
		Value Strategy 1					5						95
		Value Strategy 2							7				133
		Value Strategy 3							7				133
		Value Strategy 4						6					114
Environmental - Social	14	Baseline Concept						6					84
		Value Strategy 1						6					84
		Value Strategy 2								8			112
		Value Strategy 3						6					84
		Value Strategy 4						6					84
Constructibility	2	Baseline Concept					5						10
		Value Strategy 1				4							8
		Value Strategy 2					5						10
		Value Strategy 3				4							8
		Value Strategy 4					5						10
Maintainability	24	Baseline Concept					5						120
		Value Strategy 1					5						120
		Value Strategy 2							7				168
		Value Strategy 3					5						120
		Value Strategy 4					5						120
Construction Impacts	10	Baseline Concept					5						50
		Value Strategy 1						6					60
		Value Strategy 2				4							40
		Value Strategy 3					5						50
		Value Strategy 4					5						50
Construction Schedule	2	Baseline Concept							7				14
		Value Strategy 1						6					12
		Value Strategy 2								8			16
		Value Strategy 3							7				14
		Value Strategy 4					5						10

Overall Performance Alternative	Total Performance	% Performance Improvement	Total Cost	Value Index (P/C)	% Value Improvement
Baseline Concept	518		500.00	1.04	
Value Strategy 1 (Alts. 1, 2, 5, 7)	495	-4%	470.00	1.05	2%
Value Strategy 2 (Alts. 1, 2, 6, 8)	653	26%	510.00	1.28	24%
Value Strategy 3 (Alts. 3, 9, 10)	554	7%	480.00	1.15	11%
Value Strategy 4 (Alts. 3, 4, 11)	533	3%	500.00	1.07	3%

Fig. 10-1

Introduction

In the introduction phase of the briefing, the following questions should be answered.

- **What was the scope of the value study?** Briefly describe the project scope and the value study scope—remember they may not be the same.
- **Who was involved?** Consider not only the value team members, but also any others who have made significant contributions (i.e., other departments or community representatives involved with the study).
- **What were the objectives or goals of the value study?** List the objectives or problem areas that motivated the study.
- **What was the value study process?** The value specialist should conduct a brief overview of the value methodology process, especially if there are members of the audience that were not present for the kick-off meeting.

Prepare the audience for the value alternatives that they will be hearing by identifying the number of proposals and the area of the project they impact. This information serves as a transition into the body of the presentation.

Body

The body of the presentation contains the specific value alternatives the team wants the decision makers to act upon. Each value alternative should include a discussion of WHAT, WHY, WHEN, and WHO. These four elements are detailed below.

- **What is the alternative concept?** Explain in sufficient detail so the concept can be clearly understood. Avoid

getting too detailed, as this will make the alternative confusing. Be prepared to answer questions if additional information is needed. Graphics are very beneficial in presenting the ideas.
- **Why should the alternative be accepted?** Describe the improvements over the baseline concept and state the impacts on project performance. Once these benefits have been clearly established, the effect on cost should be presented. Here the impact on both initial and life cycle cost should be presented. It is also important that any other concerns related to the alternative be addressed at this point.
- **When can these value improvements be realized?** The decision makers will want to know how long it will take for the improvements to be integrated into the project. An implementation schedule for the proposal showing the steps necessary to make the change should be prepared.
- **Who should implement the alternative?** In most cases, with the approval of the alternatives the involvement of the value team may end, and the implementation is assigned to the line organization or the designer. The value team should identify those that may be involved in the implementation.

The value team is selling the proposals in the body of the presentation. Identify the important features of the proposals. Do not dwell on the present situation. Discuss other projects that may be impacted by the proposals but were out of the scope of the study. *Figure 10-2* provides example slides from a PowerPoint presentation summarizing a value alternative for a construction staging plan.

8.0 - Modify Construction Staging Plan

- ► Close the entire interchange during construction.
  - Temporary hook ramps would be constructed at Catawba Ave. for the westbound ramps.
  - Traffic using the eastbound ramps would be detoured to either the Cherry Ave. or Sierra Ave. Interchanges.
  - Citrus Ave. will closed (which is the same assumption for the baseline concept).
- ► Cost Savings: $348,000
- ► Highway-User Savings: $3,445,000
- ► Performance: +3%
  - Reduces the construction schedule by 6-months
  - Separates construction activities from vehicular traffic
  - The detour at Catawba Ave. may require additional environmental studies – potential schedule impacts
  - May increase "loss of business" mitigation costs for properties at Slover/Citrus Intersection

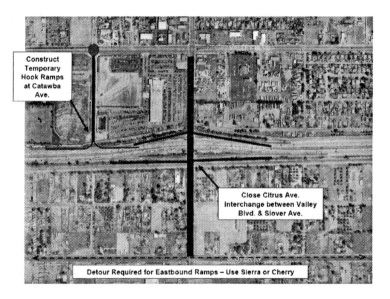

Figure 10-2

CONCLUSION

After all the value alternatives have been presented, the objective is to get the decision makers to initiate action. In the conclusion of the presentation, summarize the impact of all of the alternatives, and ask the decision makers to identify future implementation action. An implementation meeting should be scheduled after sufficient time has been allotted to review the value study report.

Presentation Considerations

The selling of alternatives is often dependent on not only the facts of the study but how the facts are presented. A clear and concise presentation is much more effective than a long, wordy, detailed one. Consideration will need to be given with respect to who will be doing the presenting. This will depend greatly upon the nature of the project, the abilities of the value team members, the amount of time available to make the presentation, and the confidence of the team in its presentation skills.

If time is particularly constrained, or much of the team does not feel confident in their presentation skills, the value specialist may want to handle the entire presentation for consistency and clarity. Otherwise, it is always preferable to have the value team participants be directly involved in the presentation. In this case, the team members should present those value alternatives that they had the biggest role in developing.

The presentation can be enhanced by the following:

- Talk in a relaxed, conversational mode; do not try to make the report too formal. A relaxed mode of presentation stimulates a relaxed atmosphere, demonstrates confidence in the alternatives, and promotes good dialogue between the audience and the value team.

- Speak rapidly, but articulate clearly, leaving pauses between paragraphs. Rapid delivery has higher interest rate.
- Reveal major points to be remembered early in the presentation.
- Learn the presentation point by point, not word by word. Careful preparation and a great deal of practice are required to create a smooth, effective presentation. Mark Twain once said, "It takes three weeks to prepare a good ad-lib speech."
- Concentrate on proposed concepts; do not dwell on existing situations.
- Key on the concepts that are being presented, not the concepts that did not work out.
- Be enthusiastic about the proposals; think positively about receiving management approval.
- Use examples, visual aids, drawings, sketches, or sample parts whenever possible to help make a point.
- When questions are asked, the speaker should not feel that it is necessary to answer all the questions personally. Questions should be responded to by the team member who is most informed about the subject matter.
- Visual aids will only be effective if they can be seen by all. Check out the room ahead of time to see how the room arrangement can be used to its best advantage. Determine where the decision makers will be sitting with respect to the speaker and visual aids.
- If projectors are being used, be familiar with their controls and be prepared to finish the presentation in the event of technical difficulties with the equipment.
- Check out the presentation material on the equipment to be used. Will it be clear and visible to the audience? How should the room lights be set to assure the visuals can be seen? You can dim the lights but do not shut them off! The audience needs to see the speaker. If the

- image appears washed out on the screen, removing a few ceiling bulbs directly over the screen generally resolves the problem.
- When using visuals, face the audience and talk to them. Often presenters tend to turn toward the visuals and talk to the screen. Feet should be pointed toward the audience and the hand closest to the screen should be used for gesturing to avoid this problem.

PREPARE AND SUBMIT VALUE STUDY REPORT

Following the exit briefing and the conclusion of the formal value study, the value specialist must prepare the written value study report for submission to the project decision makers. The value specialist is primarily responsible for gathering the documentation generated during the study and compiling it systematically into a report.

The VA Study Report should be organized in sections, preceded by a cover letter, distribution list, and table of contents. The value study report should include:

- **Executive Summary**—Provides an updated overview of the project, the value alternatives, and any other the key findings and recommendations.
- **Value Alternatives**—Documents the individual value alternatives.
- **Project Analysis**—Summarizes the findings of the value study and includes information developed using VM techniques such as cost models, FAST diagrams, Value Matrix, etc.
- **Project Description**—Narrative of the project baseline's scope, schedule and cost that formed the basis for the value study.
- **Idea Evaluation**—Lists all of the ideas generated by the value team and their evaluations.

Value Methodology Process—Summarizes the Value Methodology Job Plan, *Value Metrics* process, agenda, and participants.

Preparing a thorough value study report is essential to clearly communicate the results of the value study to the project team and decision makers as the first step in the implementation of the value alternatives.

In some cases, it may be desirable to have two iterations of the written report—a draft and a final version. In this case, the draft version need only include the executive summary and value alternatives sections. Following the implementation meeting, a final report is prepared that includes the remaining sections of the report plus an implementation section that documents the final status of the value alternatives and outlines the implementation plan, schedule and responsibilities for each.

SUMMARY

Success in the Presentation Phase requires that the value alternatives are effectively marketed to the decision makers. This requires attention to not just the content of the value alternatives, but on how they are presented. Recent research has found that persuasion works best when it is matched to the decision-making style used by management within an organization. One particular study concluded that almost 50 percent of all presentations are mismatched to the style of the executive decision maker[1].

"All too often, people make the mistake of focusing too much on the content of their argument and not enough on how they deliver that message. Far too many decisions go the wrong way because information is presented ineffectively," according to the authors.

Successfully selling a value alternative to management involves more than simply explaining the technology. It requires technical people to demonstrate how the idea will fit in a specific project's scope, schedule, and budget, or to explain how it will improve project value.

---

[1] Based on a 2002 article, "Change the Way You Persuade," by Miller-Williams, CEO Gary A. Williams and Chairman Robert B. Miller and published by Harvard Business School Publishing

Chapter 11—Implementation

Benjamin Franklin—Statesman, Inventor, Writer

Diligence is the mother of good luck.
—Ben Franklin

He that waits upon fortune is never sure of a dinner.
—Ben Franklin

Resolve to perform what you ought; perform without fail what you resolve.
—Ben Franklin

Benjamin Franklin was born in Boston on January 17, 1706. He was the tenth son of soap maker, Josiah Franklin, and but one of his 17 children. In his early years, he served as an apprentice printer in Boston and later in Philadelphia. He later went on to purchase the Pennsylvania Gazette, which soon became the most successful newspaper in the colonies. He was a prolific writer, and is famous for authoring "Poor Richard's Almanack," a collection of Franklin's witty aphorisms and lively essays.

One fascinating aspect of Franklin's life was the determination and discipline he displayed in implementing changes in his life. This trait was perhaps best demonstrated during a period as a young man where he systematically focused on improving virtuous behavior and eradicating bad habits. Specifically, Franklin would focus on one of thirteen virtues each week and methodically practice it in his daily life while keeping records of his progress.

Franklin had a strong inclination toward public service and was the catalyst for implementing many civic programs within Philadelphia. These include the "Junto," a young man's self-improvement organization; the founding of the Library Company—the nation's first subscription library; the launching of the Philosophical Society; and the foundation of the Pennsylvania Hospital to provide care to the sick and infirm. Franklin is also credited with establishing the city's first fire company.

Franklin also shone as an inventor. He is well known for some of humankind's first experiments with electricity. He invented the Franklin Stove, swim fins, the glass armonica (a musical instrument), and bifocals. Franklin is perhaps most famous for his role as one of the nation's Founding Fathers. He is in fact credited with much of the authorship of the Declaration of Independence, which is generally overshadowed by Thomas Jefferson's role in its creation. He also served in the Second Continental Congress and served as the U.S. Ambassador to France.

Perhaps Franklin's most impressive trait was his ability to implement his ideas. He is an excellent example of the importance of following through with change. Having an idea is not enough—it must be carried out and acted upon with due diligence. Benjamin Franklin provides an excellent introduction to the importance and need for the Implementation Phase.

IMPLEMENTATION PHASE

The Implementation Phase focuses on determining the disposition of the value alternatives and validating their benefits. Once the decision makers have had a chance to review the value study report and, hopefully, have provided their written analysis of each value alternative to the value specialist, an Implementation Meeting is scheduled to agree upon the disposition of each value alternative. The Implementation Phase includes the following steps:

- Review value alternatives

    o Improve decisions—*Value Metrics*

- Resolve value alternatives

    o Conduct Implementation Meeting

- Develop implementation plan
- Track and audit results

MANAGING CHANGE

The Implementation Phase is all about change, as the acceptance of a value alternative by decision makers will require the project team to integrate the associated changes into the ongoing project and may even require a systemic change within an organization to be successful. The key to dealing with the changes that come about as a result of a value study, big or small, is to successfully manage them. This requires developing a basic understanding of the nature of change itself.

The Stages of Change

The capacity of individuals and organizations to cope with change varies dramatically, depending on the size and nature of the change, as well as an awareness of the risks associated of not accepting the change. Depending on the nature of an organization's approach to implementation, the value specialist or project manager will need to assist others in adjusting to the changes brought on by value alternatives. There are essentially four stages of change. These include:

- **Stage 1: Shock**—Most people interpret impending change as a threat. Much like physiological shock, the tendency is to shut down thinking, and as many other systems as possible, in order to cope with the attendant fear. Just as people need warmth and rest when in physical shock in order to initiate recovery, they need emotional support, information, and an opportunity to gather with others in order to begin recovering the shock of change.

   Coping Strategy: The shock and stress of change can be minimized by building a support network in the form of a detailed implementation plan, and by providing as much information as possible with respect to the change. Upper management should provide support and, more importantly, maintain a visible level of involvement in seeing the changes through. A sense of safety can be provided by clearly communicating organizational expectations and by properly allocating time and resources to implement the change.

- **Stage 2: Defensive Retreat**—Many times, those that are most directly affected by a change will attempt to hold on by maintaining their old ways. Individuals and organizations can get stuck here or return to Stage 1 as each element of the change is introduced.

   Coping Strategy: Assistance can be rendered by identifying what those individuals who are resisting change are holding on to; provide insight on how to modify old behaviors in the context of the new situation; or how to simply let go of the old ways altogether if they are now inappropriate or obsolete. Identify areas of stability (i.e., things that are not changing). Provide information continually and consistently. Ask "what is risky?" and provide safety in response to discomfort with risk taking.

- **Stage 3: Acknowledgement**—This stage may include a sense of grief and sadness over what has been lost. This aspect of change may be pronounced in those that have had a major hand in the creative and/or technical development of the project's baseline concept. For these individuals, it is important to start letting go; begin to see the value of what is coming; and look for ways to make the changes work. The project team will need to begin taking risks again in order to implement the change. It takes the form of risk taking and exploring new ways to look at things and to do things. This can lead to high energy if it is managed well.

  Coping Strategy: Involve people by working with them to explore options and by planning through the use of an implementation plan and schedule. The value specialist or project manager should encourage and support risk taking at this stage by pointing out ways that it will be supported by the organization. Emphasize that everyone is facing the same learning curve.

- **Stage 4: Adaptation and Change**—At this stage, the transformation is in full motion. Be prepared to establish new routines and to help others. Risk taking comes into full bloom at this stage relative to changing methods, products, or whatever is called for by the change.

  Coping Strategy: Stick to the implementation plan. Encourage and support risk taking using the supports and structures developed in Stage 3. Establish feedback loops so that information travels in all directions, new learning occurs, and mid-course corrections can be made when necessary.

The Forces of Change

The next element in managing change is developing an understanding of the forces involved in individual and organizational change. There are both positive and negative forces at work that tend to work at cross-purposes. These forces include:

Positive Forces (Catalysts of Change)

Changes in an organization's environment, such as the introduction of new procedures, standards or regulations, rapidly increasing competition, or unpredictable changes in the economy, may require the organization to implement new organizational structures or systems of recognition.

- The development of new products or product selection resulting from improvements in technology, changes to the competition or the industry, or unusual requirements of a new client may impact the organization.
- Changes in the workplace, such as employee demographics or the introduction of more technically trained management, may call for new forms of communication and chains of decision making.
- Reductions in productivity, product quality, customer satisfaction, commitment, or an increase in employee turnover or absenteeism may call for changes in internal relations (i.e., the relationship between different departments within an organization). Sometimes, one or two specific events outside of the organization precipitate the change.

Negative Forces (Resistance to Change)

- Resistance to change occurs when a change ignores the needs, attitudes, and beliefs of the members of an organization.
- Individuals resist change when they lack specific information about the change. This ignorance hinders them from developing an understanding of when, how, or why the change is occurring.
- Individuals may not perceive a need for change; they may feel that their organization or project is currently operating effectively and/or profitably. In such a case, change may not be voluntary or requested by organizational members.
- Members of an organization may suffer from an "us vs. them" mentality that causes them to view the change agent as their enemy. These individuals may also feel inconsequential in the face of the change, especially if it is imposed by representatives from "headquarters" or of an outside entity such as a consulting firm or regulatory agency.
- Members of an organization may view the change as a threat to the prestige and security of their manager. They may perceive the change in procedures of policies as a commentary that their manager's performance is inadequate.
- Members of an organization may perceive the change as threats to their expertise, status, or security. The introduction of a new computer system, for example, may cause some individuals to feel that they lack sufficient knowledge to perform their jobs; the revision of an organization's structure may challenge their relative status in the organization; the introduction of a new reward system may threaten their feelings of job security.

In order for controlled, managed, and effective change to occur, the value specialist or project manager must confront each of these negative forces and strive to overcome them.

Implementing Change

The successful implementation of the changes related to value alternatives requires that the strategies outlined in the implementation plan succeed. Although careful preparation for change, including the proper documentation of the value alternatives and a sound implementation plan, increases the chances of success, it does not guarantee effective action. Implementation requires an ongoing assessment of the reactions of the project team to the change. Strategies for the successful implementation of change include:

- The use of a steering or oversight committee to monitor the change may increase the likelihood of success.
- The dynamic nature of organizational systems requires flexibility. The implementation plan must include contingency plans for unanticipated costs, potential risks, or unforeseen resistance.
- A strong commitment to the change on the part of top management can buffer change efforts for such difficulties and can ensure the transfer of needed resources to the implementation plan.

REVIEW AND ASSESS VALUE ALTERNATIVES

The project team and decision makers will be faced with the task of reviewing and assessing the value alternatives once the value study report has been submitted. The purpose of this assessment is to provide the project stakeholders and the value team with the assurance that the alternatives contain accurate information and that the assessments are based on their merits with the current information. During the assessment of alternatives, the project manager, key project team members, technical reviewers, and external project stakeholders review the value study report and document their comments and implementation positions on all value alternatives. It is not uncommon for the various reviewers of the value study report to have different positions regarding the acceptability of the value alternatives. For this reason, these comments should be collected and submitted to the value specialist so that proper preparation for the implementation meeting can be accomplished.

A decision to implement a value alternative constitutes the intent to incorporate it into the present or subsequent project development phase, based on current information. This final decision is made at the implementation meeting. It is recommended that a standardized form be used to capture the comments of the report reviewers for each value alternative in order to provide a consistent level of documentation regarding each value alternative.

The Value Alternative Implementation Action form is designed as a standard means for reviewers to record their comments relevant to the value alternatives. The reviewers should complete one of these forms for each of the value alternatives that appear in the value study report. These should be collected by the project manager and forwarded on to the value specialist prior to the implementation meeting. An example of this form has been provided in *(Fig. 11-1)*. This form includes placeholders for the following information:

- **Title**—The title of the alternative as shown on the Value Alternative form.
- **Alternative No.**—Alternative number as shown on the Value Alternative form.

- **Responses**—Written comments on criteria chosen by the reviewer:

    o **Prepared by**—Identify who is preparing the response and date.
    o **Technical Feasibility/Validated Performance**—Agree/disagree with the technical feasibility of the alternative based on project-specific criteria, and record agreement/disagreement with initial performance ratings.
    o **Implementable Portions**—If the alternative is not implementable in its entirety, identify *portions* of the alternative that may be selectively implemented.
    o **Validated Cost Savings**—Agree/disagree with the estimated cost savings; substantiate revised implemented savings.
    Project Development Cost Savings—Savings (increases) to project development costs resulting from the alternative. This can be due to reduced (or increased) project development effort needed, or an earlier project delivery date.

VALUE ALTERNATIVE IMPLEMENTATION ACTION			
	Bridge Replacement		
TITLE:	Modify Highway Alignment	NUMBER	1.1
RESPONSES			
Prepared by:	David Sumner, Project Mgr.	Date:	6/15/04

Technical Feasibility / Validated Performance	DISPOSITION
This alternative was accepted by the project team. The alternative alignment will significantly improve the horizontal sight distance of the highway. In addition, this alignment is preferred by the U.S. Forest Service, as there will be less environmental impact compared to the baseline concept. The project team, therefore, concurs with the value team's initial performance assessment.	☑ Accept ☐ Conditionally Accept ☐ Reject
Implementable Portions	**Validated Performance**
This alternative will be implemented as initially presented by the value team.	*+12%*
Validated Cost Savings	**Validated Savings**
The initial cost savings identified by the value team were found to be higher than originally presented. Based on the project team's evaluation, the additional cut created by the alternative concept will increase the complexity of construction staging due to the topography and more complicated traffic management plan that will be required. The project team estimates that this will reduce the original initial cost savings amount by approximately $800,000.	$11,629,000
	Project Cost Savings
	($150,000)

Project Schedule Impact	Project Phase	No Change	Reduced by	Increased by
The modifications to the highway alignment will require approximately three additional months of time for design and approval by regulatory agencies.	Planning	☑		
	Prelim. Concept	☐		
	Final Concept	☑		
	Acquisition	☑		

Other Comments
This alternative will help build consensus with the U.S. Forest Service, which has been problematic in the past for projects in this region.

Fig. 11-1

- o **Project Schedule Impact**—Check boxes to designate if the alternative has no change to the project phase, or indicate the time saved or increased for each phase. Discuss the areas in which these schedules will be impacted.
- o **Other Comments**—Comments on other issues relating to the alternative. Note any concerns or controversial items.

- ♦ **Implementation Disposition**—Choose one of the following dispositions:

  - o **Accept**—Acceptance of the alternative denotes the intent to implement in the given project development phase.
  - o **Conditionally Accept**—Alternative is desired but requires added technical analysis and/or stakeholder agreement before final disposition can be made.
  - o **Reject**—Alternative is not acceptable as presented. For rejected alternatives, check the appropriate box to note whether or not rejection is due to the fact that the value study took place too late in the Project Development Process.

- ♦ **Validated Performance**—Validated performance.
- ♦ **Validated Savings**—Validated initial cost savings in dollars.

This form should be modified to meet the specific needs of the project that is being studied. Obviously, different types of information will be needed for a management process project vs. a construction or manufacturing project.

Improve Decisions—*Value Metrics*

The information developed during the value study with respect to performance and value provides the project's decision makers with additional information in considering all the options. The detailed performance rating rationale generated during the development phase will be of particular benefit in the decision-making process. The consideration of potential implementation strategies within the context of value improvement provides project stakeholders with a means for considering the contribution of both cost and performance in achieving total value.

The project team can continue to use the Value Matrix as a means of auditing performance improvements during the implementation of the alternative concepts. A revised Value Matrix can be developed that shows the net benefits of the accepted alternative concepts *(Fig. 11-2)*.

RESOLVE VALUE ALTERNATIVES

An implementation meeting should be scheduled to develop consensus and resolve the implementation dispositions of the value alternatives. The meeting(s) include(s) pertinent value team members and the individuals with the authority to determine the alternatives' implementation decisions, the project manager, key project team members, relevant technical reviewers, and any appropriate external project stakeholders.

VALUE MATRIX - FINAL
Bridge Replacement Project

Attribute	Attribute Weight	Concept	Performance Rating 1	2	3	4	5	6	7	8	9	10	Total Performance
Mainline Operations	29	Baseline Concept					5						145
		Accepted Alts.					5						145
													0
													0
													0
Environmental - Natural	19	Baseline Concept					5						95
		Accepted Alts.						6					114
													0
													0
													0
Environmental - Social	14	Baseline Concept						6					84
		Accepted Alts.							7				98
													0
													0
													0
Constructibility	2	Baseline Concept					5						10
		Accepted Alts.				4							8
													0
													0
													0
Maintainability	24	Baseline Concept					5						120
		Accepted Alts.						6					144
													0
													0
													0
Construction Impacts	10	Baseline Concept					5						50
		Accepted Alts.						6					60
													0
													0
													0
Construction Schedule	2	Baseline Concept							7				14
		Accepted Alts						6					12
													0
													0
													0

Overall Performance Alternative	Total Performance	% Performance Improvement	Total Cost	Value Index (P/C)	% Value Improvement
Baseline Concept	518		500.00	1.04	
Accepted Alternatives (1, 2, 6)	581	12%	480.00	1.21	17%

Fig. 11-2

The meeting should be an informal working meeting to encourage the exchange of opinions, supporting data, and discussion. The implementation disposition for each alternative is discussed with the project manager, relevant project team members, and other project stakeholder representatives. The meeting results in the resolution of the dispositions for every alternative, categorized by one of the following: "accepted," "conditionally accepted," or "rejected." The value team is challenged to modify rejected alternatives when it is possible that a modification could facilitate acceptance of the alternative.

Any alternatives noted as "conditionally accepted" should include the action required, responsibilities, and timing of the final decision. The value specialist, project manager, or value program manager (if one exists within the organization) will review the resolution of the conditionally accepted alternatives at a later date to complete the reporting on the study.

All relevant comments and dispositions during this activity should be documented by the value specialist and included in the final value study report, if it is included as one of the value study deliverables in the value study scope established in the Preparation Phase. A "master" implementation action form should be prepared that summarizes the comments from the reviewers. In some cases, it may be desirable for the value team to meet prior to the implementation meeting in order to review the comments prepared by the value study reviewers. This will allow the value team to discuss the comments and possibly develop strategies or solutions to address potential problems or issues with the value alternatives.

DEVELOP IMPLEMENTATION PLAN

Those alternatives that have been selected for implementation into the project will require a plan to ensure that the changes are integrated properly. An implementation plan should be developed for each value alternative that was identified as "accepted." The implementation plan will need to identify implementation responsibilities, action dates, modifications to the project schedule, and additional project development activities that may be required.

The project manager must take the lead in developing the implementation plan, and be assisted by the value specialist as necessary. Modifications to the project's work breakdown structure and project development schedule should be developed and circulated to the project team in a timely fashion.

Some organizations, especially those with established value programs administered by a value program manager, will have established procedures for developing implementation plans. In such cases, the project manager's efforts will be greatly reduced.

Implementation plans will vary widely and depend upon the unique nature of the changes themselves, as well as the organization involved in implementing the changes. There are, however, a number of common elements that will usually need to be considered in implementing the change. Most of these elements should have been identified in the Implementation Action form identified above. These considerations include:

- *Responsibility*—Who will be responsible for managing the changes called for in the value alternative? What authority do they have? Who will they report to? What resources will be assigned to them to implement the change?
- *Design/System Integration*—How will the changes be integrated into the project? What approvals, clearances or testing will be necessary to implement the change? Will the changes necessitate modifications to other aspects of the system or design?
- *Schedule*—How will the project schedule be impacted by implementing the change? What other projects or

processes will be affected by any anticipated delays? Will critical budgeting or funding milestones be affected?
- *Implementation Costs*—What will it cost the project to implement the changes? Will there be redesign or testing costs? Will there be impacts to existing supplier or consultant contracts already in place?

TRACK AND AUDIT RESULTS

It is generally the responsibility of the project manager or value program manager to track and audit the results of the value alternatives. In some cases, the value alternative will run into problems during the implementation process. It may be that unanticipated technical problems arise, or perhaps an external stakeholder will refuse to approve the change. Regardless, problems will arise that will need to be addressed. It is incumbent upon those monitoring the implementation process to respond proactively so that the issues can be resolved.

In many cases, there will be numerous alternatives that will have been selected for implementation. In such a situation, it is recommended that a database be developed that identifies the alternatives' information, responsible parties, latest status, and action dates. Depending upon the organizational structure of the company or agency, this may be an essential tool in ensuring that implementation is carried successfully through to completion. An example of a status report generated from such a database is provided in *Fig. 11-3*.

Transit System—VM Alternatives Status Report

VM Study Title	LRT Blue Line Extension Project
Alternative #	3.0
Alternative Title	Use Aerial Structure over Jackson Expressway with Elevated Blanton Station
Proposed Cost Savings	$33,168,000
Proposed Performance	+6%
Validated Cost Savings	TBD
Validated Performance	TBD
Current Status	Under Review
Status Narrative	Based on preliminary engineering analysis, this VM alternative should result in initial cost savings of approximately $35 million. The Baseline Estimate was revised to reflect additional details, which resulted in a cost increase. A meeting with the General Manager is scheduled for October 27th to discuss these two alternatives.
Status Date	0/20/2004
Agency Contact	Jon Withers
VMS Contact	Rob Stewart

VM Study Title	LRT Blue Line Extension Project
Alternative #	4.0
Alternative Title	Locate LRT Alignment over Wagner Blvd.
Proposed Cost Savings	$12,091,000
Proposed Performance	8%
Validated Cost Savings	TBD
Validated Performance	TBD
Current Status	Under Review
Status Narrative	This alternative is being considered in conjunction with VM Alternative 3.0.
Status Date	10/20/2004
Agency Contact	Jon Withers
VMS Contact	Rob Stewart

Figure 11-3

SUMMARY

The Implementation Phase is where all of the efforts of the value team will pay off. To ensure that this happens, the value specialist must be diligent in responding to problems or issues that may arise during the review process and work with the project team in developing an implementation plan.

The project manager will also play a critical role in the success of the implementation plan. Management involvement in the implementation process will reinforce the efforts of the project manager in seeing the changes through the project development process. Implementation is all about managing change. It is the objective of the value specialist to help others adapt to the changes that will result from a successful value study.

Chapter 12—Value Leadership

Dwight D. Eisenhower—General, President

Leadership is the art of getting someone else to do something you want done because he wants to do it.
—Dwight D. Eisenhower

A sense of humor is part of the art of leadership, of getting along with people, of getting things done.
—Dwight D. Eisenhower

Dwight David Eisenhower was born in Texas in 1890 and grew up in Abilene, Kansas. He was the third of seven sons. He excelled in both academics and sports in high school, and received an appointment to West Point. In his early Army career, he excelled in staff assignments, serving under Generals John J. Pershing, Douglas MacArthur, and Walter Krueger. After Pearl Harbor, General George C. Marshall called him to Washington for a war plans assignment. He commanded the Allied Forces landing in North Africa in November 1942; on D-Day, 1944, he was Supreme Commander of the troops invading France.

After the war, he became President of Columbia University and then took leave to assume supreme command over the new NATO forces being assembled in 1951. Republican emissaries to his headquarters near Paris persuaded him to run for President in 1952.

During his two productive terms as President, he promoted Atoms for Peace; dealt with crises in Lebanon, Suez, Berlin, and Hungary in foreign affairs; saw Alaska and Hawaii become states; continued key social programs established during the Roosevelt Administration; and supported the process of the desegregation of public schools and the Armed Forces.

Bringing to the Presidency his prestige as commanding general of the victorious forces in Europe during World War II, Dwight D. Eisenhower obtained a truce in Korea and worked incessantly during his two terms to ease the tensions of the Cold War. He pursued the moderate policies of "Modern Republicanism," pointing out as he left office, "America is today the strongest, most influential, and most productive nation in the world."

President Eisenhower proved to be one of the greatest leaders in American History, through times of both war and peace. Much of his success can be attributed to the value he placed on his fellow citizens, which is eloquently illustrated by his famous quote "There must be no second class citizens in this country." President Eisenhower embodies the characteristics of leadership and provides an excellent role model in this chapter's discussion of Value Leadership.

VALUE LEADERSHIP

There are just as many styles of leadership as there are leaders. It can further be stated that different leadership styles are appropriate for different types of situations. What style of leadership, then, is best suited for the value specialist? To answer this question, it is useful to develop a basic understanding of leadership styles through a series of leadership models. There are two fundamental leadership models that are fairly well recognized. These include the Leadership Framework model and the Managerial Grid model.

The *Leadership Framework*[1] model infers that leaders display leadership behaviors in one of four types of leadership styles, or "frameworks." These include the structural, human resource, political, and symbolic frameworks. The effectiveness of each leadership framework is largely determined by the behavior of the leader in applying a particular leadership style within a particular setting or environment.

- *Structural Framework*—Leaders that focus on strategy, implementation, adaptation, and environment best describe leaders that fit the Structural Framework approach to leadership. Leaders who are effective using the Structural Framework approach can be best described as social architects who lead through analysis and design. Leaders who are ineffective using this approach are generally perceived as petty and tyrannical by those working under them.
- *Human Resource Framework*—Leaders that focus on individuals, communication, team empowerment, and consensus demonstrate characteristics that describe the Human Resource Framework. Leaders who are effective using the Human Resource Framework approach act as a catalyst for empowering others that are part of their team. Indeed, the term "coach" is a fitting description for this leadership style. On the other hand, leaders that are ineffective using this approach are often perceived as being "spineless" and others will tend to walk all over them.
- *Political Framework*—Leaders that focus on power, diplomacy, and negotiation describe those that represent the Political Framework leadership approach. Leaders who are effective using the Political Framework approach rely first upon persuasion followed by negotiation and finally by coercion if all else fail. Successful leaders using this style rely heavily on negotiating coalitions. Ineffectual leaders using this approach are seen by others as manipulative, deceiving and even "back-stabbing."
- *Symbolic Framework*—Leaders that focus on role playing, creativity, and future outcomes best describe

the Symbolic Framework approach to leadership. Leaders who are effective using the Symbolic Framework approach find ways to harness the power of symbolic meaning set the stage for inspiring others to reach for a far-reaching vision. "Fools" and "fanatics" are terms that are often used to describe those leaders that fail in following this path.

The Leadership Framework model suggests that all leaders can be put into one of these frameworks at any given point in time, depending upon their behavior. It is important to keep in mind that there are strengths and weaknesses related to each approach, and that there will be times when one approach is more appropriate than the others.

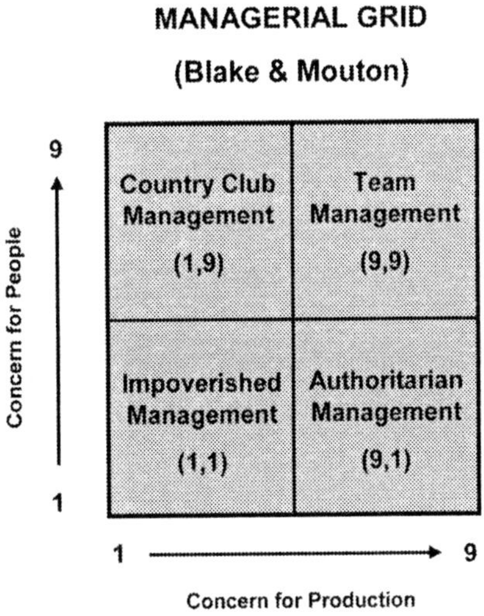

The value specialist will need to call upon all four of these frameworks to be successful. You can probably already begin to see where each of these may be appropriate in conjunction with the Value Methodology Job Plan. For instance, the value specialist might lean heavily on the Symbolic Framework during the Speculation Phase, while relying more upon the Political Framework during the Presentation Phase.

MANAGERIAL GRID
(Blake & Mouton)

	Concern for People	
9	Country Club Management (1,9)	Team Management (9,9)
1	Impoverished Management (1,1)	Authoritarian Management (9,1)
	1 → 9	

Concern for Production

Fig. 12-1

The *Managerial Grid*[2] considers two dimensions *(Fig. 12-1)*. These include "concern for people," which is plotted along the vertical axis and "concern for production," which is plotted along the horizontal axis. Both are given numerical ranges between 1 to 9 that represent the relative strength of preference for each of these two concerns. There are essentially four management (leadership) archetypes that provide reference points in describing the relevant styles.

- *Country Club Management*—Concern for Production = Low. Concern for People = High. This management style emphasizes personal relationships over task management. There is a great deal of reliance on goodwill and trust on the part of the manager that those working under him or her will get the job done. This approach can be effective when those on the team are self-directed and highly motivated. It can be a disastrous approach if this is not the case.
- *Impoverished Management*—Concern for Production = Low. Concern for People = Low. This management style describes the executive that delegates his or her authority and then stays out of sight. This is without question the weakest form of leadership and is consequently the approach that is least likely to be effective.
- *Authoritarian Management*—Concern for Production = High. Concern for People = Low. This management style focuses strictly on the efficient operations of a team in meeting its task, and tends to be autocratic in dealing with others. Managers using this approach are generally indifferent to the people under them and do not tolerate questions or dissent. This can be an effective approach when applied to tasks that require little team communication or interaction. It is generally an inappropriate style when dealing with projects involving many stakeholders or those that require consensus building.
- *Team Management*—Concern for Production = High. Concern for People = High. This type of leader leads by deed. He or she is focused simultaneously on both production and the people involved. The team manager

(or team leader) seeks to foster an environment in which all team members can reach their highest potential through good communication and hard work.

In addition to these four archetypes, there is a fifth category into which most leaders and managers fall. These individuals show an average concern for people and production. The value specialist must strive for the Team Management archetype. The brevity and substantial goals of most value studies requires a strong focus on production, while the human dynamics related to dealing with a multi-discipline team, as well as a collection of diverse stakeholders, requires extreme sensitivity to people. The value specialist must demonstrate what I would call *"value leadership."*

It could be argued that phrases such as "value management" or "value facilitation" might be more appropriate; however, I believe the term "leadership" is correct. Although the value specialist may not be the CEO of a company, the deputy director of a government agency, or even a member of the organization that is sponsoring the value study, he or she will be responsible for leading the effort in creating positive change within an organization through the improvement of value. Change requires a catalyst to overcome the inertia of the status quo of a project or organization. The value specialist must be the catalyst for change.

VALUE METHODOLOGY PROFESSIONALS

Since the time of the creation of Value Methodology in the 1940s, the job of the value practitioners has evolved into several unique professions and career paths. Today, value practitioners serve in virtually every type of organization, large and small, public and private. Some manage value programs while others earn a living as professional VM consultants. Some have been officially certified by the SAVE International Certification

Board while others have not. Irrespective of the organization or certification, they are all professionals involved in the improvement of value.

Professional value practitioners that have been certified by SAVE International have met an established level of mastery through training, applied experience, and testing. SAVE International recognizes three levels of certification. These include:

- *Certified Value Specialist (CVS)*—CVS certification represents the highest level of training and experience and recognizes those individuals whose principal career is Value Methodology. Within this certification level, there are two different classifications. These include:

    o *Value Specialist*—A value specialist is an individual whose career is primarily involved in leading value studies. A professional value specialist may either operate as a part of a larger organization or as a consultant hired by an organization to conduct value studies.
    o *Value Program Manager*—A value program manager is an individual responsible for managing a value program within an organization. It is their responsibility to identify projects for value studies, organize and manage the value studies, and to monitor the implementation of value alternatives. Value program managers may or may not be involved in conducting value studies.

- *Associate Value Specialist (AVS)*—AVS certification recognizes those individuals who have decided to become professional value specialists but who have not yet acquired all the experience or technical skills expected of a CVS. The AVS is a stepping-stone to becoming a CVS.

- *Value Methodology Practitioner (VMP)*—VMP certification recognizes those individuals who acquired the basic skills of Value Methodology but whose careers are not principally related to VM. Value methodology practitioners often frequently participate as value team members. They may be members of a larger organization, part of a VM department, or independent consultants that are hired by an organization to participate on value studies.

Related to these certification levels, there are essentially three Value Methodology professions. These include the value specialist, value program manager, and value team member.

Value Specialist

The value specialist's primary responsibility is in conducting value studies. As previously mentioned, the value specialist may work within an organization or may be a consultant that works with a variety of organizations. Value specialists that work within an organization may or may not be required to hold professional certification, depending on the organization's specific needs and requirements. Consultants, on the other hand, should always be professionally certified, as they will be working with organizations whose needs and requirements will vary widely. As such, the consulting value specialists must have a complete understanding of the Value Methodology and its many applications.

Most value specialists tend to focus in one of three areas of application—Industrial, Construction, or Management. Industrial value specialists generally come from manufacturing backgrounds and have a solid understanding of the application of VM to industrial applications. Construction value specialists generally come from one of the design or construction disciplines and are well versed in the application of VM to facilities. Management value specialists come from administrative or management backgrounds and have a good understanding of the application of VM to processes and procedures.

There is an increasing number of consulting value specialists that have developed a high level of expertise in applying VM to all applications. These individuals generally have the highest level of understanding of VM while also possessing broad experience in the areas construction, manufacturing, and management. This pairing of knowledge and diverse experience makes for a powerful combination in leading value studies.

Value Program Manager

The value program manager will be responsible for running an organization's value program. Depending on the nature of the organization, this may include performing a variety of activities including:

- Maintaining up-to-date knowledge of the Value Methodology.
- Identifying projects for value studies.
- Selecting value team members.
- Leading and coordinating value studies
- Assisting management in setting annual program goals.
- Reporting regularly on progress for active value studies and projects.
- Planning and conducting value training to assure that trained personnel are available for value studies.
- Conducting management orientations and briefings as appropriate to educate those in the organization about the value program and Value Methodology.
- Working with the procurement organization to involve vendors, suppliers, and subcontractors in the program. This

includes the development of methods and reward programs for inviting recommendations for improving value.
- Tracking the implementation of accepted value alternatives to assure the maximization of potential benefits.
- Representing the organization in value improvement. Contributing to the VM profession's growth through participation in technical conferences, public speaking, etc.

It is strongly recommended that value program managers achieve CVS certification, although this may not be an absolute requirement.

Value Team Member

Value team members are usually involved with VM on a part-time basis. Value team members have usually undergone formal VM training and may also hold VMP certification. Having trained and experienced value team members on a value study will greatly enhance the outcome of value studies. Value team members will already have the proper mindset and attitude required to perform the various activities involved in the VM job plan, in addition to bringing their specific technical expertise to bear on a project. Many professionals normally engaged in engineering, programming and architecture have received formal VM training and are frequently employed as value team members, especially those that already maintain consulting practices.

THE ART AND SCIENCE OF VALUE LEADERSHIP

The facilitation of a value study requires not only a thorough understanding of the Value Methodology, but also an intuitive ability to use the right techniques at the right time. The capacity to quickly adapt and adjust to the changing nature of the value study is critical. Problems and challenges will crop up unexpectedly during the VM process, and the value specialist will need to act decisively in order to maintain the flow of the value study and maximize the positive potential benefits to the project.

Characteristics of Value Specialists

The skills and characteristics necessary to be a successful value specialist are very similar to those required to be a successful project manager. These include:

- *Communication Skills.* Value specialists must be fluent in oral and written communications. They must be able to speak before large groups and articulate their thoughts clearly and concisely.
- *Organizational Skills.* Value specialists must have strong planning and organizational skills. Both involve the ability to manage and organize large quantities of information, coordinate schedules, handle logistical considerations, put teams together, and organize meetings.
- *Budgeting Skills.* Value specialists must be able to request, collect, analyze and assemble financial information. They must be fluent with financial terminology and have a basic grasp of cost estimating relevant to the type of product or project with which they are involved.
- *Facilitation Skills.* Facilitation refers to the ability of a value specialist or project manager to lead people, either individually or in groups, through processes and techniques in order to achieve a specific objective. Value specialists must be able to do this, whether it means facilitating the evaluation of competitive bids or leading a value team through a creativity session. Not only is it necessary to possess an understanding of the application

of processes and techniques, but ideally the behavioral psychology behind them.
- *Leadership Skills.* Leadership speaks to the ability of an individual to provide strategic vision and direction, inspire confidence, and motivate others to achieve high levels of performance. There has been much written concerning the role of project managers and value specialists as leaders. Management, facilitation, and leadership all mean different things, but they are all interrelated. A successful project manager or value specialist should possess all three of these skills. For example, a value specialist will need to motivate the value team to be creative while facilitating a brainstorming exercise. A project manager will need to apply his or her leadership skills to keep the project team focused on the "big picture" while managing a risk response meeting.
- *Problem Solving Skills.* Project managers must be able to identify, predict, resolve and hopefully avoid, through proper planning, a variety of problems that will crop up during the project development process. Value specialists, on the other hand, must welcome and even thrive on problems, since the very nature of Value Methodology is based on creative problem solving. Both project managers and value specialists must view problems as challenges, and enthusiastically rise to meet them rather than acquiesce.

Roles of the Value Specialist

The value specialist must play a variety of roles in leading a value study. It is useful to draw analogies between commonly identifiable roles and the roles that the value specialist will have to play during the course of a value study. These analogies are not unlike those used in the excellent and insightful work of the noted psychologists David Keirsey and Marilyn Bates in their research on character and temperament types.³ These diverse roles include, but are not limited to the following:

- *General*—The value specialist is like a general. He or she must lead by example; command respect by giving respect; provide strategic vision in not losing sight of the war in the midst of the many smaller battles that will be fought; weigh risks and develop contingencies; rally the troops when morale wanes in the face of adversity; and demonstrate courage in the face of overwhelming odds.
- *Diplomat*—The value specialist is like a diplomat. He or she must create a sense of goodwill; make peace between rival factions; act a messenger between parties; negotiate agreements; understand the political landscape; understand the value of protocol; utilize all available lines of communication; anticipate and avoid potential hostilities; and utilize tact, cunning and etiquette to win friends and influence people.
- *Manager*—The value specialist is like a manager. He or she must create plans; manage and organize time, resources and funds; understand organizational hierarchies; respect and maintain scope, schedule and cost; master the science of logistics; and ensure projects are delivered on time, within budget and meet or exceed customer requirements.
- *Devil's Advocate*—The value specialist is like the devil's advocate. He or she must challenge the status quo; question everything; endlessly ask the question "why?' and validate or disprove assumptions.
- *Jester*—The value specialist is like a jester. He or she must not take himself or herself too seriously, but must take their work seriously; use humor to break down

barriers; create a sense of fun; instill creativity through the use of metaphor and wit; be self-deprecating; and make people feel good about themselves.

Salesman—The value specialist is like a salesman. He or she must sell new ideas; persuade others of the merits of an idea; motivate others to consider change; display enthusiasm in communicating new products; create excitement; and sell change.

Facilitation Advice for the Value Specialist[1]

Successful facilitation of VM is as much of an art as it is a science, but it begins with a basic respect for the Value Methodology Job Plan and solid preparation before the value study itself.

Each phase of the job plan has its purpose and prepares the value team to progress to the next phase. A successful value study depends on getting the right people together to focus on the required functions. It is essential to identify opportunities or mismatches between cost, function, and performance, and then to select those ideas which offer the most benefit to the owner and/or customer. But it is not sufficient to generate great ideas. The value study must objectively document the case for acceptance of value alternatives and try to quantify any impacts on cost and performance as well as the project schedule. Many sound value alternatives will not survive due to poor presentation or lack of credibility.

Each step in the Job Plan has its risks, pitfalls, and missteps. It is wise to plan for them proactively and to structure the value study to avoid or mitigate them. Provided below on *Table 12-1* is a list of some of the more common pitfalls and potential remedies and means to avoid them.

Pitfalls	Remedies
Compromising the VM Job Plan	
♦ Skipping or abbreviating steps to meet the project's accelerated timeframe.	♦ Explain the VM process and agenda and set realistic expectations by matching the value study scope to the time allotted; don't over-promise; include stakeholder concerns.
♦ Not analyzing or overanalyzing functions.	♦ Functions must be used to disengage from current solutions and open the door to new ideas; however, don't extend this past identification of value mismatches.
♦ Not managing time well, leaving inadequate time to fully document value alternatives.	♦ Keep careful track of time and remember that it is a precious commodity, especially in the limited time of the value study.
Inadequate Pre-Study Preparation	
♦ Misunderstanding the project/process elements.	♦ Thoroughly interview the owner, customer or user, stakeholders, and project team.
♦ Unnecessarily constraining the value team's scope.	♦ Identify key issues, concerns, and constraints. Differentiate between project performance attributes and requirements.
♦ Missing needed expertise on the value team.	♦ Properly set the value study's objectives during the Preparation Phase in order to identify the proper disciplines required on the value team.
♦ Lack of pre-study time or project documentation.	♦ Communicate to the project sponsor that the value effort may be severely hindered without adequate time and project information.
Neglecting Team Dynamics	
♦ Inadequate range of disciplines to address the project scope.	♦ Brainstorm across disciplines during the Speculation Phase.
♦ Lack of team synergy.	♦ The value specialist must encourage full participation and focus. Team building exercises can be employed if necessary.
♦ Insufficient local knowledge to generate credible ideas.	♦ Include a representative of the owner or customer on the value team that will have specific knowledge of requirements, regulations, and/or codes.
Targeting the Unimportant / Wasting Resources	
♦ Unstructured creativity.	♦ Adhere to the basic rules for creativity sessions. Categorize and enumerate ideas by function.
♦ Neglecting to offer alternatives for critical components or issues.	♦ Target problem areas and find improvements. Conduct creativity sessions that target these areas specifically.
♦ Using vague generalizations.	♦ Be specific and constructive in generating and evaluating ideas.
♦ Lack of focus on basic function(s).	♦ Remember that only the basic and required secondary functions are truly necessary. Other secondary functions can be eliminated by identifying alternative ways of providing the basic function.

FUNDAMENTALS OF VALUE METHODOLOGY

Pitfalls	Remedies
Failing to Select the Best Ideas for Development	
• Developing too many ideas superficially.	• Match the quantity of ideas to be developed to the value team's capacity. Prioritize the development of ideas according to their total impact to value improvement.
• Ignoring the owner's best interest in generating and evaluating ideas.	• Ensure that the owner's and/or customer's performance attributes and requirements have been thoroughly identified and addressed. Be sure to utilize key performance attributes in the Speculation and Evaluation Phases.
• Recommending ideas that are not credible.	• Include the owner or customer in the evaluation of ideas. Plan for a mid-point (technical) review meeting early in the Development Phase.
Failing to Make the Case	
• Inadequately developing ideas.	• Include a thorough discussion / justification for all value alternatives. Document assumptions used for calculations.
• Not being objective with disadvantages and associated costs.	• Use the same diligence in documenting the shortcomings of value alternatives that is used in documenting their benefits.
• Providing insufficient documentation, such as sketches, references, and examples.	• Review value alternatives for objectivity, sensitivity, and completeness.

Pitfalls	Remedies
Overemphasizing Cost Reduction	
• Promising a targeted cost reduction in advance or "cheapening" the project.	• The focus of a value study should always be on value improvement, not mere cost reduction.
• Considering only initial costs.	• Consider long-term costs and operational functionality. Consideration must also be given to additional project development costs that may be required.
• Predicting total of potential cost reductions before implementation.	• Costs may not be additive and all value alternatives may not be accepted.
Botching the Exit Briefing	
• Sarcasm or implied insults.	• Maintain the highest level of professionalism in presenting value alternatives. Demonstrate empathy in dealing with the project team.
• Being disorganized or unprepared.	• Ensure that enough time is allotted to review the value team's presentation strategy for the exit briefing and prepare accordingly.
• Boring the audience with exhaustive detail.	• Keep the value team focused on presenting only the basic facts—details will be discussed in the written report.
• Not acknowledging the assistance and hard work of others.	• Give full credit where it is due. Express appreciation for the efforts of others during the exit briefing.
• Entering into a debate with project team members.	• Emphasize at the start of the exit briefing that it will not be a decision-making meeting. Keep the participants focused on presenting the value alternatives.

Table 12-1

PROFESSIONAL STANDARDS OF CONDUCT

Those working within professions related to Value Methodology must do so ethically, as is the case with professions in other disciplines. Maintaining a high level of professionalism and ethical behavior is of the greatest importance for anyone applying the Value Methodology. This is because value work involves the review and refinement of work developed by others. Value practitioners must, therefore, ensure that high standards are maintained in order to avoid discrediting the discipline and the profession.

The following Standards of Conduct is administered by SAVE International to its members and to those it certifies as value professionals.

- *Uphold* the high ideals and level of personal knowledge attested by Society membership or certification, and to participate in none but honest enterprises.
- *Serve* the interests of employers and clients loyally, diligently and honestly through worthy performance and fidelity.
- *Maintain* a broad and balanced outlook and recognize merit in the ideas and opinions of others.
- *Refrain* from any conduct or act which is discreditable to the reputation or integrity of the VM profession, and be guided in all activities by truth, accuracy, fair dealing, and good taste.
- *Promote* at every opportunity the public understanding of VM, and apply their specialized knowledge for public good.
- *Keep* informed on the latest developments in value techniques and applications, and recommend or initiate improvements to increase the effectiveness of VM.
- *Pledge* to all fellow value specialists, integrity and fair dealing, tolerance and respect, devotion to standards, and dignity of the profession.

- *Support* efforts to strengthen the profession through training and education, and help others reach personal and professional fulfillment.
- *Earn* and carefully guard their reputation for good moral character and good citizenship, recognizing that leadership is a call to service.
- *Recognize* that Society membership or certification as a value specialist is not the sole claim to professional competence.

Ethical Considerations—Design & Construction

Value studies that deal with facilities has special considerations with respect to abiding by the ethical codes set forth by professional engineers and architects who are subject to local, state and federal laws. Value practitioners that anticipate working on such projects should pay special attention to this section, especially those who are licensed engineers or architects.

The review by a value specialist or value team member of another professional's design, or the submission by a contractor of a value change proposal, causes some architects and engineers to become highly protective of their work and to posit that such activities are unethical. Actually, the ethical problems involved have been carefully reviewed by both the American Institute of Architects (AIA) and the National Society of Professional Engineers (NSPE). Both organizations have issued statements making it clear that, with due regard for the established standards of ethical practice, the review by one consultant of the work of another constitutes ethical and acceptable practice. The restrictions are generally that the original designer shall be made aware of the review being made by another and that the reviewer shall not be malicious or have ulterior motives.

The Board of Ethical Review (BER) of the NSPE published the following cases on the National Institute of Engineering

Ethics website[5]. (Note: these opinions are based on data submitted to the Board of Ethical Review and do not necessarily represent all of the pertinent facts when applied to a specific case. The opinions are for educational purposes only and should not be construed as expressing any opinion on the ethics of specific individuals.)

1. BER Case No. 68-6

Subject:

Value Engineering—Section 12(a)—Code of Ethics; Section 12(b)—Code of Ethics.

Facts:

A government agency entered into a contract with an engineering firm to design a facility. Following completion of the design, bids were received from contractors for the construction, and a contract was entered into with the low bidder. The construction contract contained a value engineering clause to the effect that the contractor could submit to the contracting officer of the government agency suggested changes in the plans or specifications for the purpose of reducing the cost. The suggested changes would be submitted by the contracting officer (Engineer "B") to the Engineer ("C") for comment, following which the contracting officer would make the decision whether to approve the suggested changes, in whole or in part. The saving resulting from approved changes would be divided equally between the contractor and the government.

Engineer "A", employed by the contractor, proposed a change in the plans and specifications in accord with the value engineering clause. His employer transmitted the proposed change to Engineer "B", the contracting officer. He submitted the proposed change to Engineer "C", a principal in the design engineer firm. Engineer "C" recommended that the change not be approved and further objected that the actions of Engineers "A" and "B" were unethical.

Question:

Is it unethical for engineers employed by contractors and government agencies to present, review, or approve changes in engineering designs prepared by another engineer?

References:

Code of Ethics—Section 12(a)—An engineer in private practice will not review the work of another engineer for the same client, except with the knowledge of such engineer, or unless the connection of such engineer with the work has been terminated.

Section 12(b)—An engineer in governmental, industrial, or educational employ is entitled to review and evaluate the work of other engineers when so required by his employment duties.

Discussion:

The review of the plans and specifications prepared by the engineering firm by Engineers "A" and "B" were within the permissible scope of Section 12(b), as in both cases their activities were required by their employment duties under the construction contract. Each was acting for his respective employer.

A different question would arise if the government agency had retained a second firm in private practice to review the work of the design firm. In that case Section 12(a) requires that such review not be performed without the knowledge of the design firm. While we are not faced with this precise question in this case, we note that value engineering clauses are now being uniformly inserted in construction contracts issued by some federal agencies and by some state agencies. The use of such clauses has been widely publicized to the engineering profession and where used are in accordance with agency regulations, which are public documents. Accordingly, we express the view for future guidance that engineers in private practice have constructive knowledge of the existence and use of value engineering clauses. It becomes incumbent upon engineers in private practice, who may not wish to be subject to value engineering arrangements of the type described, to check with the governmental (or private) agency or organization to determine if a value engineering clause will be used in the construction contract in order to decide whether the design engineer is willing to accept the engineering engagement on that basis. Failure to do so will remove any later objection by the engineer on ethical grounds that his work was reviewed by another engineer in private practice without his knowledge.

Conclusion:

It was not unethical for Engineers "A" and "B" to present, review, or approve the changes in the engineering designs prepared by the design engineering firm, "C".

2. BER Case No. 69-2

Subject:

Value Engineering—Contingent Contract

Facts:

An engineering firm with extensive experiences in the design of industrial equipment proposes to establish a Value Engineering Division under which it would offer to clients a value engineering service. The plan of operation contemplates offering to clients in the industrial field a review of their design, equipment, products,

FUNDAMENTALS OF VALUE METHODOLOGY 325

processes, etc. Following such review, the firm would suggest to the client revisions in the design or production mechanisms which would produce the same result at less cost to the client without sacrifice of quality or safety. If such savings are realized the client would pay the firm a percentage of the savings, determined by negotiation prior to the rendition of the service in accordance with the extent of work involved. If the client determines that the proposed changes are not feasible or desirable for any reason and does not utilize the suggested changes, he is not obligated to pay the firm any compensation.

Question:

Is the method of operation ethical?

References:

Code of Ethics—Section 11(d). An Engineer shall not request, propose, or accept a professional commission on a contingent basis under circumstances in which his professional judgment may be compromised, or when a contingency provision is used as a device for promoting or securing a professional commission.

Discussion:

The proposed method of operation is clearly a contingent contract. Section 11(d) of the code, as recently revised by the NSPE Board of Directors, in effect permits contingent contracts with two limitations as indicated in its text.

Taking these limitations in order:

We do not believe that the proposed method of operation would tend to necessarily compromise the professional judgment of the engineers preparing the proposed changes. The incentive, in fact, would be to search out even more diligently areas of potential saving to the client, otherwise the firm will not receive any compensation for its work. The only possible danger might be if in its zeal to find areas of saving to the client and thereby earn its fee the engineers of the firm might be tempted to suggest changes inimical to quality or safety. In the absence of any indication to this effect, however, we assume that the ethical duty of the engineers to serve the interests of the public and client would be honored. In addition, the client is entitled to and presumably would check carefully the proposed changes to ensure maintenance of quality and safety for which he would be responsible.

The second limitation raises the question of whether the proposed method is one which is used as a device for promoting or securing a professional commission. We believe that this limitation is intended to safeguard the public and clients from projects which are unsound from a technical or economic standpoint. There is no basis in the facts to assume that these safeguards would be jeopardized in this case under the circumstances. The firm is not promoting a particular project about which the client is uninformed and would not be retained for the service unless the client on his own initiative determines that the value engineering review might produce economies.

Conclusion:

The proposed method of operation is ethical.

3. *BER Case No. 77-10*

Subject:

Value Engineering—Contingency Fee

Facts:

John Doe, P.E., a principal in a consulting engineering firm, attended a public meeting of a township board of supervisors which had under consideration a water pollution control project with an estimated construction cost of $7 million. Doe presented a so-called "cost-saving plan" to the supervisors under which his firm would work with the engineering firm retained for the project to find "cost-saving" methods to enable the township to proceed with the project and thereby not lose the federal funding share because of the township's difficulty in financing its share of the project.

Doe further advised the supervisors that his proposal contemplated providing his "cost-saving" services on the basis of being paid ten percent of the savings, but his firm would not be paid any amount if it did not achieve a reduction in the construction cost. Doe added that his firm's value engineering approach would be based on an analysis of the plans and specifications prepared by the design firm and that his operation would not require that the design firm be displaced.

Question:

Were Doe's presentation and offer consistent with the Code of Ethics?

Reference:

Code of Ethics-Section 11(d)—"An Engineer shall not request, propose, or accept a professional commission on a contingent basis under circumstances in which his professional judgment may be compromised, or when a contingency provision is used as a device for promoting or securing a professional commission."

Discussion:

In Case 69-2 we decided what on the face of it appears to be an almost identical issue, concluding that it was ethical for a firm to offer clients in the industrial field a value engineering service with payment based on a percentage of the savings achieved in the design or production mechanisms of the client. In that case the percentage of savings to be paid the engineering firm would be based on negotiation prior to the rendition of the value engineering service, and with the understanding that the client would have the unilateral right to not utilize the proposed changes. It is important to note that we based our conclusion, in part, on the understanding that under the prevailing facts the client was informed and competent to judge the proposed changes. Consequently, the engineering firm would have the incentive to avoid compromising its professional judgment.

Subsequently, in Case 76-11 we dealt with another related case in which a private engineering firm sought a contract to prepare an independent design for a major bridge to compare with an in-house design. The engineering firm offered to provide its services on the basis that it would not be paid if its design did not save the state the amount of its proposed fee by at least five percent of the construction cost for the in-house design.

In that situation we reached a contrary result and held the procedure to be in conflict with the Code of Ethics because the engineering firm "may be tempted to specify an inferior design concept and materials to produce a lower construction cost" (in order to secure its fee). But the discussion in Case 76-11 recognized that there was an arguable view to reach a contrary result because of the possible benefit to the public if a substantial saving of money could be realized without the sacrifice of safety or quality. In rejecting that arguable premise, however, we said that on its face §11(d) bars contingency contracts when used as a device for promoting or securing a professional commission.

If the differing results reached in the two previously decided cases can be reconciled, the rationalization would be that in Case 69-2 the engineering firm was offering a value engineering service on a contingency basis in general; whereas in Case 76-11 we were dealing with a very specific project directly related to the public health and safety. Further, as previously observed, in Case 69-2 we commented that the client was informed and would have the capability to protect its own interests by careful review, with right of rejection, of any proposed changes to achieve a saving.

The facts before us are more nearly akin to those set forth in Case 76-11, pertaining to a specific project clearly related to the public health and safety. Even more urgent, the facts before us indicate a relatively small community as the client; and we may assume, on the basis of practical experience, that such a client would not likely have the expertise of its own to judge and be in a position to recognize if the changes in the design as proposed by Doe's firm would entail dangers or a serious loss of quality for the project. True, the township fathers could call upon the original design firm for comment and recommendation before acting favorably on the changes in the design intended to effect a construction cost reduction. But in that event the township supervisors would possibly be confronted with opposing opinions of two engineering firms and not be in a position to make a qualified judgment.

The final clause of §11(d), as noted in Case 76-11, is absolute on its face in barring a contingency provision as a device for promoting work. We chose to interpret that clause liberally in Case 69-2, being influenced by the expertise of the client. But we chose to treat the clause literally in Case 76-11 because we were then, as now, of the view that the final clause of §11(d) should be taken literally in all cases when it is clear, as it is in the facts before us, that the motivation for the contingency provision is as a device to secure work. If that is too strict a rule it is for the Society to consider a revision of the code provision.

Conclusion:

Doe's presentation and offer were not consistent with the Code of Ethics.

SUMMARY

The numbers of individuals choosing careers related to Value Methodology has been increasing steadily in recent years. Value Methodology professionals can be found managing value programs for government agencies and major corporations throughout the world. We live in a time of shrinking budgets, growing competition, and ever-scarcer resources. As these economic trends continue, the role of value professionals in improving the value of goods, services and facilities will grow more critical.

Many management improvement processes and fads have come and gone in the last century. Value Methodology has withstood the test time as a proven means of improving value. It is one of a handful of methodologies to have been formally legislated by governments at all levels. This is because it is soundly grounded in the fundamental source of all human endeavors—the elements of cost, performance, and function as they relate to value.

Ultimately, the successful application of Value Methodology, as with any knowledge, greatly depends upon your attitude. I would like to conclude this text with a quote from noted business writer, Robert R. Updegraff, who is perhaps most famous for his character *Obvious Adams*[6]. Please remember it the next time an unexpected challenge arises in the workplace.

> ## *LOOK FOR MORE TROUBLES*
>
> *Be thankful for the troubles of your job. They provide about half your income. Because if it were not for the things that go wrong, the difficult people you have to deal with, and the problems and unpleasantness of your working day, someone could be found to handle your job for half of what you are being paid.*
>
> *It takes intelligence, resourcefulness, patience, tact, and courage to meet the troubles of any job. That is why you hold your present job. And it may be the reason you'll be asked to handle an even bigger one.*
>
> *If all of us would start to look for **more** troubles, and learn to handle them cheerfully and with good judgment, as **opportunities** rather than irritations, we would find ourselves getting ahead at a surprising rate. For it is a fact that there are plenty of big jobs waiting for men and women who aren't afraid of the troubles connected with them.*
>
> —Robert R. Updegraff

---

[1] Bolman, Lee and T. Deal (1991). Reframing Organizations. San Francisco: Jossey-Bass.

[2] Blake, Robert R. and Jane S. Mouton (1985). The Managerial Grid III: The Key to Leadership Excellence. Houston: Gulf Publishing Co.

[3] Keirsey, David & Bates, Marilyn (1978) "Please Understand Me: Character & Temperament Types," Prometheus Nemesis Books Co.

[4] Woller, Jill (2004) "Value Engineering (VE) 401: Pitfalls and Missteps and How to Avoid Them," 2004 SAVE International Conference Proceedings. This section is condensed from Ms. Woller's excellent paper. She has managed the VE Program for the City of New York's Office of Management and Budget for nearly 20 years.

[5] http://www.niee.org/cases/

[6] Updegraff, Robert (1953) "Obvious Adams: The Story of a Successful Businessman," Reprinted by Kessinger Press, 2004.

Appendix A—Glossary

This glossary includes terms that are commonly used in this text. Those terms that are shown in italics refer to definitions excerpted directly from the Project Management Institute's *"A Guide to the Project Management Body of Knowledge, 2000 Edition."*

A

Activity—An element of work performed during the course of a project. An activity normally has an expected duration, an expected cost, and expected resource requirements.

Alteration Costs—Those costs for anticipated modernization or changing of a facility or space to provide a new function.

Alternatives—The different choices or methods by which functions may be attained. Alternatives that are developed as part of a value study are referred to as *value alternatives*.

Annualized Method—An economic method that requires conversion of all present and future expenditures to a uniform annual cost.

Annuity—A series of equal payments or receipts to be paid or received at the ends of successive periods of equal time.

Associated Costs—These costs may include functional use, denial of use, security and insurance, utilities (other than energy), waste disposal, start-up, etc.

Assumptions—Assumptions are factors that, for planning purposes, are considered to be true, real, or certain. Assumptions affect all aspects of project planning, and are part of the progressive elaboration of the project. Project teams frequently identify, document, and validate assumptions as part of their planning process. Assumptions generally involve a degree of risk.

B

Baseline—The original approved plan (for a project, work package, or an activity), plus or minus approved scope changes.

Brainstorming—A widely used creativity technique for generating a large quantity and wide variety of ideas for alternative ways of solving a problem or making a decision.

C

Consensus—A decision that is reached which all stakeholders can accept.

Constant Dollars—Dollars that have not been adjusted for the effects of expected future inflation or deflation; sometimes referred to as of a specific date (i.e., "2005 dollars").

Constraint—Applicable restriction that will affect the performance of a project.

Cost—The expenditure necessary to produce a product, service, process, or facility.

Cost/Benefit Analysis—A technique intended to relate the economic benefits of a solution to the costs incurred in providing the solution.

Cost, Design to—A procedure which establishes an estimated cost objective for each project, then designs to that cost objective to produce a reliable product or service.

Cost, Life Cycle—The sum of all acquisition, production, operation, maintenance, use and disposal costs for a product or project over a specified period of time.

Cost Model—A diagramming technique used to illustrate the total cost of families of systems or parts within a total complex system or structure.

Creativity—The development of new ideas which will satisfy an expressed or implied need.

Customer—The word "customer" refers to anyone who receives a product "downstream". Customers are also sometimes referred to as a "user," depending on the application.

Customer Value Analysis—A marketing oriented discipline that focuses on identifying, measuring, and improving customer value for the purpose of improving the profitability of an organization.

D

Deliverable—Any measurable, tangible, verifiable outcome, result, or item that must be produced to complete a project or part of a project. Often used more narrowly in reference to an external deliverable, which is a deliverable that is subject to approval by the project sponsor or customer.

Denial of Use Cost—Extra costs incurred or income lost because occupancy or production is delayed or interfered with by a prior decision.

Depreciation—An accounting device that distributes the monetary value (less salvage value) of a tangible asset over the estimated years of productive or useful life.

Discount Factor—The factor for any specific discount rate that translates expected cost or benefit in any specific future year into its present value. The discount factor is equal to $1/(1+r)t$, where r is the discount rate and t is the number of years since the date of initiation, renewal, or expansion of a program or project.

Discount or Interest Rate—The minimum acceptable rate of return for the client for investment purposes, or the current prime or borrowing rate of interest.

E

Economic Life—The period over which an investment is considered for satisfying a particular need.

Engineering Economics—A discipline that focuses on the evaluation of engineering alternatives by considering their economic consequences over time, recognizing the time value of money.

Equivalent Dollars—Dollars both present and future, that is expressed in a common baseline reflecting the time value of money and inflation. (See Present Worth and Annualized Method.)

Equivalent Full-Load Hours—Total energy consumption divided by the full-load energy input. This gives the number of hours a piece of equipment would need to operate at its full capacity to consume as much energy as it did operating at various part-loads.

Escalation—A rate of inflation above the general (differential) rate devaluation of the purchasing power of the dollar.

Evaluation Matrix—A specialized form for organizing and recording information concerning the analysis of ideas during the Evaluation Phase. The evaluation matrix must include an analysis of the performance attributes and cost impacts, a discussion of the advantages and disadvantages of the idea relative to the baseline concept, and an overall rating based upon these factors.

Exit Briefing—a Meeting organized for the purpose of presenting to a project team an overview of the value alternatives developed by the value team. It is typically held as the last activity of the formal team study.

F

Financing Costs—The costs of any debt associated with the facility's capital costs.

Function—The natural or characteristic actions performed by a product or service. That which the product, facility or service does as it is currently designed or conceived.

Function, Basic—The specific purpose(s) for which a product, facility, or service exists. The basic function must always exist, although methods or designs to achieve it may vary.

Function, Secondary—A function that supports the basic function and results from the specific design approach to achieve the basic function. As methods or design approaches to achieve the basic function are changed, secondary functions may also change. There are several kinds of secondary functions:

> *Required*—A secondary function that is essential to support the performance of the basic function under the current design approach.
>
> *Higher Order*—The specific need(s) that the basic function(s) exists to satisfy. It answers the "why" question

of the basic function, and is depicted immediately outside the study scope to the left on a FAST diagram.

Lower Order—The function that is required to initiate the project and is depicted farthest to the right, outside the study scope. For example, if the value study concerns an electrical device, the "supply power" function at the electrical connection would be the lowest order function. Also referred to as an "assumed function."

Aesthetic—A secondary function describing esteem value.

Unwanted—A negative function caused by the method used to achieve the basic function such as the heat generated from lighting, which must be cooled.

Sell—A function that provides primarily esteem value. For marketing studies it may be the basic function.

Function Analysis: The process of defining, classifying and evaluating functions. First developed by Larry Miles.

Function Analysis System Technique (FAST)—A horizontal chart depicting functions within a project, with the following rules:

- The sequence of functions on the critical path proceeding from left to right answer the questions "How is the function to its immediate left performed?"
- The sequence of functions on the critical path proceeding from right to left answer the question "Why is the next function performed?"
- Functions occurring at the same time or caused by functions on the critical path appear vertically below the critical path function.

- The basic function of the study is always farthest to the left of the diagram of all functions within the scope of the study.

G

Gantt Chart—*A graphic display of schedule related information. Activities or other project elements are listed down the left side of the chart, dates are shown across the top, and activity durations are shown as date-placed horizontal bars.*

I

Implementation Meeting—A decision-making meeting organized for the purpose of determining the disposition of value alternatives.

Implementation Plan—A formal plan for integrating accepted value alternatives into the ongoing project development process. This should be part of a project's integrated change control plan.

Inflation—A continuing rise in the general price levels, caused usually by an increase in the volume of money and credit relative to available goods.

Initial Costs—Costs associated with the initial development of a facility, including project costs (fees, real estate, site, etc.) as well as construction cost.

Interest Rate—See Discount Rate.

J

Job Plan—A structured series of steps to carry out a value study.

K

Kick-Off Meeting—A meeting organized for the purpose of acquainting the participants of a value study with the project baseline, the value study objectives, and the VM process. It is held at the beginning of the formal team study.

L

Life Cycle Cost Comparisons—An economic assessment of an item, area, system, or facility and competing design alternatives considering all significant costs of ownership over the economic life, expressed in terms of equivalent dollars.

M

Maintenance Costs—The regular custodial care and repair, annual maintenance contracts, and salaries of facility staff performing maintenance tasks.

Mental Roadblock—A subconscious, psychological habit or trait that inhibits creative or critical thinking.

Milestone—A significant event in the project, usually completion of a major deliverable.

N

Network Diagram—Any schematic display of the logical relationships of project activities. Always drawn from left to right to reflect project chronology. Also referred to as a project flow chart or PERT chart.

Nonrecurring Cost—A cost that occurs, or is expected to occur, only once.

FUNDAMENTALS OF VALUE METHODOLOGY 341

Numerical Evaluation Technique—A technique used to evaluate the importance of functions of a product utilizing the paired or scaled paired comparison evaluation method.

O

Operation (Energy) Costs—The category of items such as fuel, salaries, etc., required to operate the facility or installation.

Owner—The individual or organization that is responsible for funding and/or delivering a project.

P

Paired Comparison Method: The Paired Comparison Method is a powerful voting, prioritization and consensus technique. It can be used by an individual, but is more commonly used by a team, to prioritize a range of options or root causes (those vital and systemic for improvement). By comparing each option with every other option, scores and rankings are created.

Particle Analysis—A technique that analyzes each element of a part or component to identify what function that element is providing.

Payback Period—The time it takes the savings resulting from a modification to pay back the costs involved.

Present-Worth Method—An economic method that requires conversion of all present and future expenditures to a baseline of today's cost.

Performance—The capacity of a product to fulfill its intended function. Ideally, performance should be defined by the intended customer or user. Appropriate performance requires that the product, facility, or service have a predetermined level of quality, reliability, interchangeability, maintainability, producibility, marketability, and deliverability. These performance levels must match the customer's requirements and vary depending upon the nature of the project.

Performance Attribute—Specific characteristics that are essential in achieving a product's performance objectives. Performance attributes can possess a range of values and can be measured either qualitatively or quantitatively.

Performance Attribute Matrix—A technique using the paired comparison method of evaluating the importance of performance attributes in meeting a project's purpose and need.

Performance Parameters—The range of acceptable values for the performance attributes of a product.

Performance Requirement—Specific characteristics that are essential in achieving a product's performance objectives. Performance requirements are absolute and must be explicitly met.

Post-Study—Activities of a value study that occur after the performance of the formal team study.

Pre-Study—Activities of a value study that occur prior to the performance of the formal value study.

Pre-Study Meeting—A meeting organized by a value specialist for the purposes of preparing for the performance of a value study. Typical attendees include the project manager, project team, value team, and stakeholders.

Price—A fixed sum of money expended by the user/customer to purchase the product under study.

Product—For the purposes of value studies, a product is the subject of the study. It may be a physical product such as a manufactured item, or a facility, system, procedure, or even an organization.

Product Scope—*The features and functions that characterize a product or service.*

Project—*A temporary endeavor undertaken to create a unique product, service, or result.*

Project Life Cycle—*A collection of generally sequential project phases whose name and number are determined by the control needs of the organization or organizations involved in the project.*

Project Management—*The application of knowledge, skills, tools, and techniques to project activities to meet the project requirements.*

Project Manager—*The individual responsible for managing a project.*

Project Phase—*A collection of logically related project activities, usually culminating in the completion of a major deliverable.*

Project Plan—*A formal, approved document used to guide both project execution and project control. The primary uses of the project plan are to document planning assumptions and decisions, facilitate communication among stakeholders, and document approved scope, cost, and schedule baselines. A project plan may be a summary or detailed.*

Project Schedule—*The planned dates for performing activities and the planned dates for meeting milestones.*

Project Scope—*The work that must be done to deliver a product with the specified features and functions.*

Project Team—The people who report either directly or indirectly to the project manager.

Q

Quality—Quality refers to the conformance of design specifications during the manufacture, construction, or development of a product, facility, or service. In Value Methodology, quality is but one aspect of performance.

R

Random Function Determination—A simple function classification process that involves randomly selecting the components of a product, identifies their functions, and then determines which of those functions are basic or secondary.

Rate of Return—An interest rate which, over a period of time, equates the benefits derived from an opportunity to the investment cost of the project.

Recurring Costs—Costs that recur on a periodic basis throughout the life of a project.

Replacement Costs—Those costs which will be incurred in the future to maintain the original function of the facility or item.

Revenues, Loss of—Income lost due to delays or interference in occupancy and production. Similar to Denial of Use.

Risk—An uncertain event or condition that, if it occurs, has a positive or negative effect on a project's objectives.

Roadblock—An objection or a delaying tactic from a person or a group of people attempting to resist changes.

S

Salvage Value—The value (positive if it has residual economic value and negative if it requires demolition) of competing alternatives at the end of the life cycle period.

SAVE International—The professional society dedicated to the promotion of Value Methodology worldwide. SAVE International maintains and administers the value professional certification program.

Scope—1. The sum of the products and services to be provided as a project. 2. The limits of a value study.

Sensitivity Analysis—A technique to assess the relative effect a change in the input variables has on the resulting output.

Sensitivity Matrix—A technique commonly used in conjunction with FAST diagrams that relates performance or responsibilities to functions.

Stakeholder—Individuals and organizations that are actively involved in the project, or whose interests may be positively or negatively affected as a result of project execution or project completion. They may also exert influence over the project and its results.

Sunk Cost—A cost which has already been incurred and should not be considered in future economic decision making.

Synergism—The simultaneous action of separate agencies which, together, have greater total effect than the sum of their individual effects. In VM, for example, a team may produce results far in excess of those which would be possible by individual action.

T

Target (Cost or Energy)—A goal, expectation, budget, or estimate of the minimum an item should cost (or consume energy) during one or more phases of its life cycle. The worth of an item, as used in value engineering, is the lowest possible target for that item.

Tax Elements—Those assignable costs pertaining to taxes, credits, and depreciation. Thus, different design alternatives may have a significant impact on taxes.

Time Horizon—The ending point of the life cycle cost analysis, the cutoff, or last year, of the analysis.

Time Value of Money—A term given to the notion that the use of money costs money. Commitment of dollars to a project requires that it either be borrowed (thus incurring an interest charge) or that it be taken from owner resources (thus foregoing potential interest income). Because of these interest costs, the time at which money is required (today, next year, 10 years from now) becomes very important in economic decision making.

U

Useful Life—The period of time over which a product may be expected to give service. It may represent physical, technological, or economic life.

V

Value—A qualitative or quantitative expression of the relationship between the performance of a function, and the cost of acquiring it. Hence the term "best value" refers to the most cost effective means to accomplish a function that will meet the performance expectations of the customer.

Value, Economic—There are four classes of economic value:

> Use Value—The monetary measure of the functional properties of the product or service which reliably accomplish a user's needs.
>
> Esteem Value—The monetary measure of the properties of a product or service which contribute to its desirability or salability. Commonly answers the "How much do I want something?" question.
>
> Cost Value—The monetary sum of labor, material, burden, and other elements of cost required to produce a product or service.
>
> Exchange Value—The monetary sum at which a product or service can be freely traded in the marketplace.

Value, Functional—An expression of the value of a function (usually a basic function or functions) as a relationship between how well the function(s) are being performed compared to the cost of acquiring the performance. In *Value Metrics*, functional value is expressed by the formula $V_f = P/C$.

Value Analyst—Synonymous with Value Specialist.

Value Change Proposal—A formal proposal submitted to the project owner which requires their approval before implementing the VA change. The result will be a modification to the submitter's contract. This is often referred to as a Value Engineering Change Proposal (VECP). Many organizations maintain VECP clauses or programs that do not rely upon formal value studies. Typically, such programs are directed at contractors as a means of soliciting of value alternatives.

Value Engineer—Synonymous with Value Specialist.

Value Incentive Clause—A contractual mechanism for providing a cash-based incentive to contractors and vendors for the development of Value Change Proposals.

Value Index—The ratio used to determine the maximum opportunity for value improvement. It is derived by dividing performance by cost using the *Value Metrics* process.

Value Matrix—A technique utilized to show the relationship of cost and performance to value for value alternatives compared to a relative project baseline.

Value Methodology—The systematic application of recognized techniques which seek to improve the value of a product or service by identifying and evaluating its functions, and provide the necessary functions to meet the required performance at the lowest overall cost.

Value Methodology Training—There are two levels of SAVE International approved training specifically designed to provide the minimum knowledge of VM practice. It is expected that VM professionals, as in all professional fields, will continue to keep themselves current through seminars, conferences, and associated educational opportunities. The two levels of training include:

Value Methodology Workshop—The objective is to provide Value Methodology education to the degree that participants will be able to successfully participate in future value studies under the guidance of a qualified Value Specialist with minimum additional training. This is called the Module I program.

Value Methodology Advanced Seminar—The objective of this seminar is to extend the knowledge base of those wishing to become professionals in the value methodology field. Topics include both advanced methodology and areas of management. This seminar is referred to as the Module II program. Module I is a prerequisite, and it is expected attendees will have enough practical experience in VM to contribute to the seminar.

Value Metrics—A process developed to complement the traditional Value Methodology Job Plan through the utilization of techniques that focus on quantifying both cost and performance in measuring value improvement.

Value Program Manager—The individual responsible for managing and administering the value program of an organization.

Value Specialist—One who applies the Value Methodology to improve the value of a product. This usually occurs by way of the performance of a value study.

Value Study—The application of the value methodology using the VM Job Plan, and people previously trained in VM workshops.

Value Study Charter—A document issued by the project team (usually the project or value program manager) that formally authorizes the value study. This document should include key data relevant to the value study including a list of participants, project scope, value study scope and objectives, meeting locations and dates, and project information.

Value Study Sponsor—The individual or entity responsible for commissioning a value study to be performed on a project.

Value Team—Those individuals participating on a value study on either a full-time or officially designated capacity.

W

Work Breakdown Structure—A deliverable-oriented grouping of project elements that organizes and defines the total work scope of the project. Each descending level represents an increasingly detailed definition of the project work.

Worth—1. The lowest overall cost to perform a function without regard to performance. 2. An individual assessment of value (as opposed to a consensual, or group, assessment of value) that typically reflects a subjective perception of esteem.

Appendix B—Value Study Management Plan

This management plan has been prepared for the use of project managers and value program managers who will be involved in the organization and management of value studies. It will also provide valuable information to the Value Team.

The value study management plan presented in this appendix is presented using standard elements from the project plan approach presented in the *Project Management Institute's "A Guide to the Project Management Body of Knowledge, 2000 Edition."* The process described is based on the eight-phase VM Job Plan and VM techniques presented in this text, including the *Value Metrics* system. The following elements are included:

- *Value Study Charter*—A formal initiation document authorizing the Value Study.
- *Statement of Work*—A description of the work that will be performed for the Value Study.
- *Communication Plan*—A description of formal and informal communications that will take place within the context of the Value Study.
- *Work Breakdown Structure*—A list of activities that will take place as part of the Value Study. From the WBS, a GANTT chart and network diagram can be derived.

The Value Study Management Plan presented here is for a fictional information technology project for an equally fictitious corporation called IT International, Inc. This Value Study Management Plan provides a basic template for the management of a value study and may be modified to meet the specific needs of the project and value study requirements. This particular value study is based on a five-day team study schedule, and includes all of the recommended pre-study and post-study activities.

Project Name:	VALUE STUDY CHARTER		IT International	
	Applicant Tracking System			

PROJECT IDENTIFICATION INFORMATION

Project Code:	04-HR-027	Project Initiation:	8/30/2004
Department:	Human Resources—IT	Present Milestone:	Functional Requirements
Project Manager:	Juanita Garcia		

KEY PROJECT MILESTONE DATES

Complete Functional Specs:	09/06/04	Complete Project:	12/24/2004
Complete Design:	10/8/2004		
Complete Construction:	11/19/2004		
Complete Testing:	12/10/2004		

PROJECT DESCRIPTION

New Applications: The ATS application will receive new applications as e-mails that will be parsed and stored in the database. The system will then automatically e-mail a questionnaire to the candidate to gather information regarding level of experience in various technologies. Other personal details, salary requirements, preferences of work location and availability will also be captured. Duplicates will be avoided by having the email address of the prospective candidates as one of the keys.

Search Functionality: The hiring managers of various departments will have the ability to search the ATS database for candidates that meet their requirements. The search engine will be very flexible in allowing the users to search and also construct queries. Users will have the ability to find applicants by name, skill sets, location, salary requirements and so on.

Setup Interview: The ATS system will allow the hiring managers to setup interviews by sending e-mail to the short listed candidates. Responses from candidates will automatically be stored in the database.

Interview Notes & Rating: ATS will have the ability to store interview notes and also provide managers with an option to rate the candidates.

Correspondence: Hiring managers can send email to the selected or rejected candidates through the ATS. The references provided by the candidates will be stored and emails sent to them automatically to check the employment history of candidates. When a response is not received within the due time, ATS will have the functionality to send reminders automatically.

Estimated Project Development Costs:	$375,000

PROJECT PURPOSE and NEED

IT International, Inc, is fast becoming one of the largest information technology companies in the world. The Human Resources Dept. is in the process of developing a new Applicant Tracking System (ATS) that will be used to manage the growing number of applications, and phone inquiries IT International, Inc, is experiencing. The system will support application tracking, routing and classification of prospective employees as well as serve as the foundation for a HR database. The application will enable human resource coordinators to receive, identify, verify, classify and route employment related inquires. The ATS is envisioned to be a critical component for maintaining the high quality of our personnel in meeting the challenges of the new millennium.

VALUE STUDY PURPOSE and OBJECTIVES

The purpose of the Value Study is to ensure that this critical piece of software will fully meet the needs of the Human Resources Dept. The Value Study should validate the user requirements, identify improvements that will improve the ATS's performance and better manage the work loads that the Human Resources Dept. is currently faced with.

FUNDAMENTALS OF VALUE METHODOLOGY

	VALUE STUDY CHARTER		IT International	
Project Name:	Applicant Tracking System			

VALUE STUDY PARTICIPANTS
TEAM LEADERS

Name	Department	Discipline/Position	Phone	E-Mail
Robert B Stewart	VMS, Inc.	Value Specialist	978/531-8864	rob@vms.com

VALUE TEAM MEMBERS

Name	Department	Discipline/Position	Phone	E-Mail
John Smith	Product Development	Developer	978/272-5550	jrs@it.com
Kathy Jones	Product Development	Developer	978/272-5550	kdj@it.com
Bart Cummings	Product Development	Operations Analyst	978/272-5550	bfc@it.com
Patti Enfanto	Finance	Business Analyst	978/272-5550	pse@it.com
Tom Culhane	IT Support	Systems Administrator	978/272-5550	tlc@it.com
Royce McDaniel	IT Support	Database Administrator	978/272-5550	rod@it.com

PROJECT TEAM MEMBERS

Name	Department	Discipline/Position	Phone	E-Mail
Juanita Garcia	Human Resources	Project Manager	978/272-5550	jlg@it.com
Kishore Ramachandran	Human Resources	Module Leader	978/272-5550	ksr@it.com
Xing Li	Human Resources	Developer	978/272-5550	xyl@it.com
Gordon Gerbels	Human Resources	Developer	978/272-5550	ggg@it.com
Max Ellison	Human Resources	Developer	978/272-5550	mre@it.com
Janine Avery	Human Resources	Operations Analyst	978/272-5550	jla@it.com
Wilson Koga	Finance	Business Analyst	978/272-5550	wok@it.com
Maynard Crabtree	Human Resources	Systems Administrator	978/272-5550	mic@it.com
Beverly Hines	Human Resources	Database Administrator	978/272-5550	bth@it.com

PROJECT RESOURCE ADVISORS

Name	Department	Discipline/Position	Phone	E-Mail
Muffy Bintz	Finance	Finance Manager	978/272-5550	mob@it.com
Hiram Quagmire	Human Resources	Quality Assurance	978/272-5550	hoq@it.com
Jonny Biddles	Human Resources	Tester	978/272-5550	job@it.com

PROJECT DECISION MAKERS

Name	Department	Discipline/Position	Phone	E-Mail
John Q. Public	Human Resources	Vice President	978/272-5550	jqp@it.com
Ima N. Portent	Headquarters	Exec. Vice President	978/272-5550	inp@it.com

VALUE STUDY SCHEDULE

Meeting	Dates	Times	Location
Pre-Study Meeting	9/17/2004	9:00A-11:00A	Bldg. A, RM 237
Kick-Off Meeting	9/27/2004	8:00A-12:00P	Bldg. A, RM 237
Value Study	9/27/2004-9/31/2004	8:00A-4:30P	Bldg. A, RM 237
Technical Review Meeting	9/30/2004	8:00A-12:00P	Bldg. A, RM 237
Exit Briefing	9/31/2004	1:30P-3:00P	Bldg. A, RM 237
Implementation Meeting	10/14/2004	1:00P-5:00P	Bldg. A, HR Dept. Boardroom

Project Name:	VALUE STUDY CHARTER Applicant Tracking System	*IT International*

PROJECT DOCMUENTATION

Project Documents that will be provided to the Value Team include:

- Project Scope Document
    - Scope Statement
    - Scope Management Plan
    - Functional Requirements
        - System Requirements
        - User-Interface Requirements
        - Business Requirements
        - Data Requirements
    - Project Assumptions
    - Project Constraints
    - Project Work Breakdown Structure
- Project Schedule
    - GANTT Chart
    - Network Diagram
- Project Budget
    - Project Cost Baseline
    - Resource Allocation Estimate
    - Cost Management Plan
- Quality Management Plan
- Risk Management Plan

Value Study—Applicant Tracking System Project

Statement of Work

1.0 Background

IT International, Inc. is in the process of developing a new Applicant Tracking System (ATS) that will be used to manage the growing number of applications, and phone inquiries the Human Resource Department is experiencing. The system will support application tracking, routing, and classification of prospective employees, as well as serve as the foundation for a Human Resources database. The application will enable human resource coordinators to receive, identify, verify, classify and route employment-related inquires.

2.0 Goal

The Value Team will perform a Value Study of the ATS Project through the application of the Value Methodology. The purpose of the Value Study is to identify alternative concepts that will improve the overall value of the ATS to IT International, Inc.'s Human Resource Department. The Value Study will be conducted at the beginning of the Database Design Phase, and any alternative concepts accepted by the Project Decision Makers will be implemented into the project by the end of this project phase.

3.0 Customer

The customer and sponsor of the project is John Q. Public, Corporate Vice President for Human Resources.

4.0 Project Description

4.1 *New Applications:* The ATS application will receive new applications as emails that will be parsed and stored in the database. The system will then automatically email a questionnaire to the candidate to gather information regarding his or her level of experience in various technologies. Other personal details, salary requirements, preferences of work location and availability will also be captured. Duplicates will be avoided by having the email address of the prospective candidates as one of the keys.

4.2 *Search Functionality:* The hiring managers of various departments will have the ability to search the ATS database for candidates that meet their requirements. The search engine will be very flexible in allowing the users to search and also construct queries. Users will have the ability to find applicants by name, skill sets, location, salary requirements, and so on.

4.3 *Set Up Interview:* The ATS system will allow the hiring managers to set up interviews by sending email to the short-listed candidates. Responses from candidates will automatically be stored in the database.

4.4 *Interview Notes & Rating:* ATS will have the ability to store interview notes and also provide managers with an option to rate the candidates.

4.5 *Correspondence:* Hiring managers can send email to the selected or rejected candidates through the ATS. The references provided by the candidates will be stored and emails sent to them automatically to check the employment history of candidates. When a response is not received within the due time, ATS will have the functionality to send reminders automatically.

5.0 Value Study Description

5.1   The Value Study will be facilitated by a consultant value specialist who is a Certified Value Specialist, as administered by SAVE International.

5.2   The Value Study will adhere to the formal Value Methodology process.

5.3   The Value Team will consist of team members from individuals from IT International, Inc. not currently involved on the ATS Project.

5.4   The team portion of the Value Study will be conducted during a five-day work week.

5.5   The Value Study will include a Pre-Study Meeting, Kick-Off Meeting, Exit Briefing, and Implementation Meeting.

6.0 Assumptions

6.1   All appropriate hardware and software required to develop ATS system have been evaluated and upgraded as necessary.

6.2   All appropriate interface requirements have been met and addressed.

6.3   Individuals from the business will be available for testing.

6.4   Any additional requirements will be addressed in subsequent application releases.

7.0 Constraints

7.1   In accordance with the confidentiality and privacy policies of the organization over the HR data, this project will not be outsourced.

7.2   All output generated by the ATS system must strictly comply with corporate guidelines for Equality & Fairness in the Workplace.

8.0 Deliverables

8.1 The Value Specialist will facilitate a Pre-Study Meeting to coordinate with the other value study participants as identified in the Value Study Communication Plan.
8.2 The Value Specialist will facilitate the Value Study and submit a Preliminary Value Study Report that will document the Value Team's findings and recommendations.
8.3 The Value Specialist will facilitate an Implementation Meeting. The results of the Implementation Meeting will be documented in a Final Value Study Report.

Value Study—Applicant Tracking System Project

Communications Plan

1.0 Participants

This Value Study will include approximately 21 participants. The participants will be broken down as members of the following four categories. The Value Team participants will be drawn from various departments of IT International, Inc. other than Human Resources.

1.1 Value Team (VT)

- Value Specialist
- Developer (2)
- Business Analyst
- Operations Analyst
- Systems Administrator
- Database Administrator

1.2 Project Team (PT)

- Project Manager
- Module Leader
- Developers (3)
- Business Analyst
- Operations Analyst
- Systems Administrator
- Database Administrator

1.3 Project Resource Advisors (PR)

- Finance Manager
- Quality Assurance Team Lead
- Tester

1.4 Project Decision Makers (DM)

- IT Executive Vice President
- Human Resources Vice President

2.0 Formal Communications

The formal communications for the participants of the Value Study will include the following documents and meetings:

2.1 Value Study Charter

A written Value Study Charter will be developed by the Project Manager and/or Value Program Manager. This document will formally initiate the Value Study and shall identify the following elements:

2.1.1   Project Scope & Schedule

Identify the project scope, including a brief description of the purpose and need and project objectives. Identify the current project phase and the dates of key project milestones.

2.1.2   Value Study Scope & Objectives

Identify the scope of the Value Study and primary objectives.

2.1.3   Meeting Dates & Locations

Identify the dates, times and locations of the following meetings related to the Value Study:

- Pre-Study Meeting
- Kick-Off Meeting
- Value Study

- Technical Review Meeting
- Value Study Exit Briefing
- Implementation Meeting

2.1.4 Project Contact List

Identify the names, positions, locations, and contact information for all Value Study Participants.

2.1.5 List of available documents

Identify the names and quantities of project documents and information that will be made available to the Value Team.

2.2 Pre-Study Meeting

This meeting will be conducted to review the Value Study scope and objectives, discuss the project, and make the necessary preparations for the Value Study.

2.2.1 Participants

The participants of this meeting should include the Value Team, Project Team, Project Resource Advisors, and Project Stakeholders.

2.2.2 Ground Rules

This meeting will follow the Pre-Study Meeting Agenda to be prepared by the Value Specialist.

2.3 Kick-Off Meeting

This meeting will be conducted to inform the Value Team of the specifics of the project, and to identify and discuss constraints and stakeholder issues relevant to the Value Study. Project Performance Attributes and Requirements will also be identified and discussed.

2.3.1 Participants

The participants of this meeting should include the Value Team, Project Team, Project Resource Advisors, Project Stakeholders, and Project Decision Makers.

2.3.2 Ground Rules

This meeting will follow the Kick-Off Meeting Agenda prepared by the Value Specialist. The Project Team will be responsible for preparing an informational overview of the project.

2.4 Value Study

The Value Study will follow the Value Methodology Job Plan and will be facilitated by the Value Specialist. The purpose of the Value Study is to develop alternative concepts that will improve project value.

2.4.1 Participants

The Value Team will be primarily responsible for conducting the Value Study. The Project Team, Project Resource Advisors, and Project Stakeholders will be available by phone during the Value Study for informational purposes.

2.4.2 Ground Rules

The Value Study will follow the Value Study Agenda prepared by the Value Specialist.

2.5 Technical Review Meeting

The Technical Review Meeting will allow the Technical Reviewers to conduct a mid-point review of the alternative concepts prior to their completion.

2.5.1 Participants

The Value Team will be primarily responsible for conducting the Value Study. The Technical Reviewers and will drop in at their convenience for this informal review midway through the Value Study, as identified in the Value Study Agenda.

2.5.2 Ground Rules

This will be an informal review. The Value Specialists will familiarize the Technical Reviewers with the alternative concepts and invite their comments.

2.6 Value Study Exit Briefing

The Value Study Exit Briefing will provide the Project Team with an informational overview of the value alternatives developed by the Value Team.

2.6.1 Participants

The participants of this meeting should include the Value Team, Project Team, Project Resource Advisors, Project Stakeholders, and Project Decision Makers.

2.6.2 Ground Rules

The Value Team will prepare an Exit Briefing Agenda to be distributed to all participants at the commencement of the briefing. This is not to be a decision-making meeting.

2.7 Implementation Meeting

The Implementation Meeting will serve as the decision-making meeting in determining the acceptability of the value alternatives.

2.7.1 Participants

The participants of this meeting should include the Value Team, Project Team, Project Resource Advisors, Project Stakeholders, and Project Decision Makers.

2.7.2 Ground Rules

The Value Specialist will facilitate the meeting by initiating a discussion of each of the value alternatives. The comments of all participants will be documented, and the Project Decision Makers will determine the status of each value alternative.

3.0 Informal Project Communications

Informal communications includes phone, email, fax, video conferencing, and face-to-face meetings. All Value Team members must maintain access to the following media / tools: email, voice mail, fax, Microsoft Office XP, and Acrobat Reader.

3.1 The informal communications path is as follows:

- Value Study Sponsor (Owner) to Project Manager
- Project Manager to Project Team Member

- ◆ Project Manager to Value Specialist
- ◆ Value Specialist to Value Team Member

3.2 Ground Rules

Value Team Members must document all external communications with outside information sources (i.e., vendors, contractors, etc.) to be included in the Final Value Study Report.

4.0 General Ground Rules

All communication will be in English.

5.0 Assumptions

All Value Study Participants are assumed to have access to internet, voice messaging system, fax machine, and video conference room.

6.0 Constraints

No traveling costs have been budgeted.

Value Study—Applicant Tracking System Project

Work Breakdown Structure

1.0 Value Study—Applicant Tracking System Project

   1.1 Preparation Phase

       1.1.1 Identify Project for Value Study
       1.1.2 Identify Timing of Value Study
       1.1.3 Develop Value Study Management Plan

            1.1.3.1 Prepare Value Study Charter

       1.1.4 Retain Consultant Value Specialist

            1.1.4.1 Advertise for Professional VM Services
            1.1.4.2 Select Qualified Consultant
            1.1.4.3 Negotiate Fee
            1.1.4.4 Administer Consultant Contract

       1.1.5 Conduct Pre-Study Meeting

            1.1.5.1 Collect Project Information
            1.1.5.2 Identify Project Scope, Schedule and Cost
            1.1.5.3 Identify Performance Attributes and Requirements—*Value Metrics*
            1.1.5.4 Establish Value Study Objectives and Goals
            1.1.5.5 Define Value Study Scope and Schedule
            1.1.5.6 Identify Value Study Participants
            1.1.5.7 Organize Value Study Logistics

1.2 Information Phase

    1.2.1   Review Project information

           1.2.1.1 Review and Analyze Project Scope Information

                1.2.1.1.1 Distribute Project Data to Value Team

           1.2.1.2   Review and Analyze Project Schedule Information

           1.2.1.3   Review and Analyze Project Cost Information

                1.2.1.3.1 Develop Cost Models

    1.2.2   Begin Value Study

           1.2.2.1 Conduct Value Study Kick-Off Meeting

                1.2.2.1.1   Introduce Value Study Process, Objectives and Schedule
                1.2.2.1.2   Present Project Overview
                1.2.2.1.3   Identify Project Constraints and Stakeholder Issues
                1.2.2.1.4   Identify Project Performance—*Value Metrics*
                1.2.2.1.5   Measure Project Performance

1.3 Function Phase

    1.3.1   Define Functions
    1.3.2   Classify Functions

1.3.3 Evaluate Functions

    1.3.3.1 FAST Diagram
    1.3.3.2 Relate Cost and Performance to Function—*Value Metrics*

1.4 Speculation Phase

    1.4.1 Generate Ideas

        1.4.1.1 Utilize Creativity Techniques
        1.4.1.2 Stimulate Creativity—*Value Metrics*

1.5 Evaluation Phase

    1.5.1 Evaluate Ideas

        1.5.1.1 Utilize Evaluation Techniques
        1.5.1.2 Enhance Evaluation—*Value Metrics*

    1.5.2 Select Ideas for Development

        1.5.2.1 Assign Ideas to Value Team

1.6 Development Phase

    1.6.1 Develop Value Alternatives

        1.6.1.1 Verify Technical Validity
        1.6.1.2 Determine Costs
        1.6.1.3 Assess Performance—*Value Metrics*
        1.6.1.4 Develop Narratives

1.6.2 Review Value Alternatives

    1.6.2.1 Conduct Technical Review Meeting
    1.6.2.2 Conduct Value Team Review of Value Alternatives

1.7 Presentation Phase

  1.7.1 Assess Value—*Value Metrics*
  1.7.2 Conduct Exit Briefing

    1.7.2.1 Present Value Alternatives

  1.7.3 Prepare Preliminary Value Study Report
  1.7.4 Submit Preliminary Value Study Report

1.8 Implementation Phase

  1.8.1 Review Value Alternatives

    1.8.1.1 Improve Decisions—*Value Metrics*

  1.8.2 Resolve Value Alternatives

    1.8.2.1 Conduct Implementation Meeting

      1.8.2.1.1 Review Comments from Participants
      1.8.2.1.2 Determine Disposition of Value Alternatives

  1.8.3 Develop Implementation Plan
  1.8.4 Prepare Final Value Study Report
  1.8.5 Submit Final Value Study Report
  1.8.6 Track and Audit Results
  1.8.7 Close Out Value Study Process

APPENDIX C—CASE STUDIES

This appendix provides three examples of the application of Value Methodology to actual projects. A case study has been provided representing three major areas where VM is typically applied:

- *Manufacturing and Product Design* – This case study covers the application of VM to an existing line of industrial hardware. This example demonstrates the power of the *Value Metrics* system in measuring total value improvement and the importance of distinguishing performance attributes and requirements. It also illustrates the importance of challenging performance requirements and creating a paradigm shift in the way we approach problems.
- *Design & Construction* – This case study involves the design and construction of a new emergency operations center facility. This example includes the application of the *Value Metrics* system and utilizes comparative scales in evaluating performance. The timing of the value study for this project occurred at the concept design stage prior to the development of detailed design drawings and specifications. The value study included strong participation from the user and was used to validate the project scope while identifying alternatives that will enhance value.
- *Management Processes and Procedures* – This case study involves a complicated customer service process. This example illustrates the power of FAST diagrams in simplifying complex processes and identifying areas of poor value. This particular example did not utilize the *Value Metrics* system, but still serves as an excellent example of the Value Methodology. Based on the information provided, what do you think the performance attributes might be?

These case studies include a brief discussion of the project and basic information used to develop the value alternatives and measure cost and performance in determining total value improvement. The function analysis and *Value Metrics* activities have been included. In order to keep the length of this text manageable, these case studies do not include all of the other activities related to the various phases of the VM Job Plan such as idea evaluation lists, and management presentations.

Another consideration in perusing these case studies is the fact that slightly different forms were used to organize relevant study information. The forms should always be tailored to meet the specific needs of the project and value study objectives.

PRODUCT DESIGN CASE STUDY— FM-500 SERIES FLUID MOUNT

Project Description:

Fluid mounts are rubber mounting units that encapsulate a fluid that flows through a variety of ports and orifices depending upon the dynamic characteristics needed. A generator or engine is placed on top of the fluid mounts which act as an effective vibration isolator.

The FM-500 Series fluid mounts are typically used on engine-generator sets primarily used in larger yachts to reduce noise and vibration when not underway, and to control motion of the engine-generator unit in heavy seas and during start-up and shutdown.

The use of the FM-500 Series sterndrive and inboard engine mounts reduce noise and isolate

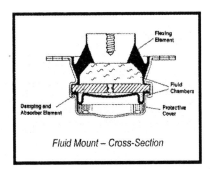

Fig. C-1

boat hulls from engine vibration. Fixed and adjustable mounts are available for both salt and fresh water environments.

Value Study Objective:

Reduce the standard cost of the FM-500 Series Fluid Mount while maintaining or improving the performance attributes and minimizing external configuration changes.

Sales History and Projection:

The current production costs are approximately $81.62 per unit. The average selling price in 2004 was $190.00 per unit. The 2005-2006 sales forecasts assume that a cost reduced version will be available in order to increase the size of the market.

	2002 (actual)	2003 (actual)	2004 (projected)	2005 (forecast)	2006 (forecast)
Units Sold	842	518	800	2000	2500
Sales ($)	155,000	100,000	150,000	220,000*	275,000*

Estimated sell price for cost reduced version: $110.00 (50% SGM)

Table C-1

Design and Development:

The FM-500 series was originally designed as a 4-1/2 Hz cab mount for Ford, Peterbuilt and Kenworth. Later, the FM-500-1 was suggested as a replacement for Alaska Diesel's costly high maintenance air spring-damper system. The FM-500-1 solved the customer's noise, vibration and motion problems at a lower cost. The FM-500 series became the new standard mounting system for marine engine-generator sets weighing from 1200-2800 lbs. Current customers include Alaska Diesel, Kilo Pack, Kelly Power, Sunpower Diesel, David Taylor

Research, Logan Mfg, Duggan Marine, Gage Marine and Mack Truck.

Future Market Opportunities:

The 2004 average selling price of $190.00 limits the market to expensive yachts. Our market analysis shows that the current market would more than triple and could include fishing and work boats if the selling price was below $125.00. If the value analysis concepts developed for the FM-500 series are incorporated in a physically smaller fluid mount series with load ratings to 75 lb (300 lb engine-generator sets), the market would be much larger. The market for the FM-500 series and a smaller version could be expanded to include vehicle-mounted engine sets and marine engine applications. Marketing has also identified the need for a failsafe option that would continue to secure critical equipment to the mounting surface even if the fluid mount fails under use. It is estimated that an additional 500 units could be sold for this new application.

Assumptions:

All savings estimates are based on the current FM-500-7 series. Engineering changes to the inertia track system and top compliance have been developed to resolve performance problems and are incorporated into the FM-500-13 series. Standard costs for these proposed changes are not available and are not included in the three value alternatives (except for conical outer member cost).

Tooling costs for the FM-500-13 conical outer member ($25,000) have been included in the value alternatives. (Implementation of the value alternatives will result in a faster payback for the required tooling.) Tooling costs for the FM-500-13 inertia track, fluid control disk, mold rework for the top compliance and inner member have not been established and are not included in the value alternatives.

Performance Requirements:

The following performance requirements were identified by the project team as essential:

- The existing external physical dimensions must be maintained in order to allow new units to be used in replacing existing units.

Performance Attributes:

The following performance attributes were identified by the project team:

- *Rated Load* – The maximum load that the fluid mount is able to support and still provide full vibration isolation. Acceptable parameters = (200 lbs. to 1200 lbs.)
- *Isolation Efficiency* – The protection of equipment from vibration and/or shock. The degree (or percentage) of isolation necessary is a function of the fragility of the equipment. Acceptable parameters = (1% to 100%)
- *Reliability* – A measure of anticipated life under normal use (i.e., use creating vibration) as measured in hours. Acceptable parameters = (10,000 to 20,000).

The existing (baseline) concept's current performance is described as follows:

- *Rated Load* – The current maximum rated load for the unit is 900 lbs.
- *Isolation Efficiency* – The current vibration isolation efficiency of the unit is approximately 65%.
- *Reliability* – The current anticipated operating life is approximately 14,000 hours.

Performance Utility Curves:

The following utility curves were derived for the three performance attributes identified above:

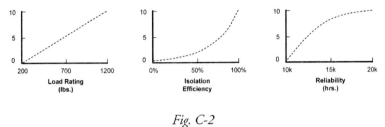

Fig. C-2

Relative Importance of Performance Attributes:

A scaled paired-comparison was utilized to determine the relative importance of the three performance attributes in meeting the customer's requirements (i.e., the product's purpose and need). Reliability was the least important of the three attributes. The scoring was adjusted by adding a point to each of the attributes scores to derive the relative attribute weights.

PERFORMANCE ATTRIBUTE MATRIX
FL-500 Series Fluid Mount

				TOTAL	%
Load Rating	A	B-1	A-2	3.0	38%
Isolation Efficiency		B	B-2	4.0	50%
Reliability			C	1.0	12%
				8.0	100%

Fig. C-3

Value of Baseline Concept:

A Value Matrix was developed utilizing the data developed for performance and cost. The Value Matrix utilized the existing units production cost rather than sales price as the basis for the cost side of the value equation.

VALUE MATRIX - Baseline Concept
FL-500 Series Fluid Mount

Attribute	Attribute Weight	Concept	Performance Rating 1	2	3	4	5	6	7	8	9	10	Total Performance
Load Rating	38	Baseline Concept							7				266
													0
													0
													0
													0
Isolation Efficiency	50	Baseline Concept				4							200
													0
													0
													0
													0
Reliability	12	Baseline Concept				4							48
													0
													0
													0
													0

Overall Performance Alternative	Total Performance	% Performance Improvement	Total Cost	Value Index (P/C)	% Value Improvement
Baseline Concept	514		81.62	6.30	

Fig. C-4

Function Analysis:

The basic functions of the fluid mount are to ISOLATE VIBRATION and DAMPEN VIBRATION. The only required secondary function of the fluid mount is to SUPPORT LOAD. A design objective of the fluid mount is to ASSURE RELIABILITY. All other functions are supporting secondary functions and exist only as a result of the current design approach. The random function identification identified the following functions for the fluid mount:

Function	Type
Isolate Vibration	Basic
Support Load	Secondary (Required)
Dampen Vibration	Basic
Absorb Energy	Secondary
Mount Equipment	Assumed
Facilitate Connections	Secondary
Contain Fluid	Secondary
Protect Surfaces	Secondary (All the Time)
Reduce Noise	Higher Order
Reduce Vibration	Higher Order
Ensure Reliability	Design Objective

Table C-2

A FAST diagram was constructed using the *Value Metrics* approach. Cost (material and labor) and performance was assigned to each of the functions. From this process, the Value Team discovered that the function FACILITATE CONNECTIONS was one of the highest cost functions (36%) but had a relatively small contribution to the performance of the fluid mount, thereby revealing an area of poor value. The function SUPPORT LOAD was the highest cost secondary function and plays the most critical role in contributing the fluid mount's load rating. The Value Team focused on these two functions in the subsequent phases of the VM Job Plan.

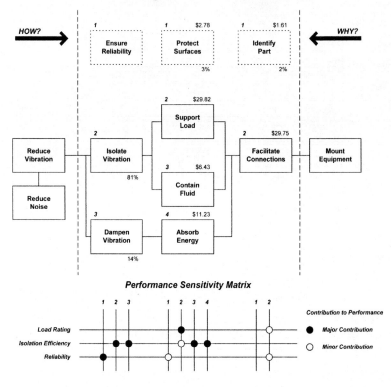

Figure C-5

Value Alternatives:

The Value Team developed two value alternatives. Value Alternative #1 met the performance requirements that were originally established by management in order to ensure that any modifications made to the unit would permit the field replacement of existing units that had reached the end of their service life. This alternative maintained all of the existing exterior physical dimensions. Once this alternative was developed, the Value Team recognized during the Speculation

Phase that there were additional improvements that would still allow for the field replacement of existing units but would require changes to the unit's exterior housing. Once this paradigm was changed, additional cost savings were realized in the form of Value Alternative #2. Value Alternative #2 also incorporated the ability of the unit to provide for a failsafe option that would now meet performance requirements for new customer requested applications, thereby increasing the number of marketable units by 500.

Value of Alternative Concepts:

A Value Matrix was developed was showing the potential for value improvement of these two value alternatives. The potential increase in value is significant for both alternatives. Value Alternative #1 has the potential to improve product value by about 60% while Value Alternative #2 can improve product value by over 100%.

VALUE MATRIX - Alternatives
FL-500 Series Fluid Mount

Attribute	Attribute Weight	Concept	Performance Rating 1	2	3	4	5	6	7	8	9	10	Total Performance
Load Rating	38	Baseline Concept							7				266
		Alternative #1							7				266
		Alternative #2							7				266
													0
													0
Isolation Efficiency	50	Baseline Concept				4							200
		Alternative #1					5						250
		Alternative #2					5						250
													0
													0
Reliability	12	Baseline Concept				4							48
		Alternative #1				4							48
		Alternative #2				4							48
													0
													0

Overall Performance Alternative	Total Performance	% Performance Improvement	Total Cost	Value Index (P/C)	% Value Improvement
Baseline Concept	514		81.62	6.30	
Alternative Concept #1	564	9.73%	55.04	10.25	62.72%
Alternative Concept #2	564	9.73%	42.13	13.39	112.58%

Fig. C-6

Implementation Plan:

The Value Team recommends implementing both alternatives using a two stage approach:

- *Stage 1:* Set up the new FL-500-13 series using the VA Value Alternative #1 (Low Impact). This will reduce the cost of the new series while providing the same fit, form and function. When purchasing tooling for the conical outer member, ensure that tooling can accommodate the extra length and bend in the outer member required by Value Alternative #2.
- *Stage 2:* After additional market analysis, introduce Value Alternative #2 with the optional failsafe cable system. Value Alternative #2 provides an extremely flexible, inexpensive design that will allow penetration into other markets.

VALUE ALTERNATIVE
FL-500 Series Fluid Mount

FUNCTION:	Dampen Vibration	**ALTERNATIVE NO.** 1
TITLE:	Low Impact Modifications to Fluid Mount	**PAGE NO.** 1 of 4

BASELINE CONCEPT:

The FL-500 Series Fluid Mounts are completely fabricated and assembled in-house. The outer housing is made of stamped steel while the inner housing is made of machined steel. The mounting studs on the bottom of the unit consist of machined and welded knurled bolts.

ALTERNATIVE CONCEPT:

The alternative concept includes a number of low impact modifications to the existing design that would require minimal tooling impacts. The changes consist of:

- Replace machined steel inner member with a cast iron inner member (exposed surfaces to be machined).
- Replace machined bolts that are welded to the bottom of the housing with standard projection welded bolts.
- Stamp inner member with the part dash number and eliminate ink stamp and clear coat (additional benefit is that customer can paint the part and still be able to read identification markings).

ADVANTAGES:

- Allows retrofit of the FM-500-7
- $26.58 cost savings per part
- Eliminates need for ink stamping part numbers
- Improves vibration isolation efficiency by 10%

DISADVANTAGES:

- Tooling costs, including new outer member tooling, is $20,000
- Additional engineering analysis required to validate strength of projection welded studs

COST / PERFORMANCE SUMMARY

	Material	Labor	Burden	TOTAL
Baseline	$ 61.14	$ 7.07	$ 13.41	$ 81.62
Alternative	$ 34.65	$ 7.07	$ 13.32	$ 55.04
Change in Cost	-32.57%		Savings Per Unit	$ 26.58
Change in Performance	+9.73%		Gross Savings (Qty. x $/Unit)	$ 53,160
CHANGE IN VALUE	+62.72%		Implementation Costs	$ 20,000
			NET SAVINGS	**$ 33,160**

VALUE ALTERNATIVE		
FL-500 Series Fluid Mount		
TITLE: Low Impact Modifications to Fluid Mount	NUMBER 1	PAGE NO. 2 of 4

DISCUSSION / JUSTIFICATION:

The Value Team thoroughly focused on identifying ways of manufacturing the unit differently while maintaining the baseline dimensions, appearance, and function. The team recommends replacing the machined steel inner member with a cast iron inner member. Using a cast iron inner member is permissible, as the exterior tolerances do not require a precision-machined component. The interior surfaces, however, would still need to be machined. The inner member will have conical rather than vertical sides, thereby reducing the amount of material required. The current method of ink stamping and clear coating the inner member can be eliminated by including the part number in the new casting. Tooling modifications for the stamping of the outer housing will be required to incorporate the changes to the inner member.

The machined knurl bolts that are currently welded to the bottom of the housing can be replaced with standard projection welded bolts. The Value Team is fairly confident that the projection welded bolts will meet torque-out strength requirements; however, additional engineering analysis will be required to validate this.

The Value Team also considered modifying the upper restraint housing; however, this effort was abandoned due to prohibitive tooling costs for stamping. It is recommended that alternate materials, methods, and suppliers for top restraint housing be continuously evaluated, as this component contributes significantly to the overall cost of the fluid mount assembly.

	SKETCHES		
	FL-500 Series Fluid Mount		
TITLE: Low Impact Modifications to Fluid Mount		**NUMBER** 1	**PAGE NO.** 3 of 4

Baseline Concept

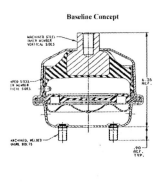

Alternative Concept

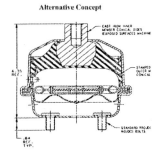

PERFORMANCE ASSESSMENT
FL-500 Series Fluid Mount

TITLE: Low Impact Modifications to Fluid Mount	NUMBER 1	PAGE NO. 4 of 4

PERFORMANCE RATIONALE for ALTERNATIVE	Performance	Baseline	Alternative
RATED LOAD: There are two modifications that were made to the unit that could affect the rated load. These include using a cast iron inner member and projection welded studs. Based on the Value Team's preliminary load calculations, there does not appear to be any change in the existing unit's maximum rated load of 900 lbs. Additional engineering analysis of the projection-welded studs will be required to validate these initial calculations.	Rating	7.0	7.0
	Weight	38	38
	Contribution	266	266
ISOLATION EFFICIENCY: There should be a slight improvement in the unit's isolation efficiency created by the design changes to the inner sleeve. The Value Team calculates that the conical sides of the inner member will achieve an improvement in vibration dampening of approximately 10%.	Rating	4	5
	Weight	50	50
	Contribution	200	250
RELIABILITY: The Value Team does not anticipate any change in the overall reliability of the unit.	Rating	4.0	4.0
	Weight	12	12
	Contribution	48	48
		514	564
	Net Change in Performance:		+9.73%

VALUE ALTERNATIVE
FL-500 Series Fluid Mount

FUNCTION:	Dampen Vibration	**ALTERNATIVE NO.** 2
TITLE:	High Impact Modifications to Fluid Mount	**PAGE NO.** 1 of 4

BASELINE CONCEPT:

The FL-500 Series Fluid Mounts are completely fabricated and assembled in-house. The outer housing is made of stamped steel, while the inner housing is made of machined steel. The mounting studs on the bottom of the unit consist of machined and welded knurled bolts.

ALTERNATIVE CONCEPT:

The alternative concept includes a number of major (high impact) modifications to the existing design that will create significant tooling impacts. The changes consist of:

- Replace machined steel inner member with a cast iron inner member.
- Replace machined bolts that are welded to the bottom of the housing with projection-welded nuts (open-ended with plastic cap). Internal threads requested by customer.
- Increase length of bottom housing by ½ inch to allow room for the capped nuts and add wire groove.
- Add length and bend to outer member and assemble by crimping outer member to bottom housing.
- Add wire and plate assembly for inexpensive failsafe function. Emboss assembly part number in top compliance and eliminate ink stamp and clear coat.

ADVANTAGES:

- Significant cost savings
- Allows retrofit of the FM-500-7
- Eliminates need for ink stamping part number
- Provides capability of adding a failsafe
- Improves vibration isolation efficiency by 10%

DISADVANTAGES:

- Tooling costs are $35,000
- Additional engineering analysis is required to validate strength of projection-welded studs, crimp strength, and cable/plate assembly
- Bolts can't penetrate more than ½" into mount

COST / PERFORMANCE SUMMARY

	Material	Labor	Burden	TOTAL
Baseline	$ 61.14	$ 7.07	$ 13.41	$ 81.62
Alternative	$ 21.96	$ 6.98	$ 13.19	$ 42.13

Change in Cost	-48.38%	**Savings Per Unit**		$ 39.49
Change in Performance	+9.73%	**Gross Savings (Qty. x $/Unit)**		$ 98,725
CHANGE IN VALUE	+112.58%	**Implementation Costs**		$ 35,000
		NET SAVINGS		$ 63,725

VALUE ALTERNATIVE
FL-500 Series Fluid Mount

TITLE:	High Impact Modifications to Fluid Mount	NUMBER	PAGE NO.
		2	2 of 4

DISCUSSION / JUSTIFICATION:

Once Value Alternative #1 was completed, the Value Team felt that additional improvements were possible if the paradigm created by the Performance Requirement of maintaining the baseline dimensions was challenged.

The Value Team recommends replacing the machined steel inner member with a cast iron inner member (the exposed surfaces would still be machined). The length of inner member would be reduced by ½ inch to accommodate the new plate and cable failsafe assembly. The top of inner member will require some additional machining to allow the slip fit of the new plate assembly.

The machined bolts that are welded to the bottom of the housing would be replaced with projection-welded nuts that would be open-ended and include a plastic cap. Internal threads have been added in response to customer requests. The plastic cap will protects diaphragm from damage. An added benefit is that the customer can provide their own bolts to allow for variations in base thickness of the mounting surface. Dome nuts are preferred, but they are expensive and must have a smooth top surface to prevent damage to the diaphragm. The bottom housing must be increased by ½ inch to allow room for the capped nuts.

Add length and bend to outer member and assemble by crimping outer member to bottom housing.* Note that the new tooling required for this alternative on the outer member should be interchangeable with tooling for the FL-500-13 outer member (i.e., it should be able to handle the extra length and bend).

A wire groove would be added to the bottom housing (can also be incorporated as part of Alternative #1).*

A wire and plate assembly can be added to provide an optional, inexpensive failsafe function.* The failsafe function will keep the equipment secured to the mounting surface in the event the fluid mount unit should fail. (This is a function that only some customers appear to be interested in – the failsafe feature is a customer option at an additional cost of $3.78). It is anticipated that the addition of this optional feature will increase the marketability of the unit by meeting customer requirements for new applications by approximately 500 more units.

The assembly part number can be embossed on the top housing, thereby eliminating the need to ink stamp and clear coat. As an additional benefit, the customer can paint the unit without covering identification markings.

Additional engineering analysis will be required to validate the torque-out strength of the projection-welded studs, crimp strength of the outer member, and installation of the cable plate assembly.

Note: Allows elimination of top restraint housing.

SKETCHES		
FL-500 Series Fluid Mount		
TITLE: High Impact Modifications to Fluid Mount	NUMBER 2	PAGE NO. 3 of 4

Baseline Concept

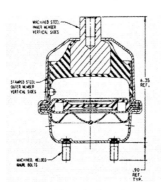

Alternative Concept

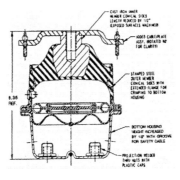

PERFORMANCE ASSESSMENT *FL-500 Series Fluid Mount*				
TITLE: High Impact Modifications to Fluid Mount	**NUMBER** 2		**PAGE NO.** 4 of 4	
PERFORMANCE RATIONALE for ALTERNATIVE	Performance	Baseline	Alternative	
RATED LOAD: There are two modifications that were made to the unit that could affect the rated load. These include using a cast iron inner member and projection-welded studs. Based on the Value Team's preliminary load calculations, there does not appear to be any change in the existing unit's maximum rated load of 900 lbs. Additional engineering analysis of the projection-welded studs will be required to validate these initial calculations.	Rating	7.0	7.0	
	Weight	38	38	
	Contribution	266	266	
ISOLATION EFFICIENCY: There should be a slight improvement in the unit's isolation efficiency created by the design changes to the inner sleeve. The Value Team calculates that the conical sides of the inner member will achieve an improvement in vibration dampening of approximately 10%.	Rating	4.0	5.0	
	Weight	50	50	
	Contribution	200	250	
RELIABILITY: The value team does not anticipate any change in the overall reliability of the unit. The addition of the failsafe (plate and cable assembly) option will keep the equipment secured to the mounting surface in the event the fluid mount unit fails; however, it will not increase the service life of the unit.	Rating	4.0	4.0	
	Weight	12	12	
	Contribution	48	48	
		514	564	
	Net Change in Performance:		+9.73%	

DESIGN & CONSTRUCTION CASE STUDY—EMERGENCY OPERATIONS CENTER

Project Description:

The subject of this value study was the design and construction of a new emergency operations center (EOC) building. This new facility will replace an existing facility that is located in the basement of a large office building. Due to significant growth in the region over the past decade, and the fact that the existing EOC is located in a building that does not meet the seismic requirements of the state's Essential Services Facility Act, a new, larger facility is required.

The purpose of the EOC is to receive and develop a response to 911 emergency calls and to coordinate and control fire and law enforcement resources during a catastrophe (i.e., earthquake, flood, etc.) Due to the criticality of this facility, it must be designed to withstand a variety of natural disasters. In addition, the facility must be resistant to terrorist threats. The information and communications systems that will be contained in this building will require a high level of physical and technological security to prevent unauthorized access.

Baseline Concept:

- Baseline Gross Square Feet = 44,805 gsf
- Cost per GSF = $300/gsf
- Total Project Costs = $25,000,000
- Structural System

  o Base isolated foundation
  o Braced steel frame
  o No fireproofing on steel frame
  o Pad footings with grade beams

- o Two stories
- o 20 foot floor to floor height

- ♦ **Exterior Enclosure**

    - o Composite metal panels
    - o Non-operable windows
    - o Flat roof with single ply membrane
    - o Formal entry feature

- ♦ **Interior Finishes**

    - o Metal studs with gypsum board sheathing
    - o Level 5 corridor finishes
    - o Suspended ceiling
    - o Raised access floors in equipment areas
    - o Ceramic tile in bathrooms
    - o Single elevator
    - o Moveable partitions in some areas

- ♦ **Plumbing**

    - o Fire sprinkler system
    - o 12 toilet fixtures
    - o bathroom and kitchen sinks
    - o Potable water system with storage tank

- ♦ **Mechanical Systems**

    - o Standard HVAC system for main building
    - o Separate HVAC system for critical areas
    - o Redundant chiller
    - o Central vacuum system
    - o Humidification system
    - o Return air plenum in ceiling

- Electrical System

  - o 1 primary power feed
  - o Emergency generator
  - o Diesel fuel tank w/capacity for 72 hours of emergency operation
  - o UPS system (30 minutes power)
  - o 3 separate electrical distribution systems for normal, emergency and critical power
  - o Recessed lighting with dimmer controls

- Internal Security

  - o Doors with card readers (multiple security levels)
  - o CPU room enclosed in fire-rated room
  - o CCTV in corridors

- External Security

  - o Perimeter fence (7-feet high)
  - o Building and pole mounted CCTV
  - o Security gate w/card reader and intercom
  - o Separate visitor parking outside security fence

- Communications

  - o 100-foot tall radio tower

- Site Work

  - o 100 staff parking spaces
  - o 20 visitor parking spaces
  - o 200 park and ride spaces
  - o Storm water retention ponds
  - o Landscaping

o   Access roadway

Value Study Objectives:

This value study was conducted at the concept stage of the design process, prior to the development of preliminary drawings and specifications. The objectives of the value study are to validate the project scope in conjunction with the user group; ensure that the current project budget will satisfy the scope; and to identify alternative concepts that will improve value.

Performance Requirements:

The following performance requirements were identified:

- Must meet Essential Service Facilities Act requirements
- Must meet state building manual (SBM) guidelines
- Building finish floor elevation must be located above the 100-year floodplain
- Building must comply with city and county planning and building standards
- The existing site location must be maintained

Performance Attributes:

Five performance attributes were identified at this stage of the design process. These include:

- *Functionality*—The capacity of the facility to meet the user's functional requirements (i.e., size and intended use of space). This attribute considers:

    o   Size of spaces relative to the original program document (total square footage)

- *Survivability*—The capacity of the facility to remain operable after experiencing a catastrophic event such as:

  o Earthquake
  o Weather event (i.e., thunder storm, high winds, flood, etc.)
  o Fire
  o Explosion or small arms fire

- *Human Factors*—The optimization of the interface between people, technology and the facility. This attribute considers such issues as:

  o Ergonomics
  o Lighting Design
  o User-Friendliness of Technology

- *Maintainability*—An approximation of the impact on the facility's annual maintenance and operations costs over a 50-year period.

- *Security*—An approximation of the overall level of security for the site and facility. Issues to be considered under this attribute include:

  o Site Lighting and Security Fencing
  o Buffer Zones / Landscaping
  o Surveillance Monitoring
  o Locks
  o Security of data and communications systems
  o Vehicular Control

Provided below is an assessment of the performance of the baseline concept.

Performance Attributes Baseline Concept	
Functionality	The baseline concept should provide a satisfactory level of functionality. The building layout will fully comply with SAM guidelines and should meet the spatial requirements for transportation, fire and police personnel.
Survivability	The baseline concept's design will meet the survivability requirements outlined in the Essential Services Act. It is anticipated that the new EOC will be a base-isolated structure in order to resist seismic events and will also include an emergency generator and potable water supply.
Human Factors	The baseline concept should perform at a satisfactory level with respect to ergonomic design features and user comfort.
Maintainability	The new EOC is anticipated to be a low maintenance facility. Finishes will be simple, yet durable and easy to maintain. The high HVAC demands of this facility will increase operational costs, however.
Security	The new EOC will meet basic security requirements. CCTV monitoring will be provided on site and in main corridors. A perimeter security fence will be installed to secure employee parking. Card key locks will be used within the building to restrict access in sensitive areas.

Table C-3

Due to the rather broad and qualitative nature of the attributes selected, a standard comparative scale was used for all five of the performance attributes where the baseline concept provides the basis for comparing the performance of the alternative concepts:

Performance Attribute Scale
10—Alternative Concept is extremely preferred. 9—Alternative Concept is very strongly preferred. 8—Alternative Concept is strongly preferred. 7—Alternative Concept is moderately preferred. 6—Alternative Concept is slightly preferred. 5—Alternative Concept and Baseline Concept are equally preferred. 4—Baseline Concept is slightly preferred. 3—Baseline Concept is moderately preferred. 2—Baseline Concept is strongly preferred. 1—Baseline Concept is very strongly preferred. 0—Baseline Concept is extremely preferred.

Relative Importance of Performance Attributes:

A scaled paired-comparison was utilized to determine the relative importance of the five performance attributes in meeting the user's requirements (i.e., the project's purpose and need). *Maintainability* was the least important of the three attributes. The scoring was adjusted by adding a point to each of the attributes scores to derive the relative attribute weights.

PERFORMANCE CRITERIA MATRIX
Emergency Operations Center

						TOTAL	%
Functionality	**A**	A	A	A	A	5.0	34%
Survivability		**B**	B/C	B	B	3.5	23%
Human Factors			**C**	C	C	3.5	23%
Maintainability				**D**	E	1.0	7%
Security					**E**	2.0	13%

A	More Important
A/B	Equal Importance

15.0	100%

Fig. C-7

Value of Baseline Concept:

A Value Matrix was developed utilizing the data developed for performance and cost. The Value Matrix utilized the total project costs (including furnishings, equipment, right-of-way and project development) for the cost side of the value equation.

FUNDAMENTALS OF VALUE METHODOLOGY

VALUE MATRIX
Emergency Operations Center

Attribute	Attribute Weight	Concept	Performance Rating 1	2	3	4	5	6	7	8	9	10	Total Performance
Functionality	34	Baseline Concept					5						170
													0
													0
													0
													0
Survivability	23	Baseline Concept					5						115
													0
													0
													0
Human Factors	23	Baseline Concept					5						115
													0
													0
													0
Maintainability	7	Baseline Concept					5						35
													0
													0
													0
Security	13	Baseline Concept					5						65
													0
													0
													0

Overall Performance Alternative	Total Performance	% Performance Improvement	Total Cost ($ millions)	Value Index (P/C)	% Value Improvement
Baseline Concept	500		25.00	20.00	

Fig. C-8

Function Analysis:

Function analysis was performed and a FAST Diagram was produced, which revealed the key functional relationships for the EOC facility. This analysis provided a greater understanding of the total project and how the issues, cost, and function requirements are related.

The FAST diagram shows TRANSMIT DATA as the basic function, with key supporting secondary functions of RECEIVE DATA, EVALUATE DATA, and VERIFY EVENT. The basic function and the three supporting secondary functions all relate directly to the EOC's primary control room. The $3.7 million cost identified on the FAST diagram for EVALUATE DATA encompasses the control room costs and would otherwise be distributed equally among these four functions. Two key project objectives included MAINTAIN SECURITY and ENSURE RELIABILITY. The FAST diagram indicates that the function PROTECT DATA is contributing greatly to the overall cost of the project while having only a minor contribution to the performance attributes of *Survivability* and *Maintainability*.

FUNDAMENTALS OF VALUE METHODOLOGY 399

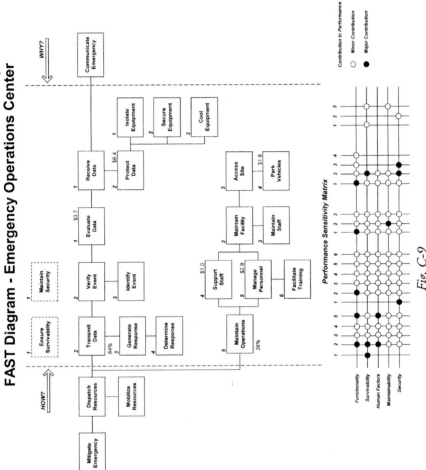

Fig. C-9

Value Alternatives:

The Value Team developed 21 value alternatives for improvement to the project. Key value alternatives included:

- Utilize a CMU Finish for the Building Exterior
- Place HVAC Distribution Below Floor
- Provide Integrated Audio/Visual System
- Provide Two Separate Power Feeds from Different Grids
- Place Vehicle Barriers Around the Building Perimeter

The net potential benefits of the recommended value alternatives would result in initial cost savings of approximately $1,850,000, life cycle cost savings of $5,050,000, performance improvements of 45%. These benefits amount to a net improvement in project value of 57%.

VALUE MATRIX
Emergency Operations Center

Attribute	Attribute Weight	Concept	Performance Rating 1-10	Total Performance
Functionality	34	Baseline Concept	5	170
		Recommended Alts.	6	204
				0
				0
				0
Survivability	23	Baseline Concept	5	115
		Recommended Alts.	8	184
				0
				0
				0
Human Factors	23	Baseline Concept	5	115
		Recommended Alts.	8	184
				0
				0
				0
Maintainability	7	Baseline Concept	5	35
		Recommended Alts.	7	49
				0
				0
				0
Security	13	Baseline Concept	5	65
		Recommended Alts.	8	104
				0
				0
				0

Overall Performance Alternative	Total Performance	% Performance Improvement	Total Cost ($ millions)	Value Index (P/C)	% Value Improvement
Baseline Concept	500		25.00	20.00	
Recommended Alternatives	725	45%	23.15	31.32	57%

Fig. C-10

Implementation Plan:

Following the submission of the preliminary written Value Study Report, the project team reviewed the content of each value alternative. An implementation meeting was held to determine which of the value alternatives would be incorporated into design development. Nine of the original twenty-one value alternatives were accepted. An implementation action form was prepared for each alternative describing the actions that will be taken. The rationale for the rejection of those alternatives that were not accepted is also identified on these forms.

Two of the alternatives that were accepted are provided on the following pages.

VALUE ALTERNATIVE
Emergency Operations Center

FUNCTION:	Enclose Space	IDEA NO. ES-17	NUMBER 1.1
TITLE:	Utilize a CMU Finish for the Building Exterior		PAGE NO. 1 of 7

BASELINE CONCEPT:

The baseline concept would provide a metal panel exterior skin for the building. The metal panels provide a durable exterior finish that is less likely to inhibit dust collection. A braced structural frame would be provided to accommodate lateral building loads.

ALTERNATIVE CONCEPT:

The alternative concept would provide a Concrete Masonry Unit (CMU) exterior for the building. A variety of finishes are available, from split face to glazed finish. The CMU walls would act as shear walls, thereby eliminating the need for the braced frame to resist lateral loads.

ADVANTAGES:
- Improves resistance to damage or intrusion
- Superior thermal performance
- No painting required
- CMU can also be used as a shear system, reducing or eliminating the need for a braced frame system
- Natural colors will hide dust better than metal panel

DISADVANTAGES:
- Requires furring
- Less "high-tech" in appearance
- Some finishes (such as split face) may collect more dust than metal panel
- Requires periodic sealing of CMU (every 10 years)
- Requires additional structural analysis

COST SUMMARY	Initial Cost	Present Value Subsequent Cost	Net Present Value
Original Concept	$ 3,737,000	$ 0	$ 3,730,000
Alternative Concept	$ 1,658,000	$ 30,000	$ 1,688,000
Savings	$ 2,079,000	$ (30,000)	$ 2,049,000

| Team Member: | David Long | Discipline: | Architect | PERFORMANCE: | +3% |

VALUE ALTERNATIVE		
Emergency Operations Center		
TITLE: Utilize a CMU Finish for the Building Exterior	NUMBER 1.1	PAGE NO. 2 of 7

DISCUSSION / JUSTIFICATION:

As an integral portion of the EOC, the building is expected to be in service for 50 years. Concrete block masonry (CMU) is a durable product which has had proven performance in excess of this time period. In the warm environment of the Southwest, CMU has superior thermal mass and will provide superior insulation value. In addition, due to recent concerns that the EOC could be a target for terrorism, CMU is more resistant to damage from projectiles and explosives.

The CMU can also act as a shear wall, providing lateral bracing for the facility and allowing the reduction or elimination of the required structural bracing.

While a number of alternative exterior finishes are being considered, CMU appears to be the most cost effective and durable product. CMU comes in a variety of finishes that should be considered during the design phase if selected. Burnished, split face, glazed and patterned block provide attractive finishes and may be considered in the latter stages of the design process.

The CMU would require sealing (waterproofing) every 10 years. Assuming a 50-year building life, this results in a present worth cost increase of only $30,000.

TECHNICAL REVIEWER COMMENTS:

PROJECT MANAGEMENT CONSIDERATIONS:

At this early stage of the design, there should be no significant project management issues to contend with.

SKETCHES		
Emergency Operations Center		
TITLE: Utilize a CMU Finish for the Building Exterior	NUMBER 1.1	PAGE NO. 3 of 7

Baseline Concept (Example of Metal Panel System)

Alternative Concept (Example of a CMU System)

PERFORMANCE ASSESSMENT			
Emergency Operations Center			
TITLE: Utilize a CMU Finish for the Building Exterior	**NUMBER** 1.1		**PAGE NO.** 4 of 7
PERFORMANCE RATIONALE for ALTERNATIVE	Performance	Baseline	Alternative
FUNCTIONALITY: Use of CMU exterior does not affect the functionality of the facility.	Rating	5	5
	Weight	34	34
	Contribution	170	170
SURVIVABILITY: Use of CMU should increase survivability of the facility due to the increased durability of the surface and its improved resistance to damage.	Rating	5	6
	Weight	13	13
	Contribution	65	78
HUMAN FACTORS: With proper use of insulation, use of CMU exterior should not affect the human factors related to the facility.	Rating	5	5
	Weight	23	23
	Contribution	115	115
MAINTAINABILITY: The CMU and metal panel systems will have similar maintenance requirements. Both systems are relatively low maintenance. The CMU will require resealing every 10 years or so; however, the metal panels will require periodic maintenance of the joints between the panels. Both will be easy to keep clean and neither should require painting. Metal panels are more likely to be dented or damaged, especially in high traffic areas.	Rating	5	5
	Weight	7	7
	Contribution	35	35
SECURITY: No significant change.	Rating	5	5
	Weight	23	23
	Contribution	115	115
		500	513
	Net Change in Performance:		+3%

ASSUMPTIONS & CALCULATIONS		
Emergency Operations Center		
TITLE: Utilize a CMU Finish for the Building Exterior	NUMBER 1.1	PAGE NO. 5 of 7

Cost Estimating Assumptions

All costs are based on similar current unit costs provided by a professional cost estimator.

Metal panel cost is assumed at $38-$40 per square foot installed, which includes a vapor permeable water-resistant substrate on an exterior gypsum sheathing behind the panel.

Metal panels are installed on a structural stud support system. Insulation is placed in the stud cavity. CMU walls are self-supporting, and insulation is placed in a lighter gauge furring stud system behind the block wall. The premium for structural studs is assumed at $4 per sf. All other components of the system are assumed to be similar.

Requirements for structural steel for the lateral bracing system are assumed at 22 lbs/sf for the braced frame system required for the metal panel building and 10 lbs./sf for the system, which relies on the CMU for shear support.

Life Cycle Assumptions

Assume the CMU would need to be resealed every 10 years at a cost of $0.50 sf for 30,000 sf of wall area, which equates to a cost of $15,000.

FUNDAMENTALS OF VALUE METHODOLOGY

INITIAL COSTS
Emergency Operations Center

TITLE: Utilize a CMU Finish for the Building Exterior					NUMBER 1.1	PAGE NO. 6 of 7	
CONSTRUCTION ELEMENT		BASELINE CONCEPT			ALTERNATIVE CONCEPT		
Description	Unit	Quantity	Cost/Unit	Total	Quantity	Cost/Unit	Total
BUILDING ITEMS							
Metal Panel Exterior walls (Architectural Finish)	SF	29,935	$38	$1,137,530			
Metal Panel structural exterior stud upgrade	SF	29,935	$4	$119,740			
CMU Exterior walls (Architectural Finish)	SF				29,935	$18	$538,830
Lateral system cost (22lb. Vs. 10 lb./SF)	Ton	495	$3,500	$1,732,500	225	$3,500	$787,500
BUILDING SUBTOTAL				*$2,989,770*			*$1,326,330*
BUILDING MARK-UP		25%		*$747,443*			*$331,583*
VA ADDED MARK-UP							
BUILDING TOTAL				*$3,737,213*			*$1,657,913*
SITE DEVELOPMENT							
SITE DEVELOPMENT SUBTOTAL							
SITE DEVELOPMENT MARK-UP							
VA ADDED MARK-UP							
SITE DEVELOPMENT TOTAL							
RIGHT-OF-WAY ITEMS							
Right-of-Way Acquisition							
Utility Relocation							
Relocation Assistance							
Demolition							
Title and Escrow Fees							
RIGHT-OF-WAY TOTAL							
ENVIRONMENTAL MITIGATION ITEMS							
CAPITAL OUTLAY SUPPORT ITEMS							
Reengineering and Redesign							
Project Engineering							
TOTAL				$3,737,213			$1,657,913
TOTAL (Rounded)				$3,737,000			$1,658,000
						SAVINGS	$2,079,000

LIFE CYCLE COSTS
Emergency Operations Center

TITLE:	Utilize a CMU Finsish for the Building Exterior				NUMBER 1.1	PAGE NO. 7 of 7
Life Cycle Period __50__ Years			Real Discount Rate __3.00%__		BASELINE	ALTERNATIVE
A. INITIAL COST					$3,737,000	$1,658,000
Service Life-Original	__50__	Years	**INITIAL COST SAVINGS:**			$2,079,000
Service Life-Alternative	__50__	Years				
B. SUBSEQUENT ANNUAL COSTS						
1. Maintenance and Inspection						
2. Operating						
3. Energy						
			Total Subsequent Annual Costs:		$0	$0
			Present Value Factor (P/A):		25.730	25.730
	PRESENT VALUE OF SUBSEQUENT ANNUAL COSTS (Rounded):				$0	$0
C. SUBSEQUENT SINGLE COSTS		Year	Amount	PV Factor (P/F)	Present Value	Present Value
					$0	
CMU Sealant		10	15,000			$11,161
					$0	
CMU Sealant		20	15,000			$8,305
					$0	
CMU Sealant		10	15,000			$6,180
					$0	
CMU Sealant		10	15,000			$4,598
	PRESENT VALUE OF SUBSEQUENT SINGLE COSTS (Rounded):				$0	$30,000
D. TOTAL SUBSEQUENT ANNUAL AND SINGLE COSTS (B+C)					$0	$30,000
			TOTAL SUBSEQUENT COSTS SAVINGS:			($30,000)
E. HIGHWAY USER ANNUAL COSTS					Present Value	Present Value
1. Accident						
2. Travel Time						
3. Vehicle Operating						
			TOTAL HIGHWAY USER ANNUAL COSTS:		$0	$0
			TOTAL HIGHWAY USER COST SAVINGS:			$0
F. TOTAL PRESENT VALUE COST (A+D+E)					$3,737,000	$1,688,000
				TOTAL LIFE CYCLE SAVINGS:		$2,049,000

VALUE ALTERNATIVE IMPLEMENTATION ACTION
Emergency Operations Center

TITLE: Utilize a CMU Finish for the Building Exterior

NUMBER 1.1

RESPONSES	**Prepared by:** Ed Snyder, Project Mgr.	**Date:** 9/15/04
Technical Feasibility / Validated Performance		**DISPOSITION**
This alternative was accepted by the Project Team. The use of CMU is compatible with the base isolation system proposed for this facility. The Project Team concurs with the Value Team's assessment of the improvement to the building's durability and survivability.		☑ Accept ☐ Conditionally Accept ☐ Reject
Implementable Portions		**Validated Performance**
This alternative will be implemented as initially presented by the Value Team.		+2%
Validated Cost Savings		**Validated Savings**
The initial cost savings identified by the Value Team is a reasonable estimate for this early stage of design development. The savings realized from this alternative will permit the implementation of other value alternatives that will increase project costs but improve performance. There will be no additional project development costs due to the early stage of the design.		$2,079,000 **Project Development Cost Savings** ($150,000)

Project Schedule Impact	Project Phase	No Change	Reduced by	Increased by
No significant change.	Planning	☑		
	Prelim. Concept	☑		
	Final Concept	☑		
	Acquisition	☑		

Other Comments
None.

VALUE ALTERNATIVE
Emergency Operations Center

FUNCTION:	Maintain Operations	IDEA NO. MO-7	NUMBER 3.0
TITLE:	Place HVAC Distribution Under Floor		PAGE NO. 1 of 9

BASELINE CONCEPT:
Project is assumed with traditional overhead duct distribution in office areas. Air distribution in computer and communication rooms is through self-contained redundant systems in the room, which supply air to equipment through an access floor system. Access flooring systems are assumed for the control room, EOC, ERC, computer rooms, and communication rooms.

ALTERNATIVE CONCEPT:
The alternative concept would increase the area of access flooring and utilize under-floor air distribution to areas beyond the equipment rooms to improve flexibility and efficiency. Individual HVAC controls would be provided at control room workstations for control of ventilation volume and enhanced control.

ADVANTAGES:
- Provides better air conditioning for equipment
- Reduces HVAC load by providing more efficient distribution of air at a higher temperature and lower velocity
- Improves flexibility in office areas
- Allows reduction in ceiling plenum height and overall building height
- Eliminates transitions between access floor and standard floor
- Provides life cycle savings
- Greater individual control at workstations
- Reduces "churn" cost associated with workstation relocation

DISADVANTAGES:
- Increases initial costs
- Requires more access floor, which increases cost

COST SUMMARY	Initial Cost	Present Value Subsequent Cost	Net Present Value
Original Concept	$ 453,000	$ 0	$ 453,000
Alternative Concept	$ 830,000	$ (2,088,000)	$ (1,258,000)
Savings	$ (377,000)	$ 2,088,000	$ 1,711,000

Team Member:	Janet Thayer	Discipline:	Mechanical Engineer	PERFORMANCE:	+27%

VALUE ALTERNATIVE			
Emergency Operations Center			
TITLE:	Place HVAC Distribution Under Floor	**NUMBER** 3.0	**PAGE NO.** 2 of 9

DISCUSSION / JUSTIFICATION:

Under-floor distribution of ventilation (known as displacement ventilation) is generally considered to be a more effective method of ventilating space. Cool air is introduced into the space from floor diffusers and rises to ceiling return diffusers using natural convection current. Cooling is more efficient because only the occupied area from the floor-to-head height needs to stay at comfort temperature. Most systems also provide vents, which can be controlled by individual occupants, allowing better comfort control and corresponding increase in productivity. Vents can also be placed at each workstation, providing ventilation right at heat sources. In addition, overall cooling loads and associated equipment and energy costs are reduced.

Also included in this alternative review is the possible integration of a workstation console in the control rooms with individual ventilation and heating panels to further enhance comfort and productivity.

TECHNICAL REVIEWER COMMENTS:

PROJECT MANAGEMENT CONSIDERATIONS:

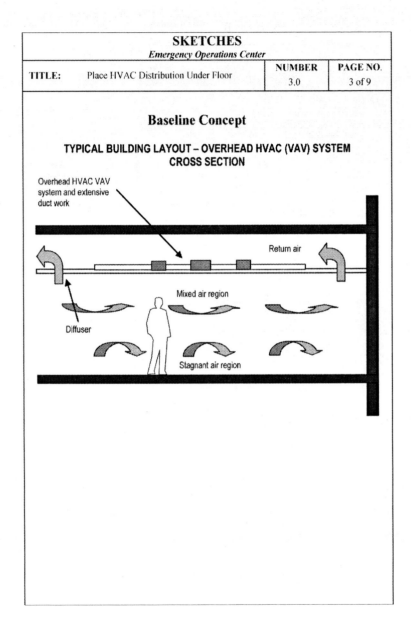

FUNDAMENTALS OF VALUE METHODOLOGY

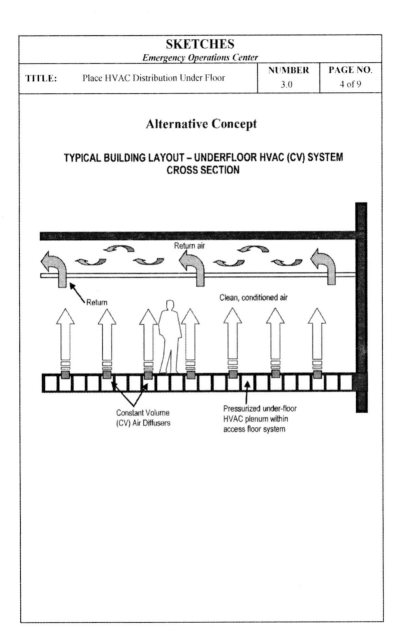

SKETCHES			
Emergency Operations Center			
TITLE:	Place HVAC Distribution Under Floor	NUMBER 3.0	PAGE NO. 5 of 9

Alternative Concept

PERFORMANCE ASSESSMENT
Emergency Operations Center

TITLE: Place HVAC Distribution Under Floor	NUMBER 3.0		PAGE NO. 6 of 9
PERFORMANCE RATIONALE for ALTERNATIVE	Performance	Baseline	Alternative
FUNCTIONALITY: Use of access floor in all work areas may increase functionality by allowing ease of reconfiguration of workstations and easier cable and power modifications if required.	Rating	5	6.5
	Weight	34	34
	Contribution	170	221
SURVIVABILITY: No significant change.	Rating	5	5
	Weight	13	13
	Contribution	65	65
HUMAN FACTORS: Allowing environmental controls at each workstation should provide a significant improvement to user comfort and productivity within the control room.	Rating	5	8
	Weight	23	23
	Contribution	115	184
MAINTAINABILITY: Access floor system increases flexibility to reconfigure workstations and provides easier access to cabling and power for future changes or repairs.	Rating	5	7
	Weight	7	7
	Contribution	35	49
SECURITY: No significant change.	Rating	5	5
	Weight	23	23
	Contribution	115	115
		500	634
	Net Change in Performance:		**+27%**

ASSUMPTIONS & CALCULATIONS
Emergency Operations Center

TITLE:	Place HVAC Distribution Under Floor	NUMBER 3.0	PAGE NO. 7 of 9

Cost Estimating Assumptions

Cost comparison is based on a reduction of building height of 12" per floor. A reduction in air conditioning equipment and ducting of 25% and a decrease in HVAC load of 20% and a base cost for access floor systems of $8.00/SF. Computer and communication rooms are assumed to have separate HVAC and access floor systems and are excluded from this survey (deduct 4,870 sf). Bathrooms, locker rooms, mechanical, electrical, and janitorial rooms are also assumed as not raised (deduct 5,000 sf). Structural reductions are based on a 40' x 40' structural grid (24 columns. total). Savings for electrical and cabling, while possible, are difficult to quantify at this early a stage and are excluded.

The cost premium for workstation consoles with individual HVAC controls is approximately $5,000.

Life Cycle Cost Assumptions

The following page includes calculations generated by a specific vendor of the underfloor air distribution system. Their calculations include an estimate of energy, as well as productivity savings. The Value Team felt that these calculations were either high or not applicable, and opted not to use all of them in the life cycle cost analysis. Those that were used include:

- Energy Savings = $11,163

Improve Productivity = Assume a reduction in absenteeism for employees working in the control room due to improved air quality and comfort equal to one full-time employee. Assume $70,000.

FUNDAMENTALS OF VALUE METHODOLOGY

INITIAL COSTS
Emergency Operations Center

TITLE	NUMBER	PAGE NO.
Place HVAC Distribution Under Floor	3.0	8 of 9

CONSTRUCTION ELEMENT		BASELINE CONCEPT			ALTERNATIVE CONCEPT		
Description	Unit	Quantity	Cost/Unit	Total	Quantity	Cost/Unit	Total
BUILDING ITEMS							
Exterior Building Walls	SF	1,228	$55	$67,540			
Access Floor	SF				36,300	$8	$290,400
HVAC Systems	SF	36,300	$8	$287,859	36,300	$6	$212,718
Raised Core	SF				5,000	$0	$950
Columns	LF	48	$145	$6,960			
Premium for Consoles w/HVAC Controls	EA				32	$5,000	$160,000
BUILDING SUBTOTAL				*$362,359*			*$664,068*
BUILDING MARK-UP	25%			*$90,590*			*$166,017*
VA ADDED MARK-UP							
BUILDING TOTAL				*$452,949*			*$830,085*
SITE DEVELOPMENT							
SITE DEVELOPMENT SUBTOTAL							
SITE DEVELOPMENT MARK-UP							
VA ADDED MARK-UP							
SITE DEVELOPMENT TOTAL							
RIGHT-OF-WAY ITEMS							
Right-of-Way Acquisition							
Utility Relocation							
Relocation Assistance							
Demolition							
Title and Escrow Fees							
RIGHT-OF-WAY TOTAL							
ENVIRONMENTAL MITIGATION ITEMS							
CAPITAL OUTLAY SUPPORT ITEMS							
Reengineering and Redesign							
Project Engineering							
TOTAL				$452,949			$830,085
TOTAL (Rounded)				$453,000			$830,000
						SAVINGS	($377,000)

LIFE CYCLE COSTS
Emergency Operations Center

TITLE:	Place HVAC Distribution Under Floor					NUMBER 3.0	PAGE NO. 9 of 9
Life Cycle Period	50 Years		Real Discount Rate		3.00%	BASELINE	ALTERNATIVE
A. INITIAL COST						$453,000	$830,000
Service Life-Original		50	Years	INITIAL COST SAVINGS:			($377,000)
Service Life-Alternative		50	Years				
B. SUBSEQUENT ANNUAL COSTS							
1. Maintenance and Inspection							
2. Operating							($70,000)
3. Energy							($11,163)
				Total Subsequent Annual Costs:		$0	($81,163)
				Present Value Factor (P/A):		25.730	25.730
		PRESENT VALUE OF SUBSEQUENT ANNUAL COSTS (Rounded):				$0	($2,088,000)
C. SUBSEQUENT SINGLE COSTS			Year	Amount	PV Factor (P/F)	Present Value	Present Value
						$0	
							$0
						$0	
							$0
						$0	
							$0
						$0	
							$0
		PRESENT VALUE OF SUBSEQUENT SINGLE COSTS (Rounded):				$0	$0
D. TOTAL SUBSEQUENT ANNUAL AND SINGLE COSTS (B+C)						$0	($2,088,000)
				TOTAL SUBSEQUENT COSTS SAVINGS:			$2,088,000
E. HIGHWAY USER ANNUAL COSTS						Present Value	Present Value
1. Accident							
2. Travel Time							
3. Vehicle Operating							
				TOTAL HIGHWAY USER ANNUAL COSTS:		$0	$0
				TOTAL HIGHWAY USER COST SAVINGS:			$0
F. TOTAL PRESENT VALUE COST (A+D+E)						$453,000	($1,258,000)
					TOTAL LIFE CYCLE SAVINGS:		$1,711,000

VALUE ALTERNATIVE IMPLEMENTATION ACTION
Emergency Operations Center

TITLE:	Place HVAC Distribution Under Floor	NUMBER 3.0

RESPONSES	Prepared by: Ed Snyder, Project Mgr.	Date: 9/15/04
Technical Feasibility / Validated Performance This alternative was accepted by the Project Team. The use of under-floor air distribution, per the Value Team's alternative, will significantly improve user comfort, improve flexibility, and reduce operating costs.		**DISPOSITION** ☑ Accept ☐ Conditionally Accept ☐ Reject
Implementable Portions This alternative will be implemented as initially presented by the Value Team.		**Validated Performance** *+27%*
Validated Cost Savings The initial cost savings identified by the Value Team is a reasonable estimate for this early stage of design development. The additional initial construction costs will be more than offset by long-term operational savings. The manager of the current 911 call center concurs with the assessment of reduced absenteeism, based on past experience.		**Validated Savings** ($377,000) *$1,711,000 LCC* **Project Development Cost Savings** $0

Project Schedule Impact	Project Phase	No Change	Reduced by	Increased by
No significant change.	Planning	☑		
	Prelim. Concept	☑		
	Final Concept	☑		
	Acquisition	☑		

Other Comments
None.

MANAGEMENT PROCESSES & PROCEDURES CASE STUDY – HELP DESK

Project Description:

The subject of this value study was the Information Systems (IS) Help Desk Operations for a major state agency that supports computer systems for over 2,600 state employees. IS supports computer operations and network problems with personal computers, Apple computers, Unix workstations, networks, some mainframe applications, and printers throughout the state.

When users experience a computer or network problem, they contact the Help Desk, where the problem is recorded and resolved or assigned to someone on the IS Staff to follow-up on and resolve. Currently, the response times to the user are poor due to the large volume of calls and the limited staff size of IS. In addition, it is believed that there is a pent-up demand for Help Desk services, and that many employees that experience problems do not contact the Help Desk due to their perception that response will be slow.

Value Study Objective:

The objectives of the value study are to improve the IS Help Desk operations so that user "lost time" is reduced by 50%, all calls are responded to within 24 hours, and problems are resolved in a timeframe more acceptable to users. The analysis of the Help Desk log revealed that user "lost time" due to computer problems that are reported to the Help Desk personnel totals over 56 person years (PY) per year. This equates to over $4,000,000 per year.

Analysis of Problem:

Analysis of the Help Desk problem log revealed that over 7,100 calls were logged and resolved annually in District 7. The major sources of problems relate to the e-mail system (projected to be even worse with Lotus Notes versus Groupwise), printers and the network.

The cost model revealed that over $4,000,000 in "lost productive time" is caused because of computer system problems in D-7 annually. This equates to an annual loss of over 56 person years (PY's). In addition, it is consuming almost 15 PY's annually just to respond to and correct these problems.

Existing Process Flow Chart:

A flow chart was developed of the existing Help Desk process as a means for developing a better understanding of how it currently operates.

Function Analysis:

Function analysis was performed and a FAST Diagram was produced, which revealed the key functional relationships for the project. This analysis provided a greater understanding of the total project and how the issues, cost, and function requirements are related.

The FAST diagram shows SUPPORT USERS as the basic function, with key secondary functions of SOLVE PROBLEMS, MAINTAIN SYSTEMS, UPGRADE SYSTEMS, COORDINATE USER RELOCATIONS, and UNDERSTAND USER NEEDS. The discussion during the development of the FAST Diagram revealed the majority of time is spent SOLVING PROBLEMS, and IS has little time available to address their required other functions. Most of the work in these areas comes as a result of user problems instead of pro-active steps that avoid user problems and downtime.

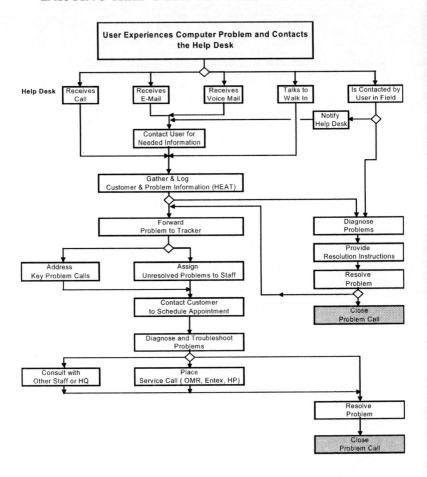

Fig. C-11

FUNDAMENTALS OF VALUE METHODOLOGY 423

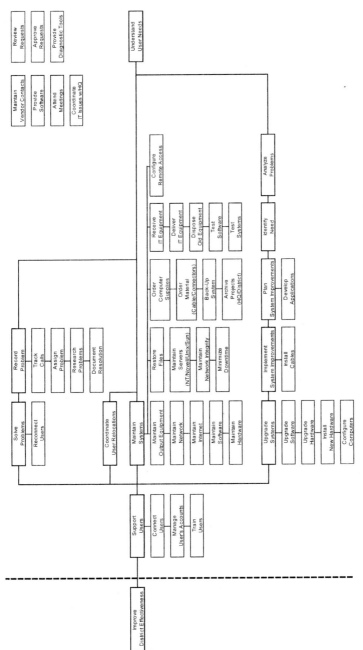

Fig. C-12

Value Alternatives:

The Value Team developed thirty-one value alternatives for improvement to the project. The value alternatives affect six areas:

- IT – Information Technology/Information Services Actions
- U – User Group Actions
- Pr – Procedures
- H – Hardware
- B – Building Related Items

Implementation of the value alternatives could result in exceeding the target to reduce lost time by over 50%, and as much as $3,800,000 in annual productivity improvements could be realized. The value alternatives address actions that will:

1. Reduce or avoid the occurrence of current problems
2. Allow problems to be resolved more quickly
3. Respond quicker to user's problems

Much of the lost time cost is due to the fact there is not enough personnel in IS Help Desk to support the number of calls being received. For each qualified person added to the IS Help Desk, the net reduction in "lost time" costs to the state is ~$300,000. Three of the most critical value alternatives are included in this section.

Implementation Plan:

Four priorities have been established for the implementation of the value alternatives. The priorities are based on the resources required to implement and the level of decision necessary to proceed. These priorities are:

1. What IS can do within their current operating constraints.
2. Requires upper management involvement or approval – low implementation cost/risk.
3. Requires upper management involvement or approval – higher implementation cost/risk.
4. Requires state agency director's approval.

Once the stakeholders have reviewed the alternatives and provided their feedback regarding each item, IS Help Desk will finalize the implementation plan for the approved value alternatives.

A recommended way to reach consensus between the stakeholders on which value alternatives will be implemented and the priority given that alternative for implementation, is to conduct a facilitated implementation meeting with all stakeholders present. Inviting selected Value Team members to the meeting will ensure a full understanding of the value alternatives. The value specialist guides the decision-making process so the stakeholders can agree to accept, conditionally accept, or reject each idea presented in the Value Study Report. Other implementation categories may be appropriate, depending on the status of the design effort.

It is important to note that resources are needed to accomplish the implementation of these items, and currently the lack of resources is the main concern of the IS group. Considering the benefits, management may need to approve added resources in order to gain the benefits of the study.

VALUE ALTERNATIVE
Help Desk

TITLE: Develop Broad Knowledge Base in IT Personnel	NUMBER IT-1	PAGE NO. 1 of 3

ALTERNATIVE CONCEPT:
Provide extensive on-the-job and formal training to all desktop and Unix support staff. The training will cover all areas that support staff might encounter when responding to and solving end user problems. The goal is to make each staff person self-sufficient and capable of individually supporting a small to medium IS shop. Build skill level in desktop, network, server, Unix, and telecommunications support.

CURRENT PROBLEM THIS WILL RESOLVE:
The problem is that the staff has not obtained the knowledge to self-sufficiently handle all problems encountered. The staff relies on each other to resolve some problems that increase the time and resources necessary to find resolutions.

ADVANTAGES:
- More efficient service
- Increases overall staff IT knowledge
- Increases capability
- Reduces use downtime
- Improves IT image and professionalism
- Better response to more complex problems

DISADVANTAGES:
- Increases time necessary to develop training plan
- Increases time necessary to provide training
- Increases time necessary to attend training
- Adds cost of formal training

COST / PERFORMANCE SUMMARY

Benefit Summary	User Time Lost (Annual $)	IT Time Expended (Annual $)	Cost to Effect Change	Total First Year Cost
Current Situation	$ 4,175,700	$ 1,125,000	$ 0	$ 5,300,000
Alternative	$ 3,758,130	$ 1,125,000	$ 48,300	$ 4,931,000
Savings/Increased Benefit	$ 417,570	$ 0	$ -48,300	$ 369,000

FUNDAMENTALS OF VALUE METHODOLOGY

VALUE ALTERNATIVE			
Help Desk			
TITLE: Develop Broad Knowledge Base in IT Personnel		**NUMBER** IT-1	**PAGE NO.** 2 of 3

DISCUSSION / JUSTIFICATION :

Developing a broad knowledge base in IT personnel increases the capability of the staff, thereby increasing productivity and improving overall customer service and relations. Ultimately reduces IT response time by 25%. This could be accomplished in one year. Reduces total user lost time by an added 10%. Due to the high workload, training has not been practical for IT staff. IT has a good, hardworking staff with diverse skills, but the skills of each person need to be broadened.

IMPLEMENTATION PLAN:

Sharing Key Skills and Lessons Learned

1. IT managers and staff determine and prioritize sharing of common problems and fixes – 2 PD

2. Identify a lead staff member for each problem area to document fixes and lessons learned – 10 issues @ 1.5 PD/issue)

3. Establish monthly 2-hour staff meetings to share key skills and lessons learned (11x.25 PD x 12 months)

Formal Training

1. Identify any formal training needed and develop a formal training plan – 2 PD

2. Develop a training schedule for formal training – 3d/class x 4 classes x 6 people

On-the-Job Training

1. Identify and plan on-the-job training for the staff – 1 PD

2. Staff rotate through on-the-job the training – 30 PD (120 calls at 2 hours per call)

COST WORKSHEET
Help Desk

NAME: Develop Broad Knowledge Base in IT Personnel
ALTERNATIVE NO. IT-1
PAGE NO. 3 of 3

DEPARTMENT Description	Unit	BASELINE CONCEPT			ALTERNATE CONCEPT		
		Quantity	Total Cost Cost/Unit	Total	Quantity	Total Cost Cost/Unit	Total
Labor Cost				$5,300,700			$4,883,130
User Time	PD	13,919.00	$300	$4,175,700	12,527.10	$300	$3,758,130
IT Time	PD	3,750.00	$300	$1,125,000	3,750.00	$300	$1,125,000
Labor Cost to Implement				$0			$48,300
IT Time	PD			$0	161.0	$300	$48,300
					0.0		
Other Costs				$0			$0
	EA			$0			$0
				$0			$0
				$0			$0
TOTAL				$5,300,700			$4,931,430
SAVINGS	$						$369,270
SAVINGS	PD						1,231

VALUE ALTERNATIVE
Help Desk

TITLE: Assign Division IS Support to work Under IT Supervision	NUMBER IT-3	PAGE NO. 1 of 3

ALTERNATIVE CONCEPT:
IT hires and trains IS support staff for primary support positions in Divisions. Some of the problems reported to the Help Desk are assigned to the IS Division support person. The IS Division support person is located in the Division but reports to the IT shop (matrix-type organization) for technical support and to maintain standards. The IS Division support person is trained by the IT shop and attends IT staff meetings to discuss problems and solutions.

CURRENT PROBLEM THIS WILL RESOLVE:
It takes too long to respond to calls due to the workload for the existing staff. The IT staff is not knowledgeable of and capable of supporting Division-specific applications.

ADVANTAGES:
- IS support follows IT guidelines and procedures
- Timelier service
- Less downtime
- Adds resources to solve problems
- Division IS support can draw on IT team support

DISADVANTAGES:
- Adds time to train new staff
- Division cost to acquire IS support person
- Division's loss of control of Division resource

COST / PERFORMANCE SUMMARY

Benefit Summary	User Time Lost (Annual $)	IT Time Expended (Annual $)	Cost to Effect Change	Total First Year Cost
Current Situation	$ 4,175,700	$ 1,125,000	$ 0	$ 5,300,700
Alternative	$ 3,340,560	$ 1,125,000	$ 96,000	$ 4,562,160
Savings/Increased Benefit	$ 835,140	$ 0	$ -96,000	$ 738,540

VALUE ALTERNATIVE
Help Desk

TITLE: Assign Division IS Support to work Under IT Supervision	NUMBER IT-3

DISCUSSION / JUSTIFICATION :

The Division will have an IT trained designated IS support person who addresses and coordinates the Division's IT related issues, especially software and applications. Problems will be responded to faster. Procedures and solutions will be consistent for the entire District.

IS support personnel need not be full-time in IS but should be available to provide other Division support as well. These people should not be "direct production," or their IS support function will not be properly executed.

Reduces customer down time due to software by 50 %

Reduces IT workload (assume IS support will handle 50% of software and application support)

IMPLEMENTATION PLAN:

- Divisions without IS support need to fill this position
- Establish roles and responsibilities for IS/IT with clear delineation and workflow procedures – 2 PD
- Establish training/indoctrination meetings with IS support personnel – 3 PD x 10 IS x 10 IT
- Maintain regular lessons learned and coordination meetings with IS personnel

COST WORKSHEET

Help Desk

NAME: Assign Division IS Support to Work Under IT Supervision
ALTERNATIVE NO. IT-3
PAGE NO. 3 of 3

DEPARTMENT Description	Unit	ORIGINAL CONCEPT			ALTERNATE CONCEPT		
		Quantity	Total Cost Cost/Unit	Total	Quantity	Total Cost Cost/Unit	Total
Labor Cost				$5,300,700			$4,465,560
User Time	PD	13,919.00	$300	$4,175,700	11,135.20	$300	$3,340,560
IT Time	PD	3,750.00	$300	$1,125,000	3,750.00	$300	$1,125,000
Labor Cost to Implement				$0			$96,600
IT Time	PD			$0	62.0	$300	$18,600
Division Staff	PD				260.0	$300	$78,000
Other Costs				$0			$0
	EA			$0			$0
				$0			$0
				$0			$0
TOTAL				$5,300,700			$4,562,160
SAVINGS	$						$738,540
SAVINGS	PD						2,462

VALUE ALTERNATIVE
Help Desk

TITLE:	Maintain Inventory of Replacement Hardware	**NUMBER** H-1	**PAGE NO.** 1 of 3

ALTERNATIVE CONCEPT:

Maintain inventory of replacement CPUs, hard drives, mice, keyboards, and monitors to allow IT to swap out key components when one of the user's systems goes down. This will minimize downtime. IT can repair the original CPU without delay.

CURRENT PROBLEM THIS WILL RESOLVE:

Hard drives and CPUs are the most time-consuming hardware problems to resolve. Lost productive time waiting for a replacement CPU or hard drive will be minimized. Having the other key hardware items to replace will also reduce lost time for users.

ADVANTAGES:

- Gets user back to work quicker
- Allows IT better management of time

DISADVANTAGES:

- Funding for parts inventory

COST / PERFORMANCE SUMMARY

Benefit Summary	User Time Lost (Annual $)	IT Time Expended (Annual $)	Cost to Effect Change	Total First Year Cost
Current Situation	$ 751,158	$ 43,974	$ 0	$ 795,132
Alternative	$ 75,116	$ 48,000	$ 14,600	$ 137,716
Savings/Increased Benefit	$ 676,042	$ -4,026	$ -14,600	$ 657,416

VALUE ALTERNATIVE			
	Help Desk		
TITLE:	Maintain Inventory of Replacement Hardware	NUMBER H-1	PAGE NO. 2 of 3

DISCUSSION / JUSTIFICATION :

When CPUs go down, users are experiencing longer than needed downtime due to replacement parts. Having CPUs and hard drives on hand will improve this lost time factor significantly. When combined with Alternative Pr-14, the majority of the user lost time due to PC hardware problems can be eliminated.

IMPLEMENTATION PLAN:
- Purchase 8 CPUs and have them on hand and ready to replace bad ones
- Purchase 12 hard drives and have them loaded and ready to be installed and ready for use
- Purchase 6 each of mice, keyboards and monitors

COST WORKSHEET
Help Desk

NAME: Maintain Inventory of Replacement Hardware
ALTERNATIVE NO. H-1
PAGE NO. 3 of 3

DEPARTMENT Description	Unit	ORIGINAL CONCEPT			ALTERNATE CONCEPT		
		Quantity	Total Cost Cost/Unit	Total	Quantity	Total Cost Cost/Unit	Total
Labor Cost				$795,132			$123,116
User Time	PD	2,158.50	$300	$647,550	215.85	$300	$64,755
IT Time	PD	139.60	$300	$41,880	150.00	$300	$45,000
Unlogged Time - User	PD	345.36	$300	$103,608	34.54	$300	$10,361
Unlogged Time - IT	PD	6.98	$300	$2,094	10.00	$300	$3,000
Labor Cost to Implement				$0			$1,500
IT Time	PD			$0	5.0	$300	$1,500
Other Costs				$0			$13,100
CPUs	EA			$0	8	$1,000.00	$8,000
Hard Drives	EA			$0	12	$200	$2,400
Monitors	EA			$0	6	$400	$2,400
Keyboards	EA			$0	6	$40	$240
Mice	EX			$0	6	$10	$60
TOTAL				$795,132			$137,716
SAVINGS	$						$657,416
SAVINGS	PD						2,191

Index

A

Analytical Hierarchy Process 152, 154
Aristotle 42, 207, 230, 231
Associate Value Specialist 310

B

Bacon, Francis 69
Bytheway, Charles 176, 200

C

California Department of Transportation 32, 33
Certified Value Specialist 310
Chamberlin, Thomas 58, 59, 66, 233
Chanel, Coco 268, 269
Change
    forces of 290
    implementing 292
    selling 270
    stages of 287
City of New York, OMB 31, 34, 35, 138
Cost 11, 12, 13, 14, 16, 17, 20, 25, 26, 27, 30, 31, 32, 33, 34, 36, 40, 41, 42, 43, 44, 45, 46, 47, 48, 50, 58, 61, 73, 75, 76, 77, 78, 79, 80, 82, 83, 87, 88, 89, 90, 91, 92, 93, 94, 95, 97, 98, 99, 102, 106, 107, 109, 120, 126, 127, 128, 129, 130, 131, 132, 133, 134, 135, 136, 137, 138, 140, 141, 143, 144, 145, 155, 156, 159, 163, 164, 166, 167, 168, 184, 200, 201, 202, 204, 227, 240, 244, 245, 247, 251, 252, 256, 272, 274, 275, 278, 282, 294, 296, 297, 301, 302, 314, 316, 317, 322, 325, 327, 328, 329, 330
    cost models 89, 90, 129, 130, 131, 159, 282
Creativity 26, 58, 70, 71, 76, 83, 158, 159, 176, 200, 207, 208, 209, 210, 211, 212, 213, 214, 215, 216, 218, 227, 228, 233, 242, 306, 314, 317
    roadblocks 211
    roadblocks to 211
Creativity Techniques
    brain sketching 219, 221

brain writing 219, 220, 221
brainstorming 111, 219, 228
checklists 219, 223
morphological analysis 219, 222
Curie, Marie 67, 68
Customer 13, 15, 16, 21, 40, 41, 42, 43, 44, 45, 46, 47, 48, 49, 50, 51, 52, 53, 61, 65, 73, 75, 79, 80, 98, 101, 118, 120, 128, 129, 142, 144, 149, 150, 158, 163, 164, 167, 168, 176, 182, 184, 214, 290, 316, 317

D

da Vinci, Leonardo 161, 162, 225
De Marle, David 44, 46, 66

E

Edison, Thomas 249, 250
Einstein, Albert 71, 206, 207, 208, 218, 223
Eisenhower, Dwight 304, 305
Evaluation Techniques
  by comparison 240, 241
  nominal group technique 240, 242, 243
  simple rating 240

F

Fallon, Carlos 44, 66, 150
Fowler, Ted 150, 160
Franklin, Benjamin 227, 285, 286
Function
  aesthetic 169
  assumed 182, 188
  basic 75, 94, 100, 167, 168, 169, 170, 171, 172, 173, 174, 175, 176, 181, 182, 183, 184, 185, 188, 202
  higher-order 168, 215
  independent 185
  ladder of abstraction 172, 173
  numerical evaluation technique 163, 173, 174, 176
  required 15, 17, 76, 198, 200, 317
  secondary 100, 163, 167, 168, 169, 173, 174, 175, 177, 181, 188, 189
  unwanted 92, 169, 200
  work 164

Function Analysis 53, 54, 75, 99, 111, 173, 176, 197, 200, 204, 205, 250
  numerical evaluation technique 163, 173, 174, 176
  Random Function Determination 170, 173
  random function determination 170, 173
Function Analysis Concept Design 99
Function Analysis System Technique 75, 91, 109, 111, 163, 173,
    176, 177, 178, 179, 180, 181, 182, 184, 187, 188, 189, 190, 197,
    198, 200, 201, 202, 204, 205, 227, 282
  flow charts 80, 98, 177, 179, 189, 190, 197, 198, 200, 218, 252

H

Heuristics
  anchoring 233, 234
  availability 234, 236, 237
  confirmation 237
  representativeness 238, 239, 270

J

Job Plan 14, 34, 46, 53, 67, 68, 69, 70, 71, 72, 76, 81, 82, 83, 85, 88,
    100, 105, 106, 107, 109, 118, 120, 155, 173, 213, 216, 227, 243,
    250, 283, 307, 313, 317
  Development Phase 78, 83, 94, 241, 243, 247, 250, 251, 259, 267,
    272
  Evaluation Phase 77, 78, 83, 213, 231, 232, 243, 250, 251, 254,
    267
  Function Phase 75, 76, 83, 162, 163, 204, 213, 227
  Implementation Phase 72, 83, 106, 266, 275, 286, 287, 303
  Information Phase 73, 83, 118, 119, 120, 123, 155, 156, 158, 159,
    257
  Preparation Phase 72, 83, 88, 102, 109, 120, 121, 155, 299
  Presentation Phase 81, 83, 269, 283, 307
  Speculation Phase 76, 77, 83, 153, 173, 204, 207, 208, 213, 231,
    232, 240, 307
Jobs, Steven 117, 118, 159

L

Laws & Regulations
  Defense Authorization Act 17
  National Highway System Designation Act 17
  OMB Circular A-131 17, 31
  Water Resources Development Act 17

Life Cycle Cost 30, 92, 94, 132, 133, 134, 137, 140, 141, 144, 159, 252, 256, 278
    time value of money 137, 138
Lombardi, Vincent 86, 87

M

Meeting
    exit briefing 266, 270, 271, 273, 274, 275, 280, 282
    kick-off 120, 144, 198, 277
    pre-study 73, 88, 97, 100, 145
Meetings
    exit briefing 280
    kick-off 120, 144, 198, 277
Miles, Lawrence 11, 12, 20, 23, 24, 25, 26, 27, 37, 43, 44, 45, 66, 70, 71, 72, 85, 170, 177, 212, 232, 248

N

Need and Purpose 31, 73, 77, 98, 99, 100, 120, 150, 153, 167, 168, 170, 174
Network diagrams 113

P

Paired Comparison 154, 174, 175
Pareto Analysis 90, 92, 129
Performance 13, 14, 15, 16, 19, 20, 28, 30, 40, 41, 42, 44, 45, 46, 48, 49, 52, 58, 73, 75, 76, 77, 79, 80, 82, 83, 94, 95, 97, 100, 144, 147, 148, 149, 150, 151, 152, 153, 155, 156, 159, 163, 164, 168, 174, 184, 189, 200, 201, 202, 204, 210, 217, 227, 237, 243, 244, 245, 251, 254, 255, 257, 258, 259, 272, 274, 275, 278, 291, 294, 296, 297, 315, 317, 320, 330
Program Requirements Clause 95, 96
Project
    constraints 146
    overview 111, 145
    schedule 113, 124, 296
    scope 31, 41, 51, 53, 54, 97, 98, 99, 100, 101, 102, 120, 121, 159, 252, 277
Project Management 19, 20, 41, 100, 121, 124, 133, 270
Project Manager 18, 19, 20, 73, 92, 112, 122, 123, 124, 145, 158, 287, 289, 292, 293, 297, 299, 300, 301, 303, 314, 315
Project schedule 113, 124

R

Rosenthal, Robert 217, 229

S

Saaty, Thomas 152
SAVE International 28, 29, 30, 37, 116, 205, 309, 310, 320, 332
Smith, Adam 38, 39, 43

T

Teambuilding 23, 113
Teamwork 21, 22, 23, 25, 267

U

U.S. Army Corps of Engineers 30, 31, 95, 96
Updegraff, Robert 330, 331, 332

V

Value
  esteem 168
  functional 46, 47, 82, 167
  indicators 92
  theory 47
  use 163, 168
Value Alternatives
  forms 251
  implementation 81, 283, 287, 288, 289, 292, 293, 299, 300, 303
  technical validity 254
Value Change Proposal 96, 321
Value Incentive Clause 95, 96
Value Leadership 12, 28, 304, 305, 313
  leadership framework 305, 307
  managerial grid 305, 307, 331
Value Methodology
  history 11, 12, 23, 24, 25, 26, 27
Value Methodology Practitioner 311
Value Metrics 46, 52, 53, 54, 82, 83, 97, 100, 144, 147, 149, 159, 163, 200, 227, 232, 240, 243, 244, 254, 257, 270, 272, 273, 283, 287, 297
  absolute scales 152
  assessing performance 257

assessing value 273
comparative scales 152
cost-function matrix 201, 202
evaluation matrix 240, 244
performance attribute matrix 153, 154, 155
performance Attributes 73, 75, 77, 83, 97, 100, 147, 148, 149, 152, 153, 154, 155, 159, 174, 189, 203, 227, 237, 243, 244, 257
performance function matrix 202
performance parameters 100, 102, 140, 141, 148, 149, 151, 257
performance Requirements 73, 79, 100, 148, 237
performance sensitivity matrix 202
utility curves 150, 151
value matrix 155, 156, 282, 297
Value Metrics, evaluation matrix 240, 244
Value Program Manager 310, 312
Value Specialists 19, 310, 311, 312, 315, 320
  characteristics of 314
  ethics 321
  facilitation skills 22, 34, 221, 309, 313, 315, 317
  roles of 315
  standards of conduct 320
Value Study
  logistics 110
  objective & goals 101
  participants 103
  report 259, 275, 280, 282, 283, 286, 292, 293, 299
  schedule 105
  scope 102
  site visit 112, 120, 158, 159
  timing 92
Value Team Member 204, 313
von Oech, Roger 208, 211

W

Work Breakdown Structure 123
Worth 17, 25, 47, 75, 82, 130, 133, 141, 143, 218, 232, 233, 243, 249, 274